# Measure of Engagement, Independence, and Social Relationships (MEISR™) Manual

## Research Edition

# Measure of Engagement, Independence, and Social Relationships (MEISR™) Manual

## Research Edition

by

**R. A. McWilliam, Ph.D.**
The University of Alabama

and

**Naomi Younggren, Ph.D.**
Department of Defense Army Educational and
Developmental Intervention Services (EDIS)
Early Intervention Programs

*With invited contributors*

·P A U L·H·
BROOKES
PUBLISHING C°®

Baltimore • London • Sydney

**Paul H. Brookes Publishing Co.**
Post Office Box 10624
Baltimore, Maryland 21285-0624
USA

www.brookespublishing.com

Typeset by Absolute Service, Inc., Towson, Maryland.
Manufactured in the United States of America by
Sheridan Books, Inc., Chelsea, Michigan.

Cover photo © iStockphoto.com.
All examples in this book are composites. Any similarity to actual individuals or
circumstances is coincidental, and no implications should be inferred.

Measure of Engagement, Independence, and Social Relationships (MEISR™), Research Edition, booklets
(ISBN: 978-1-59857-642-9) are available for separate purchase. To order, contact Brookes Publishing Co.,
1-800-638-3775; http://www.brookespublishing.com

ISBN-13: 978-1-59857-641-2

**Library of Congress Cataloging-in-Publication Data**

Library of Congress Cataloging in Publication Control Number: 2019005517

British Library Cataloguing in Publication data are available from the British Library.

2023    2022    2021    2020    2019

10      9      8      7      6      5      4      3      2      1

# Contents

# About the Authors

**R. A. McWilliam, Ph.D.,** Professor and Department Head, Department of Special Education and Multiple Abilities, The University of Alabama, Tuscaloosa, Alabama

Robin McWilliam is the originator of the Routines-Based Model, implemented in 10 countries and many states in the United States. He is a professor of special education at The University of Alabama, where he founded and directs the Evidence-based International Early Intervention Office (EIEIO). He is also the founder and leader of The RAM Group, an international community of practice fostering the Routines-Based Model.

**Naomi Younggren, Ph.D.,** Early Childhood Consultant, Department of Defense Army Educational and Developmental Intervention Services

Dr. Naomi Younggren is currently the Part C/Comprehensive System of Personnel Development (CSPD) Coordinator for the Department of Defense Army Educational and Developmental Intervention Services (EDIS) Early Intervention Programs. She is also an independent consultant focusing on early intervention and preschool processes and best practices and has served as a consultant with the Early Childhood Technical Assistance Center (ECTA). She is a developer on the Universal Online Part C Early Intervention Curriculum workgroup, a longstanding member of the Division for Early Childhood, a member of The RAM Group, and an adjunct early childhood faculty member with Central Texas College–Europe Campus, and she has recently joined the Lead Inclusion team. Dr. Younggren's years of experience in early childhood special education include being a direct provider working with children with disabilities and their families in early intervention and preschool programs, providing technical assistance, developing early intervention guidance and training materials, and serving in a program development and leadership capacity.

# About the Contributors

**Tânia Boavida, Ph.D.,** Researcher, Centro de Investigação e Intervenção Social, ISCTE-Instituto Universitário de Lisboa, Portugal

Dr. Boavida is a researcher at Centro de Investigação e Intervenção Social (CIS-IUL), ISCTE-Instituto Universitário de Lisboa (ISCTE-IUL), Portugal, and a member of The RAM Group, a global group of individuals with expertise in the Routines-Based Model. As a physiotherapist and an educational psychologist, she has a path of practice and research in early childhood intervention and collaborates with different institutions, providing parent workshops, professional training and workshops, and team supervision. Her main interest is professional development in recommended and evidence-based practices, particularly with the Routines-Based Model for Early Intervention Birth to Five.

**Cami M. Stevenson, M.S.,** Assistant Administrator, Multnomah Early Childhood Program, Portland, Oregon

Ms. Stevenson is a supervisor and team leader of a large team of service providers using the MEISR at the Multnomah Early Childhood Program. She serves as Associate Director for Evaluation for the Routines-Based Interview Certification Institute, the Routines-Based Home Visiting Certification Institute, and the Collaborative Consultation to Children's Classrooms Certification Institute. She has been working in early intervention and special education for 20 years.

# Preface: The Need for the MEISR

The Measure of Engagement, Independence, and Social Relationships, or MEISR™, is a uniquely designed tool organized by family routines. As such, it fills the functional assessment void found in the field of early intervention. Current conventional assessment tests, such as the Battelle Developmental Inventory (Newborg, 2005) and the Bayley Scales (Bayley, 1993), are primarily organized around developmental domains and consist of contrived tasks. Those tasks work to produce a summated score that differentiates children along a norm-referenced scale. Items that work well for that purpose are not necessarily skills children need to participate meaningfully in their everyday routines. Therefore, teams have to infer that if a child is able to do something on the test, he or she can probably transfer that ability to a functional setting, and if the child is not able to do a test item, he or she is probably not able to apply the underlying function of that skill to a meaningful routine. Yet we know this is not always the case. When we have to rely on inference about a child's abilities, we compromise the objective understanding of a child's functioning that is critical for making many decisions in early intervention. Because the MEISR is focused on a child's functioning within the context of common family routines, we can eliminate the need for teams to presume or even guess about a child's functioning capacity.

The MEISR is structured around 14 everyday home routines and designed to be used with children from birth to 36 months of age. Items reflect the functional skills infants and toddlers typically display in each routine; for each item, a typical starting age is listed. To complete the MEISR, parents or other caregivers rate each item with a 3 (if the child does the skill often or has progressed beyond it), a 2 (if the child does it sometimes), or a 1 (if the child does not yet do it). If an item is rated 3, the child is considered to have mastered the skill. The intervention professional uses the caregiver's ratings to determine the percentage of items mastered for each routine and then to complete a scoring summary. In this way, the MEISR provides a profile of child functioning in everyday life. This profile helps caregivers monitor progress and identify areas to work on.

The MEISR provides different types of information about a child's functioning, depending upon the team's assessment purpose. It can generate a profile of the child's functioning organized around routines and by age. Items are also crosswalked to McWilliam's (2008) foundations of learning (engagement, independence, and social relationships), to developmental domains, and to the three national child outcomes, thereby providing additional information about the child's functioning.

The MEISR is organized around children's functional abilities—that is, what the child does to participate within the context of common family routines—rather than the five domains of development, which inadvertently align with specific early intervention team disciplines. That is, the communication domain aligns with speech-language pathology; the gross motor domain aligns with physical therapy; adaptive and fine motor domains often align with occupational therapy; the cognitive domain is most aligned with early childhood special education; and the social domain is also frequently aligned with education, social work, or other mental health professions represented on an early intervention team. The challenge this often presents is that when a child demonstrates a particular delay in one or more of the five developmental domains, the team tends to think that the child's area(s) of delay requires services from the discipline frequently aligned with the delayed domain(s). This can happen too when a child has a diagnosed condition and service decisions are made based on the child's diagnosis. For example, a child with a diagnosis of autism requires services from speech and occupational therapy, at least; a child with a diagnosis of Down syndrome, with the potential for global developmental delays, requires services from all disciplines.

But early intervention is not a "got a need, get a service" program. Early intervention is designed to address the needs Congress defined in the Individuals with Disabilities Education Act (IDEA) Part C (2004, PL 108-446,), which are as follows:

> (1) to enhance the development of infants and toddlers with disabilities, to minimize their potential for developmental delay, and to recognize the significant brain development that occurs during a child's first 3 years of life; (2) to reduce the educational costs to our society, including our Nation's schools, by minimizing the need for special education and related services after infants and toddlers with disabilities reach school age; (3) to maximize the potential for individuals with disabilities to live independently in society; (4) to enhance the capacity of families to meet the special needs of their infants and toddlers with disabilities; and (5) to enhance the capacity of State and local agencies and service providers to identify, evaluate, and meet the needs of all children, particularly minority, low-income, inner city, and rural children, and infants and toddlers in foster care. [(IDEA Title I, Part C, SEC 631, (a) (1-5)]

To effectively accomplish these defined needs, the holistic nature of the child in the context of the family must be regarded and respected.

Teams need information about a child's performance in five domains of development to help determine the child's eligibility for these services. Beyond that, the team needs information about a child's functioning that cuts across the five domains of development and occurs within the context of the child and family day-to-day routines and activities. This information helps the family identify their true priorities for their child and family.

The MEISR assesses a child's engagement in common family routines. It is designed to develop a profile of the functioning of a young child (birth to 3 years of age) and to monitor progress within that profile. As opposed to traditional assessments, the MEISR combines important perspectives: It is family centered, because families (not professionals alone) rate their children's functioning; it is ecological, because the profile is organized by everyday routines; it is functional, because the skills assessed are those commonly needed for successful participation in daily routines; and it is developmental, because the items are organized according to the ages at which the skills usually begin (Boavida, Aguiar, & McWilliam, 2014). Furthermore, each item is coded according to:

- The corresponding functional area (engagement, independence, and social relationships)

- The five developmental domains (cognitive, communication, motor, adaptive, and social)

- The national child outcomes (have positive social relationships, acquire and use knowledge and skills, and take appropriate action to meet needs)

These characteristics make the MEISR an ideal tool to help professionals shift to a functional way of viewing children and using the family's knowledge of their child to complete the assessment.

## THE ROUTINES-BASED MODEL AND DOCUMENTATION OF CHILD PROGRESS

*Routines-Based Early Intervention* (McWilliam, 2010) describes a model for providing early intervention in natural environments. This model was previously termed Routines-Based

Early Intervention (RBEI); however, its use is not limited to children ages birth–3 years. For this reason, the model is now known as the Routines-Based Model for Early Intervention Birth–Five, or more simply, the Routines-Based Model or RBM. The MEISR provides the most salient method for measuring child progress for professionals using the RBM, because the three child constructs, engagement, independence, and social relationships, are central to the RBM and formative in the MEISR. Chapters 2 and 3 of this manual describe in detail the relationship between the MEISR, the RBM, and the RBM component most aligned with the MEISR, the Routines-Based Interview (RBI). In brief:

- The MEISR dovetails with the five components of the RBM—understanding the family ecology; developing a functional, family-centered plan (RBI); integration of services; support-based home visits; and collaborative consultation to child care—as discussed in Chapter 2.

- Both the RBI and the MEISR are methods for assessing child functioning, in the context of routines.

- The MEISR can be used as a tool for helping conduct an RBI and to help with other aspects of quality early intervention, as discussed in Chapter 3.

## INFLUENCE OF ROUTINES-BASED INTERVIEWS

Where did the items on the MEISR come from? Most came from listening to families talk about their daily lives as we conducted RBIs. One of us (McWilliam) estimates he has conducted over 300 RBIs, which amounts to listening to families, only in the context of an RBI, for over 600 hours. We sought input from others who nominated skills to include, and we included them only if they were typical skills children used to participate meaningfully in the routine. Weird, "therapeutic," or "educational" activities, designed by professionals, that abnormalized the routine were excluded. One category of such activities includes those designed to prime the pump for function, such as oral-motor exercises before eating (or talking). Such warm-up activities are not normal in routines and, in the case of nonspeech oral-motor exercises, have a poor evidence base. These two problems would double-eliminate the activity.

## ORGANIZATION OF THE MANUAL

This manual is organized in three sections comprising nine chapters. The first section, "Context and Conceptual Framework," presents the fundamentals needed to understand and implement the MEISR in early intervention. Chapter 1 provides an overview of assessment in early intervention. Chapter 2 lays out the MEISR's conceptual framework: engagement theory, functioning and participation, and the RBM. The MEISR is a different way of looking at a family's needs, so some explanation is probably needed. Chapter 3 presents the rationale for the RBI and explains how to conduct it and integrate it with the MEISR.

The title of Section II, "Ways to Use the MEISR," is self-explanatory. In this section, Chapter 4 describes the MEISR's purpose and states how to use the MEISR. It has various uses—most related to assessment of needs. This chapter also provides an overview of the MEISR's organization and identifies potential misuses of the tool. Chapter 5 describes how the MEISR can inform federal child outcome reporting.

The third section, "Implementation, Scoring, and Working With Data," presents more detailed guidance on how to implement the MEISR when developing an intervention plan and how to interpret and use MEISR results. An effective intervention plan is based on a functional needs assessment. The MEISR obtains the family's ratings of child functioning in routines, so it satisfies the need to get information the family can use to choose meaningful goals. Chapter 6 explains how to introduce the MEISR to families and work with them throughout the intervention process. Chapter 7 describes the scoring of the MEISR in detail. Chapter 8 explains other ways MEISR results can be interpreted and analyzed, and Chapter 9 describes how to use the MEISR for program evaluation. Finally, the book's appendix discusses the MEISR's psychometric properties.

## REFERENCES

Bayley, N. (1993). *Bayley Scales of Infant Development manual.* San Antonio, TX: Psychological Corporation.

Boavida, T., Aguiar, C., & McWilliam, R. A. (2014). A training program to improve IFSP/IEP goals and objectives through the Routines-Based Interview. *Topics in Early Childhood Special Education, 33,* 200–211.

Individuals with Disabilities Education Act (IDEA) of 2004, PL 108-446, 20 U.S.C. § 631, (a) (1-5). (IDEA Title I, Part C, SEC 631, (a) (1-5).

McWilliam, R. A. (2008). The engagement construct. In R. A. McWilliam & A. M. Casey (Eds.), *Engagement of every child in the preschool classroom* (pp. 125–134). Baltimore, MD: Paul H. Brookes Publishing Co.

McWilliam, R. A. (2010). *Routines-based early intervention.* Baltimore, MD: Paul H. Brookes Publishing Co.

Newborg, J. (2005). *Battelle Developmental Inventory* (2nd ed.). Itasca, IL: Riverside.

# Acknowledgments

Our first acknowledgment is a mutual one. Naomi and Robin have known each other for over two decades and have exchanged ideas, tools, practices, experiences, bottles of wine, and travel stories. Our professional partnership, from an informal one to, with this book, a formal one, has been mutually rewarding and a testament to the saying that two heads are better than one.

But it hasn't been only our heads. Other people along the way have made substantial contributions to the development of the MEISR™. An earlier version of the MEISR was developed by R. A. McWilliam and Shana Hornstein at Vanderbilt University in 2007. Colleagues who have helped create and improve the instrument include Amy Casey, Pau García-Grau, Amy Jenkins, Catalina Morales Murillo, Marisú Pedernera, Cami Stevenson, and the early interventionists at Siskin Children's Institute in Chattanooga, Tennessee. We thank Terri Strange-Boston and her colleagues in Virginia for piloting the MEISR, Richard Corbett for his hours of work on an electronic sorting component currently being developed to complement the MEISR paper protocol, and earlier MEISR system pioneers, such as David Munson and his colleagues in Montana. Finally, our colleagues at Brookes Publishing have provided detailed and sensible contributions in editing this manual.

# Context and Conceptual Framework

CHAPTER 1

# Assessment in Early Intervention

To understand the context in which the Measure of Engagement, Independence, and Social Relationships (MEISR™) was developed and the need it fulfills, it is helpful for readers to have a broader understanding of assessment. This chapter discusses assessment in the context of early intervention in natural environments. It addresses assessment questions, assessment postulates, evaluation and assessment in Part C early intervention under the Individuals with Disabilities Education Improvement Act (IDEA) of 2004 (PL 108-446), assessment on the individualized family service plan (IFSP), the current level of functioning or present levels of development (PLOD), and service coordinator roles. It concludes with a checklist for infant–toddler assessment.

## ASSESSMENT QUESTIONS

Infants and toddlers need different types of assessment: assessment for diagnosis, assessment for determining eligibility, assessment for monitoring progress, and assessment for intervention planning. Each of these types might require a different way of conducting the assessment, and different types of people might be involved. A problem in early intervention is that many systems confuse the different assessment purposes or try to take shortcuts by using the method for determining eligibility as the assessment of *needs*. Standardized tests might successfully sort out children who are eligible for services under the delay criterion. These tests have items that do well for the purposes intended, but those items are not necessarily meaningful for children and families in everyday life.

Assessment can be accomplished through formal testing, informal testing or clinical judgment, observation, or report. When using report, one can ask closed-ended questions, open-ended questions, or a combination. A closed-ended question might be, "Does he sleep through the night?" Not all closed-ended questions are yes–no questions. For example, a forced-choice question such as, "Does he prefer oatmeal or cold cereal?" is closed-ended. The answer is closed—determined by the question. An open-ended question might be, "What does he like for breakfast?" The questioner puts no limits on the possible answers. A combination is when the questioner begins with an open-ended question and follows with closed-ended questions, such as asking, "What does he like to play with?" (open-ended), and, after the answer, asking, "Does he always choose the same train?" (closed-ended). A mistake interviewers sometimes make is to ask the two types of questions together, such as, "How does he like bath time? Does he fight getting his hair washed?" The skilled interviewer would wait for the answer to the open-ended question before posing a closed-ended question.

3

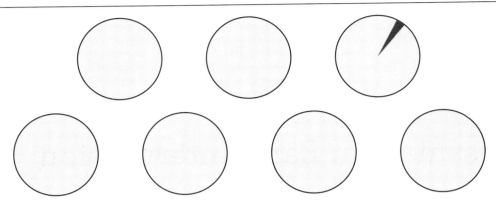

**Figure 1.1.** Time a home visit represents in a child's week. Each circle represents a day of the week. The sliver in the third circle indicates the brief amount of home visiting time on just one day of the week.

An interview can be used to ask such questions and to elicit a report. In fact, the distinction between direct observation and interview is worth discussion. Direct observation by a professional other than a classroom teacher is based on a very small slice of life. Figure 1.1 shows the typical amount of time a professional spends on a home visit during a child's week. Therefore, what the home visitor observes is hardly a reasonable time sample of the child's typical behavior. Despite the premise behind Malcolm Gladwell's *Blink* (2005), quick, one-time observations of children's behavior provide limited information. In a study of the amount of observation needed to produce stable engagement data, McWilliam and Ware (1994) discovered that eight 15-minute observations on different days were necessary.

But what if you interview caregivers of children—people who have spent hours with them, day after day? What they report is their *observations* across much time, across multiple settings, with many people, and with many objects. To get a good picture of children's and families' functioning this way requires a skillful interview. Elsewhere in this book, we have proposed the Routines-Based Interview (RBI) as an assessment method for obtaining an observational report.

## ASSESSMENT POSTULATES

The field faces three challenges to assessment in early intervention. First, ***we overemphasize assessment, especially diagnosis, and underemphasize intervention***. For example, documentation of the child's "disorder" is often considered a major activity in a family's journey through early intervention. The diagnosis is expensive: in our experience, often upward of $600. In addition to the cost, professionals might actually like the professional cachet that comes with being able to administer a test or, even better, a battery of tests and proclaiming what is wrong with the child. Admittedly, many families do want to know what is "wrong" with their child, so these diagnostic assessments can be helpful. It is often said that diagnostic assessments open the gate to intervention services. Sometimes this is true, but, more often, testing for eligibility can be done relatively more cheaply and quickly. For professionals and parents who have a strong belief in diagnosis-specific "treatments," rather than a belief that intervention principles can cut across most learning requirements, the diagnosis is supreme.

A second challenge is the common, misguided reason given for multiple specialists making regular home visits to a child and family: Assessment should be ongoing, and only the specialist can really do the assessment. Our proposal is that ***we should provide support (i.e., intervention) and work in assessment rather than assess constantly and work in intervention***. The emphasis should be on intervention that provides ongoing information about the child's learning and progress (i.e., assessment information).

The third challenge is the view that effective intervention depends upon ongoing input from multiple experts. Our proposal is that ***high-level expertise from multiple experts*** *does not need to be applied to intervention for infants, toddlers, and families all the time*. As long as families have one competent professional providing ongoing support, the high-level expertise might be needed from time to time, as the child makes changes or as the family and primary service provider run into situations outside their scope of knowledge and skill. However, this rarely means sending an educator, an occupational therapist, a physical therapist, and a speech-language pathologist into the home every single week. Weekly visits by a primary service provider are an effective method of supporting families. Less frequent visits make it hard to build capacity and to address child and family needs.

## EVALUATION AND ASSESSMENT IN PART C

In many communities, children in Part C are being tested for reasons other than eligibility determination. Four types of children are potentially eligible for Part C services:

1. Children with established conditions (sometimes known as medical conditions) are automatically eligible. States define what conditions are applicable but often include chromosomal abnormalities and physical impairments. These children do not need developmental testing for eligibility. All children in Part C need a multidisciplinary evaluation that must cover five domains, but this can be accomplished without formal testing. Nevertheless, some states and communities have "simplified" the process by telling professionals to test the children to get this information. Perhaps they did not realize that other forms of assessment can produce the required "current level of functioning." The case for using the RBI as the method for assessment of these children will be made in Chapter 3.

2. Children with developmental delays require testing to document that the delay actually exists. Consequently, states have established criteria about the number of months for the delay or the number of standard deviations below the mean and the number of domains. These children do not have known, established conditions. For example, a child with Down syndrome should not need testing, but a child with delayed language and no known etiology would. "Testing" usually means that a standardized instrument needs to be scored. States vary in the types of tests they allow. Some restrict testing to norm-referenced tests such as the Bayley (1993) or the Battelle (Newborg, 2005), whereas others allow norm-referenced tests such as the Hawaii Early Learning Profile (Parks, Furono, O'Reilly, Inatsuka, & Hosaka, 1997). Depending on the test, it might be possible to score most of an eligibility test from the information gained in an RBI (McWilliam, Casey, & Sims, 2009), as described in Chapter 3.

3. Children with "atypical development" but no documented delay or established condition are also eligible if a qualified professional makes the determination through informed clinical opinion. This eligibility category is usually used for children with challenging behaviors not directly related to a disability. Although testing might not be required to establish eligibility under this category, these children are often tested to rule out a delay. Some children with autism or challenging behaviors do not exhibit enough of a delay on the developmental test but have serious functioning problems, so, in states where informed clinical opinion is used, this category is their ticket to eligibility.

4. The final eligibility category is used only by those states that elect to serve children at risk for delays or disabilities. States decide on the risk factors that can be used for such children, who do not meet any of the other three criteria. Risk factors usually include environmental or biological conditions. Again, testing is usually used to rule out delay, so, although it is not required for eligibility, most of these children in fact are tested.

## ASSESSMENT ON THE IFSP

The IFSP requires documentation of the child's PLOD in five domains: cognitive, communication, physical, social or emotional, and adaptive performance. The purpose is to be able to monitor that outcomes have been developed and services have been planned to match performance needs in these domains.

Usually, IFSP forms are designed with a box in which to write some information for each domain. This box is good for prompting basic information, so the paperwork burden is reduced. The downside, however, is that the service coordinator might be so cryptic that the information is useless. For example, a service coordinator might write, "No words," in the communication space. A better description might be, "Orlando communicates at meals, during play time, and at bath time by gesturing. He understands simple directions, such as 'Come here,' during outings, outside time, and bedtime. He does not yet use words." With most IFSPs now completed electronically, service coordinators can type as much as they want, unless the form has a character number limit.

Policy organizes the PLODs on the IFSP by traditional domains. Understandably, the five domains were chosen because standardized instruments producing scores in these areas exist. To establish developmental delay, states can establish criteria for the amount of delay necessary to be eligible for services, so one might expect to see similar information in this section of the IFSP. The link back to standardized evaluations is logical, but the link forward to outcomes is not as logical. Better ways exist for organizing assessment of function needs. One way is discussed in Chapter 3 on the RBI, which explains how functional areas of development (engagement, independence, and social relationships), rather than domains, can be used to assess children's needs. The terminology is important: Tests and domains tend to focus on deficits—what the child cannot do—and functional areas of development tend to focus on needs—what the child needs to do to participate meaningfully.

On some IFSPs, only positive comments are made in the PLOD boxes, such as, "Ben crawls, sits independently, and pulls to stand," presumably to emphasize the positive (Jung & McWilliam, 2005; McWilliam et al., 1998). But this does not help anyone understand why the outcomes were chosen. Ben was 18 months old and not yet standing independently. It would have been better to add that fact to the positives.

On other IFSPs, only scores are placed in the boxes, sometimes because eligibility for specific services is based on domain scores. For example, a child might be able to receive speech-language services only if there is a 15-point difference between his or her language score and his or her cognitive score. This, by the way, is a flawed policy, because it can make children with cognitive impairments ineligible for services (Cole, Dale, & Mills, 1992). Another example would be in places where the discrepancy criterion is not used, but the absolute or base score is. For example, a child might be eligible for speech-language services based on a delay of 25%. This implies that the age-equivalent score is accurate and that the delay has something to do with functional needs. For a host of reasons, the rules and culture around this section of the IFSP result in scores being entered into the boxes.

The notion of monitoring the match between the information in these evaluation result boxes and the outcomes has some problems. First, just because there is a delay does not mean the family has chosen to address it. The family might have more pressing needs that are even more important than the delay. For example, suppose the family is more concerned about a child's communication and getting along with others than the child's fine motor awkwardness when playing with small toys. Or the family may have basic needs, such as reliable housing, access to healthy food, or diapers, that trump focusing on child development. This is a difficult idea for professionals who are schooled in the child-centered early intervention philosophy that we should address delays as soon as possible. Second, the method for obtaining evaluation information (e.g., a standardized test, for some children) does not necessarily reveal a problem in everyday functioning, so it would be foolish to expect an outcome to match failures on those evaluations.

The policy, to ensure that systems were not denying needed supports to families, is well intended. However, it does not account for the possibility that needs found in the evaluation might be met through support from a generalist. For example, a delay in adaptive performance could be addressed by the same person who is addressing delays in cognitive and communication performance, to use domain terms. An occupational therapist and a speech-language pathologist might be involved, but the rationale that the child needs separate specialists for each of these testing domains is defective (Rapport, McWilliam, & Smith, 2004; Shelden & Rush, 2013). One cannot tell simply from information about delay whether specialists are needed, let alone the extent to which they are needed. ***This is one of the most common fundamental blunders made in the IFSP process—assigning the valuable resources of specialist time on the basis of the wrong data.***

Instead, the IFSP could consider the truly functional data, which are found in the answers to the following questions:

- What child and family needs have been indentified?

- If a primary-service-provider (PSP) model is used, who is that service provider?

- Given the child and family in question, what help does the PSP need to support the family in reaching the stated outcome? What intensity of support is needed?

If a multidisciplinary model is used, functional assessment data are less likely to be used. In fact, the reason nonfunctional data (e.g., standardized test results) are used so much is that they conform to the multidisciplinary approach: If a delay is found in a given domain, the service ostensibly related to that domain is slapped on the IFSP. For example, a delay is found in the fine motor section of the Battelle, so occupational therapy almost automatically is put on the IFSP. Nevertheless, there are ways to use functional data with multidisciplinary "teams." Beginning with the top-priority outcome, the service coordinator and family decide what service might best meet that need. They need to be prepared, however, to revisit this once the whole list of outcomes has been considered.

The next question is whether the same service provider can support the family in accomplishing the second outcome. If not, they must decide what service could address it. This process proceeds through the outcomes. Needless to say, the beauty of functional outcomes can be sabotaged when they are divided among different professionals who might not communicate with each other. This method also results in the family having to deal with many professionals, often. This process of adding services only to the extent that the existing providers need help is known as the additive approach (McWilliam, 2010).

## PRESENT LEVELS OF DEVELOPMENT

IDEA requires "(1) a statement of the infant's or toddler's present levels of physical development, cognitive development, communication development, social or emotional development, and adaptive development, based on objective criteria" (IDEA 1990, Sec. 636 (d)). This information is needed for a number of reasons. First, it is the short form of an assessment report, so monitors can determine whether the plan of action (i.e., outcomes, strategies, and services) matches the assessed needs. Second, the report serves some systems as the place to document the delay that made the child eligible by virtue of his or her delay. In many systems, the age equivalence scores are entered in this part of the IFSP. Third, some people use it as the place to document progress. From year to year, they can see how the data change.

It can be assumed, therefore, that these reasons for documenting the PLOD will require 1) developmental scores for children being served under the "delayed" category and 2) a description of salient strengths and weaknesses. Children being served under the established condition category should not need test scores, although some systems require them so they have developmental data on all children in the system. Furthermore, the test scores might be part of the information guiding the rating of children's status on the federal child outcomes

# Infant–Toddler Assessment Checklist

| Did the professional | Date | Date | Date | Date | Date |
|---|---|---|---|---|---|
| 1.  Include interview as part of the assessment? | | | | | |
| 2.  Include assessment of child needs and functioning when providing ongoing support? | | | | | |
| 3.  Check whether testing was required for children eligible under "medical" or "established" condition? | | | | | |
| 4.  Refrain from unnecessary formal testing? | | | | | |
| 5.  Test children for whom a documented delay was necessary? | | | | | |
| 6.  Provide a description of the present level of development in cognitive, communication, physical, social or emotional, and adaptive performance? | | | | | |
| 7.  Indicate clearly where the child's needs are (vs. glossing over them with positive language)? | | | | | |
| 8.  Assign services based on needs rather than using child development scores or impairment diagnoses? | | | | | |
| 9.  Set up the assessment by explaining the process to the family? | | | | | |
| 10.  Secure the family's input into how the assessment should be done? | | | | | |
| 11.  Obtain the family's signed consent to assess the child? | | | | | |
| 12.  Put assessment information (i.e., present levels of development) on the IFSP? | | | | | |
| 13.  Determine the family's needs? | | | | | |
| 14.  Have or plan to have regular (e.g., monthly) conversations with families about their aspirations? | | | | | |

**Figure 1.2.**  Infant–Toddler Assessment Checklist. (From McWilliam, R. A. [2010]. *Routines-based early intervention* [p. 66]. Baltimore, MD: Paul H. Brookes Publishing Co.)

(see Chapter 5). All children must, by law, be offered a multidisciplinary evaluation, and the results of that evaluation are usually entered in the *present level of development* section of the IFSP.

## SERVICE COORDINATOR ROLES

In the evaluation process, service coordinators have three basic roles. First, they set up the assessment, by explaining the process to families, securing their input into how the assessment should be done (this is often overlooked), and obtaining their signed consent to assess the child. In some systems, the service coordinator him- or herself might be one of the evaluators. In other systems, other employees of the program might do the evaluations. And in yet other systems, individuals are contracted to do evaluations. The service coordinator schedules these evaluations. For initial IFSPs, this step occurs following intake. Reevaluations are not required by federal law, but some states require them for some or all children in the program. In such cases, the service coordinator also schedules the annual evaluations.

The second role of the service coordinator is putting the information on the IFSP. This was discussed in the previous section, "Present Levels of Development."

The third role of the service coordinator should be the most important: determining needs with the family. Unfortunately, this role is largely overlooked for two reasons. First, service coordinators assume the multidisciplinary evaluation discovered the child's and family's needs. Therefore, they do not need to work with the family to determine needs. Second, they focus on getting services more than on determining needs and outcomes. For reasons given earlier in this chapter, the traditional multidisciplinary evaluation is usually insufficient for determining functional needs. Therefore, the service coordinator must figure out how to determine the actual needs of families and their children. Service coordinators need to have enough training and skill to be able to assess needs. In some systems, they are unprepared for this task (McWilliam, 2006). In others, they are very well prepared for this task. To help all service coordinators, it is helpful to have a method that assesses real needs and leads to a list of functional outcomes. The Infant–Toddler Assessment Checklist shown in Figure 1.2 can be used to evaluate a professional's use of effective assessment procedures with an infant or toddler.

## RATIONALE FOR USING THE MEISR

The "Agreed Upon Practices for Providing Early Intervention Services in Natural Environments" (Workgroup on Principles and Practices in Natural Environments, 2008) has been a beacon for many early intervention programs to remind professionals about why we provide this program and what it is supposed to accomplish. They read as follows:

### MISSION

Part C early intervention builds upon and provides supports and resources to assist family members and caregivers to enhance children's learning and development through everyday learning opportunities.

### KEY PRINCIPLES

1) Infants and toddlers learn best through everyday experiences and interactions with familiar people in familiar contexts.

2) All families, with the necessary supports and resources, can enhance their children's learning and development.

3) The primary role of a service provider in early intervention is to work with and support family members and caregivers in children's lives.

4) The early intervention process, from initial contacts through transition, must be dynamic and individualized to reflect the child's and family members' preferences, learning styles and cultural beliefs.

5) IFSP outcomes must be functional and based on children's and families' needs and family-identified priorities.

6) The family's priorities, needs and interests are addressed most appropriately by a primary provider who represents and receives team and community support.

7) Interventions with young children and family members must be based on explicit principles, validated practices, best available research, and relevant laws and regulations.

The MEISR can help professionals follow the agreed-upon mission because of its focus on everyday learning opportunities—routines. It is organized by everyday experiences, as mentioned in Key Principle 1. The MEISR is for everyone in early intervention (Key Principle 2), although some families might want help with reading and translation. In fact, earlier versions of the MEISR exist in Spanish, Portuguese, Arabic, and Mandarin. The MEISR has a focus on supporting families (Key Principle 3) and promotes individualized assessment and intervention (Key Principle 4). It clearly helps with the development of functional IFSP outcomes (Key Principle 5). Furthermore, it is organized by routines-based functional skills, as opposed to domains, and therefore facilitates a primary-provider approach (Key Principle 6). It is also a reliable measure of children's functioning (Key Principle 7). Therefore, the MEISR supports the way most experts believe early intervention should be carried out.

## SUMMARY

This chapter addressed questions and methods to use when assessing infants and toddlers for different purposes: diagnosis, determining eligibility, progress monitoring, and intervention planning. We outlined three challenges to assessment in early intervention and presented postulates that should inform such assessment. Children in Part C are sometimes tested for reasons other than eligibility determination; the chapter summarized four reasons children are potentially eligible for Part C services. We also described assessment in the context of developing the IFSP and outlined service coordinator roles, and then presented a checklist to use for evaluating assessment procedures with an infant or toddler. Finally, we explained how the MEISR is consistent with principles supported by many early intervention programs.

# CHAPTER 2

# Conceptual Framework for the MEISR

*With Tânia Boavida*

The MEISR is designed as a list of functional skills infants and toddlers typically display in everyday home routines. Parents or other caregivers rate each skill in terms of whether the child does it often, does it sometimes, or does not yet do it. Therefore, these ratings provide a profile of child functioning in everyday life. They help caregivers monitor their child's progress and give caregivers ideas of what they might work on in early intervention. Thus, the MEISR is like a functional snapshot of the child.

One of us (McWilliam) developed the MEISR profile as his concept of engagement theory was developing (McWilliam & Casey, 2008). The MEISR is consistent with the Routines-Based Model (RBM), which is a set of early intervention (birth–5 years of age) practices promoting children's functioning and family quality of life (McWilliam, 2010). Within the MEISR, and within the lives of children and families, children's *functioning* is organized by their participation in everyday routines. Functioning is operationally defined as children's engagement, including independence and social relationships, in everyday routines, events, or activities. It differs from skills related to developmental domains in that any number of domains might be involved in a child's engagement or functioning. For example, if a child is absorbed at breakfast time, this might mean he is paying attention to his mother (social), using a spoon to scoop oatmeal (fine motor), sitting upright (gross motor), swallowing (self-help), and letting his mother know he's finished (communication). Experts have used developmental domains as convenient artifices to sort out types of development. In reality, however, domains are not clear-cut and meld like hands of gin rummy.

Anthropologists consider routines to be especially meaningful "ecocultural niches," where parents build a commonplace activity to match values, goals, resources, and barriers (Bernheimer & Weisner, 2007). It is not always so deliberate: They often fall into these routines. But, once they are in place, they are hard to shake. To help you understand the foundational underpinnings of the MEISR, this chapter describes engagement theory, function and participation, routines, the relationship of the MEISR to the RBM, and ways to use the MEISR with other tools.

## ENGAGEMENT THEORY

Fundamental to the MEISR's rationale is the theory that the amount of time children spend interacting with their environment in the most sophisticated way possible defines their successful participation in daily life. Engagement also predicts learning, if not statistically, at least conceptually, in that it is hard for a child to learn if the child is not engaged (McWilliam,

Trivette, & Dunst, 1985). That is, we researchers do not yet have sufficient evidence that more engagement or absorption leads to better learning, but the theory that it does is supported by research (Carroll, 1989).

## What Is Engagement?

Engagement is defined as the amount of time children spend interacting with adults, peers, and materials in a developmentally and contextually appropriate manner, at different levels of competence (McWilliam & Bailey, 1992). This definition includes the duration of behavior. Generally, in early childhood, if a child is interested, participating, and busy, he or she is spending time in that interaction. The definition acknowledges that children of all ages can be engaged at different levels of competence or sophistication. In fact, McWilliam and colleagues coded nine categories of engagement that were ranked by sophistication, starting from the most sophisticated. Table 2.1 defines these nine categories and provides an example of each for a child participating in a mealtime routine (de Kruif & McWilliam, 1999; McWilliam, Scarborough, & Kim, 2003; Raspa, McWilliam, & Ridley, 2001).

One should therefore think about engagement in two ways: 1) the breadth of it, in terms of duration, and 2) the depth of it, in terms of sophistication, as shown in Figure 2.1. A child can drop a few blocks into a container and then move on to something else, or he can drop them all in, dump the container, and do it all over again. The second instance lasts longer and therefore shows higher engagement (broader). Even better would be if the child dropped in all the blocks, dumped them, and then built a tower with them. This different way of playing with the blocks is less repetitive and therefore a higher level of engagement (deeper).

Children who are engaged maximally are absorbed in what they are doing. For example, a child who has motor difficulties but persists on climbing the slide ladder, getting into position, sliding, picking himself up, and doing it again, is engaged. He is absorbed in the activity. We assume in this theory that such absorption aids learning, although children with autism

**Table 2.1.** Nine engagement categories, definitions, and child examples at meal times

| Categories of Engagement | Briefly Defined | Child Example at Meal Time |
|---|---|---|
| 1. Persistence | Makes two or more attempts to overcome a challenge. | Tries three times to scoop peas onto a spoon. |
| 2. Symbolic | Uses objects to represent different objects. Talks about things for which the referent is not present, such as things in the past or future. | Uses spoon to make airplane sounds and movement. Talks about going to Grandma's house later that day. |
| 3. Encoded | Follows rules in games and in routines; uses conventionalized language. | Says, "Don't like green food!" |
| 4. Constructive | Makes things; represents things in art. | Pokes holes in mashed potatoes for eyes, nose, and mouth, and says, "Face!" |
| 5. Focused attention | Demonstrates prolonged eye gaze, usually toward a person. | Watches a sibling talking at the lunch table. |
| 6. Differentiated | Participates as expected in a routine without displaying any of the other levels of sophistication. | Nurses at a regular pace and for appropriate duration. Sits in high chair and finger feeds. Sits at table and eats with a utensil. |
| 7. Casual attention | Looks from one thing to another. | Sits at the table, looking at Dad—who is talking—then at food on the plate, then at a dog walking by. |
| 8. Undifferentiated behavior | Demonstrates repetitive motor actions or vocalizations. | Bangs on the tray (if developmentally appropriate). Says, "ba-ba-ba-ba," in anticipation of bottle. |
| 9. Nonengaged | Passive nonengagement: Stares into space, waiting with nothing to do. Active: Cries, has a temper tantrum, displays aggression, engages in destruction. | Sits in the high chair with nothing on the tray, not paying attention to surroundings. Throws objects put on the tray. |

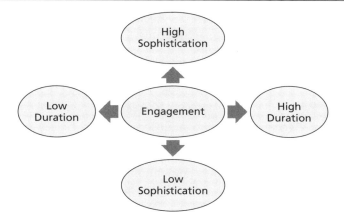

**Figure 2.1.** Breadth of duration of engagement and depth of sophistication of engagement.

have taught us to be careful about the construct of absorption: Taken too far, as in stereotyped or obsessive behavior, it might not be as valuable. In fact, the problem with obsessive behavior might be explained by engagement theory, in that such behavior is repetitive. In engagement theory, repetitive behavior is a low level of sophistication, just above nonengagement (i.e., undifferentiated behavior, Level 8).

Returning to absorption, the literature on attention and concentration is relevant. If we care about a child's absorption, we care about his or her interest, which is important to the concept of engagement. Dunst, Bruder, Trivette, and Hamby (2006) have included both interest and engagement in their notion of learning opportunities. In our work, we have long advocated for using incidental teaching for all areas of development—not just language (Casey & McWilliam, 2008). We currently define systematic incidental teaching as 1) getting a child engaged, 2) responding to the child's interest or engagement, 3) eliciting more sophisticated forms of that engagement, and 4) ensuring the interaction reinforced the elicited behavior (McWilliam & Casey, 2008). Therefore, to the extent that absorption indicates a child's interest, engagement theory is about acknowledging and expanding a child's interests.

In the sections that follow, we discuss engagement in greater depth. We begin by summarizing research that demonstrates its importance. We then explain how engagement is linked to participation, what factors predict engagement, and why it is a prerequisite for learning. Finally, we address how two other aspects of child functioning assessed by the MEISR—independence and social relationships—can be considered engagement behaviors.

## Why Engagement Is Important: Research Findings

We have described the engagement construct in *Engagement of Every Child in the Preschool Classroom* (McWilliam & Casey, 2008). This construct has evolved over a series of studies, beginning with behavioral research from Todd Risley's group at the University of Kansas in the 1970s and 1980s (Doke & Risley, 1972; Hart & Risley, 1974; Quilitch & Risley, 1973). At the time, engagement was defined as the percentage of people participating in planned activities, so it was a measure of the properties of the activity, including materials and caregivers' behaviors. Early intervention researchers became interested in engagement as, essentially, on-task behavior not previously defined for a specific activity (McWilliam et al., 1985). In McWilliam's work, the construct was developed from a group measure to an individual measure, so codes were devised to record the extent and depth of one child's behavior at a time (McWilliam & Ware, 1994). This marked an important change in how engagement was operationally defined, including how different levels of sophistication of engagement were categorized.

### Children's Levels of Engagement

Because some of the nine categories of engagement occur infrequently, we often collapse them into five:

1. Sophisticated (persistence, symbolic, encoded, constructive)

2. Attentional

3. Differentiated

4. Unsophisticated (casual attention, undifferentiated)

5. Nonengagement

Across five American studies (Casey, McWilliam, & Sims, 2012; de Kruif & McWilliam, 1999; McWilliam et al., 2003; Raspa et al., 2001; Ridley, McWilliam, & Oates, 2000), we saw that young children spend time as follows:

1. Differentiated engagement (about 30%–50% of the time)

2. Attentional engagement (about 30%)

3. Sophisticated engagement (about 10%)

4. Undifferentiated engagement (less than 10%)

5. Nonengagement (less than 10%)

Using the same coding scheme used in most of those studies, however, Portuguese research showed a slightly different order: 1) differentiated engagement, 2) focused attention (attentional engagement), 3) nonengagement, 4) unsophisticated (undifferentiated) engagement, and 5) sophisticated engagement. Other studies have shown Portuguese child care environments to be of poor quality (Pessanha, Aguiar, & Bairrao, 2007), which might explain this difference. In a recent Portuguese study of toddler engagement in child care classrooms and mother–child dyadic play, we found that sophisticated engagement, but not nonengagement, was consistent across both settings (Aguiar & McWilliam, 2013). Chronological age primarily accounted for this consistency, because older toddlers were more engaged in sophisticated behavior than younger toddlers, and they were also more likely to show consistency across settings. It is useful to know that nonengagement is probably more context dependent than sophisticated engagement. In other words, poor environments can have a deleterious effect on engagement even in children who, in better environments, are more engaged.

### Variations Across Activities

The percentage of children engaged has been found to vary by a Routine-by-Classroom Program interaction (McWilliam et al., 1985). ("Routine" in this context refers to the classroom activity.) During group activities and free play, programs focused on engagement and play achieved a greater percentage of children engaged than programs focused on one-on-one task completion, and no interaction effects were found for circle time and meals. In another preschool classroom study, active engagement with adults was associated with the physical environment (negatively), the curriculum, the method of instruction, the number of children (negatively), the child–adult ratio (negatively), and child age (negatively) (Dunst, McWilliam, & Holbert, 1986). Active engagement with peers was associated with inclusion, the physical environment, the number of children, and the degree of child impairment (negatively). Active engagement with materials was associated with parent involvement, staffing patterns, scheduling, the method of instruction, the number of adults (negatively), and the degree of child impairment (negatively). These two studies, which measured engagement differently, suggested that context was important in explaining differences in engagement.

Observational research on engagement has been conducted in classrooms because of the challenges of observing in homes. Because engagement varies by routines within the classroom, we surmise that it also varies by home routines. This assumption has been borne out, anecdotally, from hundreds of interviews about home routines (McWilliam et al., 2009).

### Variations by Disability Classification and Age

A methodological study of a detailed observational coding system revealed that eight observations were needed to obtain stable engagement data (McWilliam & Ware, 1994). Some engagement categories were more dependable than others; the most dependable ones were undifferentiated and encoded. Using this type of coding, we found differences in scores between children with and without disabilities (McWilliam & Bailey, 1995). Compared to children without disabilities, children with disabilities spent less time interactively engaged with adults, attentionally engaged with peers, and engaged with materials at mastery level. Mixed-age classrooms produced less attentional engagement (a low level of engagement) when adults were involved, but same-age classrooms produced, in children with disabilities, less attentional engagement with adults.

### Developmental Age, Global Engagement, and Observed Child Engagement

de Kruif and McWilliam (1999) examined multivariate relationships among developmental age, global engagement, and observed child engagement. Global engagement was measured with a rating scale, assessing the trait dimension of engagement. Observed child engagement was measured using the microcoding system discussed earlier. One canonical function showed a relationship between children's developmental age and high levels of engagement. A second function represented the bivariate relationship between high levels of engagement, regardless of developmental age.

In a study of group engagement, with repeated measures of the percentage of children participating in child care classrooms, we found that engagement levels were associated with independent measures of program quality. From this study, we saw that environmental rating scales, our Teaching Styles Rating Scale (de Kruif, McWilliam, Ridley, & Wakely, 2000), and another interaction scale were moderately associated with group engagement. The ratio, group size, level of teacher's formal education, and years of experience did not make much of a difference.

### Variations Due to Child Care Environment and Interactions With Adults

When researchers microcode individual children's engagement, rather than examining group engagement, the extent of time spent in *unsophisticated engagement* appears to be especially susceptible to the child care environment's quality (Raspa et al., 2001). Another important finding is that affect, as measured on the Teaching Styles Rating Scale, was the strongest predictor of unsophisticated engagement. The association is a negative one: The more "warm and fuzzy" teachers are, the less time young children are likely to spend in repetitive behavior.

We have used engagement to study the value of different adult interactions. We found, for example, that elaborations and information giving were associated with participatory engagement (i.e., differentiated behavior), attention, and low engagement (negatively), whereas 1) interactions that were responsive but did not provide direction and 2) nonresponsive, directive interactions were not associated with engagement (McWilliam et al., 2003). In this study, neither chronological age nor developmental age predicted engagement.

All levels of engagement—especially the highest and lowest levels, sophisticated engagement and nonengagement—can be predicted by teachers' use of incidental teaching, the developmental quotient of the child, and the extent of the child's peer interactions. This finding shows us that if we care about children's engagement, we should ensure children receive incidental teaching, which was the method measured, and opportunities for interactions with other children. But, the child's developmental level also plays a role.

In Portugal, where engagement has been studied with good rigor for over 10 years, we found that sophisticated engagement was consistent across two settings: toddler child care classrooms and mother–child dyadic play (Aguiar & McWilliam, 2013). The primary predictor of this consistency was chronological age. This finding argues for the fact that, as children get older, if they are prone to sophisticated engagement in one setting, they are likely to transfer that behavior pattern to another setting. The study also confirmed that dyadic play was more engaging than center-based child care.

These studies have provided a strong basis for focusing on engagement as an outcome of our work and, therefore, as a worthwhile object of measure.

## The Engagement–Participation Link

In many respects, engagement is synonymous with participation. At face value, if a child is engaged during a routine, he or she is participating in an activity that occurs in that routine. For example, a child pointing to pictures in a book (showing engagement) during a parent's bedtime reading is participating in that routine. Nevertheless, some distinctions have appeared between the two concepts in other settings, such as the workplace (Billett, 2002). Generally, people consider participation to be a less involved behavior than engagement.

One of the leading researchers in participation of children with disabilities has been Lena Almqvist. She has considered this construct as a measure of the extent of children's involvement in, for example, school activities (Almqvist & Granlund, 2005). A study of young children's perceptions of health (Almqvist, Hellnäs, Stefansson, & Granlund, 2006) revealed participation's overlap with engagement. This study showed that young children perceive health as a multidimensional construct, largely related to being engaged, which was defined as the ability to perform wanted activities and to participate in a supportive everyday context.

As will be discussed in this chapter's "Functioning and Participation" section, the *International Classification of Functioning, Disability and Health: Children and Youth Version (ICF-CY)* from the World Health Organization (WHO; 2007) has been important in bringing the participation construct to the forefront. In an analysis of the ICF-CY as a tool in early childhood intervention, the investigators concluded that guidelines for defining activity and participation as separate constructs are needed (Björck-Åkesson et al., 2010).

In McWilliam's work, participation is the condition that allows a child to be meaningfully engaged. If a child is engaged, by definition, he or she is participating. But if a child is participating only to the extent that he or she is present, he or she might not be engaged.

## Predictors of Engagement

Different factors affect the amount of time a child spends in appropriate or even sophisticated behavior. These factors can be grouped into three categories:

1. The physical environment

2. The social environment

3. Intra-individual characteristics (i.e., demographic and behavioral features belonging to the child him- or herself)

*Physical Environment*　　The physical environment includes features such as the availability of objects to manipulate, space to move around, and objects and places that interest the child. In addition, some aspects of the physical environment might need to be adjusted so the child has access to that environment—for example, no stairs if the child has mobility problems, augmented handles if the child has fine motor problems, high-contrast colors if the child has low vision, and so on. Put simply, children who spend much time in boring, dark, vacant environments are likely to be less engaged.

Some people fear that overstimulation with colors, light, and many objects might negatively affect engagement. This assumption has been insufficiently tested. For example, from an engagement theory perspective, putting children with autism spectrum disorder (ASD) in distraction-free spaces might be ethically problematic. Elsewhere, we discuss how distractibility could be considered alternative engagement (i.e., the child is more engaged by one thing than another). Is requiring the child to attend to the adult or adult-presented task more important than 1) allowing the child to choose what to do, within limits, and 2) teaching the child to function in a world full of distractions?

On the other hand, the Reggio Emilia guidelines for arranging the environment make a compelling case for increasing engagement. They include natural or incandescent light and objects in natural, muted colors (e.g., unpainted wooden toys versus garishly colored plastic toys). To people used to bright rooms with primary colors everywhere, Reggio rooms can seem dim and boring. However, in the context of "provocations" (objects intended to provoke a child's interest) and other features of the Reggio approach, these rooms promote curiosity, exploration, and both independent and interdependent play (i.e., engagement) (Hewett, 2001). Reggio features include working on long-term group projects, treating the children as little scientists, and promoting children's self-expression through art.

### Social Environment

Two aspects of the social environment affect engagement: the kinds of people the child spends time with and adults' behavior. We know, for example, that children with disabilities are more engaged when they are in mixed-age classrooms than in same-age classrooms (McWilliam & Bailey, 1995). However, we have also seen consistency in a child's level of engagement between the home and classroom (Aguiar & McWilliam, 2013), where the people the child is around are obviously different. Responsive interaction behaviors from adults promote children's engagement. In contrast, when adults engage in directive interaction behaviors that interrupt children's engagement, this reduces engagement—almost by definition. Furthermore, as mentioned already, a warm affect promotes engagement more than does a cold affect.

### Intra-individual Factors

The intra-individual factors that influence engagement can be grouped into those we have studied and those we haven't. The studied predictors are disability status, age, and personality; typical development, older age, and more zestful personality are predictors of higher engagement (de Kruif & McWilliam, 1999). We haven't yet studied variables considered executive functions, such as problem solving, modifying behavior in the light of new information, generating strategies, or sequencing complex actions (Elliott, 2003). We suspect all these predictors to be part of the sequence in which engagement is pivotal to functioning and learning, as shown in Figure 2.2.

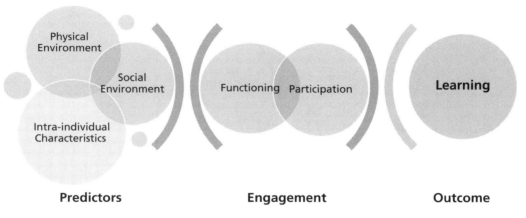

**Figure 2.2.** Predictors of engagement and outcome.

## Engagement as a Prerequisite to Learning

The level and extent of engagement are likely important for learning. That is, the amount of time a child is interacting appropriately with adults, peers, or materials is important. But so is the sophistication of those interactions. Presumably, a child who spends time in encoded, constructive, persistent, and symbolic behavior is more likely to learn than a child who spends time in repetitive behavior or casual attention. (Review Table 2.1 for levels of engagement.)

## Incorporating Independence and Social Relationships

The MEISR is a list of engagement, independence, and social relationships skills, which sounds as though these three domains might be mutually exclusive. As with most domains in child development, however, they are not. In fact, all independence and social relationship behaviors are also engagement behaviors, and independence and social relationships overlap, as shown in Figure 2.3. For example, a child who is trying to get her mother's attention by tugging on her mother's pants and saying, "Mama, Mama" is 1) engaged, 2) using independence in getting her mother's attention, and 3) using language (social relationships). For simplicity, however, each MEISR item is classified as demonstrating engagement, independence, or social relationships.

The extent of a child's engagement is important for his or her learning, and adults can modify the social and physical environments to influence the child's engagement, even though intra-individual characteristics, such as disabilities, also affect engagement. Engagement is conceptually linked to the notion that participation in home, school, and community is a key aspect of a child's functioning. Children who participate appropriately and fully in the routines for these settings are considered to be functioning well. Low levels of engagement indicate a need for intervention. At all times, responsible and caring adults aim for the most engagement possible, because this is not only good for children's learning, but also the best way for children to spend time.

This moral statement is best understood by considering the counterfactual: Who wants children to spend time nonengaged? In deciding whether a behavior is "engaged" or "nonengaged," or shows a "high level" or "low level" of engagement, we use this guiding question: *Would you want to see the child spending more time doing this?* If the answer is yes, the behavior is "engaged"; if the answer is no, it is "nonengaged." This guidance recognizes the part of the definition that is about appropriateness—in that adults generally want children to spend more time showing appropriate behavior and less time showing inappropriate behavior.

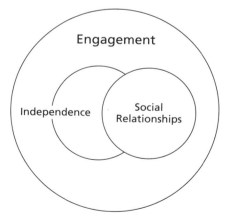

**Figure 2.3.** As shown in this figure, independence and social relationship behaviors are also engagement behaviors, and independence and social relationships overlap.

So, saying that engagement is the best way for children to spend time acknowledges two things: the learning opportunity that exists when a child is engaged and the appropriateness of the behavior.

Why is the "most engaged" time the "best" time, though? If adults were to foster engagement first and foremost, they would respect children's interests and would be less concerned with their productivity—that is, their doing things that adults have determined are important. They would see that, if a child is absorbed in something, the learning opportunity is there—especially if an adult uses it as a teaching opportunity. Children without disabilities are more likely to learn from engagement that isn't paired with a more competent person's involvement, following Vygotsky's (1978) notion of the zone of proximal development. Families with children without disabilities can provide their children many chances to experiment with opportunities that crop up in routines, and most parents do teach children in routines. In engagement theory, families with children with disabilities might need to be more mindful of their role in making routines into learning opportunities.

## FUNCTIONING AND PARTICIPATION

The MEISR assesses the extent to which children participate in their everyday routines, which is an assessment of "functioning." This is consistent with the WHO's concept of activities and participation, which are basic markers for functioning by people with disabilities.

### *The International Classification of Functioning, Disability and Health for Children and Youth*

The WHO developed the International Classification of Functioning, Disability and Health (ICF) as part of a family of international classifications constituting a framework for coding information about health; a derived classification of the ICF is the ICF-CY. Figure 2.4 shows the components of this framework.

### Why a Profile of Function Has Value

The reductionist approach to assessment, in which one score—sometimes one score per domain—is all anyone is interested in, does a disservice to *needs* assessment. When assessment is needed for determining eligibility or for research, perhaps a score is sufficient. But, for program planning and even for meaningful progress monitoring, reducing assessment to one or more scores is insufficient. A functional profile is necessary.

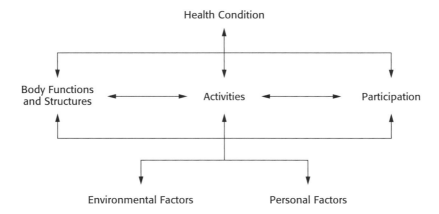

**Figure 2.4.** Components of the International Classification of Functioning, Disability and Health (ICF) framework. (Adapted from *Towards a common language for functioning, disability, and health: ICF.* WHO/EIP/GPE/CAS/01.3. World Health Organization. "The Model of ICF," Page 9, Copyright 2002.)

And yet the functional profile can't be so complicated that professionals and families can't use it for the purposes intended. It has to reveal areas needing intervention, and they have to show how intervention has improved the person's functioning in home, school, and community. The MEISR provides a structure for showing what a child does and doesn't do in routines and for showing change in the child's functioning, in home routines, over time. Therefore, it can help in families' decision making about intervention goals and in professionals' monitoring of the child's progress.

## ROUTINES

Theorists have identified how routines (everyday activities or events) are important, as shown in Table 2.2.

### What Are Routines?

Routines have been described as everyday activities, but the word also has other meanings, so professionals must be clear about what they mean—or avoid the word altogether—when speaking to families. According to one older theoretical perspective about routines, these behaviors might "protect the health and well-being of family members by providing stability and continuity during periods of stressful change" (Boyce, Jensen, James, & Peacock, 1983, p. 193). Here, family routines were predictable events in the daily life of a family. Many families, however, have routines of the sort we mean but without a high level of predictability or rote sameness; their everyday events do not occur in a predictable sequence or similarly from one day to the next. Nevertheless, we would still say the family had *routines*. In every family, people wake up, eat, change diapers, hang out, sleep, bathe, go outside, and so on. It is therefore impossible to say that a family has no routines.

### Settings, Events, and Activities

Some researchers have grouped family rituals and routines, although they differ (Fiese et al., 2002). Fiese et al. describe rituals as the established forms for a ceremony, ritual observances, ceremonial acts, or acts regularly repeated in a set precise manner, whereas routines are chunks of the day that happen every day or frequently and that might not be done the same way—depending on the family: Some families' routines are highly ritualized; others not so much. Some rituals, surely, such as praying before meals, are also routines. Rituals and routines have been correlated with parenting competence, child adjustment, and marital satisfaction (Fiese et al., 2002).

Dunst and colleagues (2006) showed that using everyday activities as sources of children's learning opportunities was associated with positive benefits, whereas professionals

**Table 2.2.** Theorists, theories, and relationships to routines

| Theorist | Theory | Relationship to Routines |
|---|---|---|
| Weisner, Matheson, Coots, and Bernheimer (2005) | Ecocultural niches | Routines are the contexts in which child and family development is played out. |
| Bronfenbrenner (1986) | Ecological framework | The family environment is a developmental "system" affecting the child and affected by more external systems, such as the neighborhood. |
| Horwitz, Chamberlain, Landsverk, and Mullican (2010) | Ecobehavioral model | Parenting stems from parent and family factors, parent–child interactions, and other external factors. |
| Dunst and Bruder (1999) | Learning opportunities framework | Families' naturally occurring activity settings provide situations for child functioning and teaching by adults. |

implementing their interventions in everyday activities showed little or no positive benefits. Earlier, these researchers had determined that family and community life each included 11 categories of learning opportunities (see family activities listed in Table 2.3). Some of the activities, such as child's bath time, toileting/going to the bathroom, and meal time, are what we would consider routines. Others are activities within routines, such as reading/looking at books, watching TV/videos, and saying grace at meals. Still others—although not very many—are skills, such as brushing teeth, dancing/singing, and cleaning up room. Some of the categories are for children 3 years of age and older, such as sports and recreational activities. Some community activities are found in some cultures and not in others, such as going shopping at the mall, participating in child play groups, and playing arcade games. This restriction makes it likely that some activities common in other cultures might be missing, such as playing in the street, carrying water from the well, and hanging out at a family member's workplace. The value of these lists might perhaps be to point out that 1) everyday life is the crucible in which young children learn and 2) families already have many resources they are using to teach children. Rather than working with children in these activities, professionals should support what adult family members do in these activities. This support should consist of providing families with emotional support, including encouragement; material support, if necessary (e.g., adaptive equipment); and informational support (how best to use these existing learning opportunities) (McWilliam & Scott, 2001).

Three reasons a routines-based approach to early intervention is helpful are as follows:

1. Families understand routines.
2. Context is everything.
3. Interventions can be blended within routines.

When families talk about their children's functioning, it is relatively easy for them to do so when describing examples from daily life. For example, a parent trying to present a picture of a child's use of language might say, "He sometimes puts words together. Like at meals, he'll say,

**Table 2.3.** Categories of learning opportunities

| Category/Activities | | |
|---|---|---|
| *Family Routines*<br>Doing household chores<br>Cooking/preparing meals<br>Caring for pets/animals<br>Doing errands<br>Shopping for food | *Literacy Activities*<br>Reading/looking at books<br>Telling child stories<br>Adult/child play times<br>Taking walks/strolls<br>Reading bedtime stories<br>People coming/going<br>(hellos/good-byes)<br>Cuddling with child | *Family Rituals*<br>Having family talks<br>Saying grace at meals<br>Reading religious/spiritual texts<br>Praying<br>Holding family meetings |
| *Parenting Routines*<br>Child's bath time<br>Child's bedtime/nap time<br>Child's wake-up times<br>Meal time<br>Fixing/cutting child's hair | *Physical Play*<br>Riding bike/wagon<br>Playing ball games<br>Playing in water/swimming<br>Roughhousing | *Family Celebrations*<br>Holiday dinners<br>Family members' birthdays<br>Decorating home (holidays)<br><br>*Socialization Activities*<br>Family gatherings<br>Picnics |
| *Child Routines*<br>Brushing teeth<br>Washing hands/face<br>Cleaning up room<br>Picking up toys<br>Toileting/going to bathroom<br>Dressing/undressing | *Play Activities*<br>Doing art activities/drawing<br>Playing board games<br>Playing video games<br><br>*Entertainment Activities*<br>Dancing/singing<br>Listening to music<br>Watching TV/videos<br>Playing alone | Playdates with friends<br>Visits to neighbors<br>Sleepovers<br><br>*Gardening Activities*<br>Doing yard work<br>Planting trees/flowers<br>Growing vegetable garden |

*Source:* Dunst, Bruder, Trivette, and Hamby (2006).

'More please.' Or, when we're hanging out in the den and the TV is on, he'll say 'Want Arthur.'" Parents can visualize (picture) their children in different contexts, at different times of the day. Routines are meaningful to families, unlike the esoteric methods professionals have for grouping skills, such as developmental domains.

Children's successful functioning largely occurs when there is a good fit between 1) the demands of a routine and 2) the child's abilities and interests. For example, a child's ability to sit independently, in and of itself, is relatively nonfunctional. It does have physiognomic benefits, such as helping the child breathe. However, the functional uses of sitting independently include looking at one's surroundings, being able to wash oneself in a bathtub, and being able to sit in a chair with less restriction than a high chair. To understand child functioning, therefore, we need to determine the demands in the child's everyday life and how well the child meets those demands. Because adults adjust the demands of routines, as in helping a child, teaching a child often means gradually changing the demands of the routine (i.e., reducing the amount of help we give). For example, when a child is playing with glue and glitter, at first, we carefully control how much glue and glitter is available. We possibly do the gluing ourselves and let the child pick up small amounts of glitter. We're teaching the child how to sprinkle glitter on glue; we're not yet teaching how to make designs with the glue. Over time, the child gets less help, more access, and more independence. That is, the demands of the routine shift with the child's changing skill level. Regardless, when we're supporting the family, we're talking about arts and crafts time, if that's a routine for the family or the child care program. We're not simply talking about fine motor skills and problem solving; we're talking about them in the context of the child's handling glue and glitter during arts and crafts time. This is a way of discussing the child's functioning in which families can participate.

Routines are also helpful because, within a single routine, the child might need a number of different skills. In traditional, domain- and discipline-specific early intervention, a speech-language pathologist might work with the family (or, heaven forbid, the child alone) on the child's ability to say words that begin with a /d/ sound. In separate sessions, an occupational therapist is working on the child's ability to grasp and release small objects. And in yet other sessions, the physical therapist is working on the child's ability to squat to retrieve objects from the floor. Each of these specialists is working on the skill identified as deficient in his or her evaluations.

First, let's assume that these skills are meaningful, which is a big assumption if they came from a typical, discipline-specific, decontextualized checklist or conventional test. What if we discovered that, at hanging-out time after dinner or supper, the following things are true:

1. The child plays with *Daddy*, with *dinosaurs* and a stuffed *doggie*, but he cannot pronounce the /d/ at the beginning of each of these words.

2. The child has difficulty handling his small dinosaurs.

3. When he drops a dinosaur on the floor, he struggles to retrieve it.

It would be very helpful for the child and his family to work on enunciating initial /d/ sounds, grasping and releasing, and squatting during hanging-out time. In fact, the child might not even know they are *working on* these skills. For him, it is just part of the routine.

This approach is no injection therapy. Injection therapy is when a professional detects a deficit and looks for routines in which to address it. In this example, the needs were there at hanging-out time. This makes the family's addressing the needs in this routine functional. If there had been no mismatch between the demands of the routine and the child's abilities and interests, it would be wrong to take so-called deficits and start working on them during this routine. First, it might ruin a perfectly good routine for the family. Second, the need would be artificial, not organic. When needs are created to provide intervention opportunities, the family's likelihood of persisting with the so-called intervention is diminished.

However, if the need is really there, the family is motivated to work on it: They recognize its authenticity.

Routines are therefore helpful because they make sense to families, they contain the stimuli around the behavior, and they accommodate working on more than one skill at a time. This rationale has been presented in *Routines-Based Early Intervention* (McWilliam, 2010), so now we discuss the relationship of the MEISR to that book and the RBM.

### *ROUTINES-BASED EARLY INTERVENTION* AND THE ROUTINES-BASED MODEL

*Routines-Based Early Intervention* (McWilliam, 2010) describes a model for providing early intervention in natural environments to promote engagement, independence, and social relationships (EISR) in children and to promote family quality of life. (As discussed earlier, this model, originally known as Routines-Based Early Intervention [RBEI], is now called the Routines-Based Model [RBM].) The MEISR is therefore helpful as an outcome measure, but it also is consistent with the Routines-Based Interview (RBI), one of the five components of the model. The RBI interviewer asks about EISR in all routines, which means the MEISR can be used to help ask those questions. (Chapter 3 explains in detail how to conduct the RBI.) In the sections that follow, we discuss how to use the MEISR to measure and document a child's progress within the RBM and examine the MEISR's relationship to the five RBM components.

### Documentation of Child Progress

The MEISR provides the most salient method for measuring child progress for professionals using the RBM approach, because the three child constructs—engagement, independence, and social relationships—are central to the RBM. At present, the MEISR is limited to home routines, whereas the RBEI also addresses collaborative consultation to child care. The RBEI component most aligned with the MEISR is the RBI. Both the RBI and the MEISR are methods for assessing child functioning, particularly needs, in the context of routines.

The MEISR has many uses, which are discussed further in Chapters 4 and 5. In line with the RBM, the MEISR can be used as a tool for helping conduct an RBI. It provides a list of common activities in which very young children are engaged in routines. If interviewers are unsure what to ask during the discussion of routines, the MEISR can give them sample questions. Chapter 3 provides more information about how the MEISR can help with the RBI.

### Relationship to Each of Five RBM Components

The five components of the RBM are as follows:

1. Understanding the family ecology

2. Developing a functional, family-centered plan

3. Integration of services

4. Support-based home visits

5. Collaborative consultation to children's classrooms

The MEISR's relationship to each component is explained below.

***Family Ecology***    The ecomap is the principal method for understanding the family ecology. It consists of a picture of 1) the people living in the home with the child, 2) the informal supports (e.g., friends, extended family, neighbors), 3) intermediate supports (e.g., work, religious supports), and 4) formal supports (e.g., professionals and agencies working with the family). The MEISR provides a picture of what goes on inside of the home (of the parent providing the information).

***A Functional, Family-Centered Plan***     The RBI is the true canvas for this picture, and the MEISR is similar to the RBI. The main differences, other than the fact that the MEISR is a rating scale and the RBI is an interview, are as follows:

1. The MEISR specifies routines, whereas the family identifies its routines in the RBI.

2. The child skills within routines are selected in the MEISR, whereas in the RBI, the parent (or other caregiver) describes skills, and the interviewer asks about skills that seem relevant, based on his or her knowledge of child development.

3. Most important, the MEISR does not produce family outcomes, whereas the RBI does.

***Integration of Services***     The connection between the MEISR and integration of services is that the MEISR creates a discipline-free platform on which to assess functioning. In American early intervention for infants and toddlers, assessment must be conducted in five domains: cognitive, communication, motor, social, and adaptive. These are too closely linked to professional disciplines. In particular, gross motor is linked to physical therapy, fine motor to occupational therapy, and communication to speech-language "pathology" (or SLP, as it's known in the United States). One indicator that professionals assume needs fall into discipline buckets is that some speak of "PT outcomes," "OT outcomes," and "speech outcomes"—or even worse "SLP outcomes." Items on the MEISR are coded by the five IDEA Part C (PL 108-446) domains mentioned earlier in this paragraph, but the tool is organized strictly by routines, thus encouraging a functional, family-centered way of assessing child functioning, rather than a discipline- or domain-based way.

***Support-Based Home Visits***     The MEISR is not designed to guide home visiting, but its inclusion in a program's process reinforces the notion that home visit discussions with families should place child outcomes in context, and context is routines. In other words, if everything you do—from needs assessment, through providing supports, to progress monitoring—is organized functionally, professionals and families are likely to stay focused.

***Collaborative Consultation to Children's Classrooms***     At this time, the MEISR is limited to home routines. A classroom version, the ClaMEISR™, exists for children age 3 to 5 years, but the usefulness of the MEISR for influencing our work in group care is limited. Some of the routines in the MEISR, however, such as play with others and meals (although rated in the context of the home), have parallels in the classroom. Early interventionists can ask about some of the same skills in the classroom setting.

 The MEISR therefore is really a part of the RBM. McWilliam developed them both, and the MEISR emerged from the need to provide a noninterview method of assessing skills occurring in home routines. As this section demonstrates, it dovetails with the original five components of the model. With that said, the MEISR also has valuable uses outside of the richness of the RBM approach, which are detailed in Chapter 4

## USING THE MEISR WITH OTHER TOOLS

The MEISR can be used with the ICF-CY (WHO, 2007), and with early learning standards, as described in the following sections.

### International Classification of Functioning

How valid is the MEISR, and what is its place in global and U.S. movements in the fields of disability and early childhood? In the disability field, across the world, professionals are now focusing on function rather than deficits in body structures, including the brain, as we have mentioned earlier. In particular, the WHO's (2007) ICF-CY has been adopted in many countries, sometimes as a required framework. In Portugal, for example, every child in early intervention (for children birth–6 years of age) must have an ICF profile.

The ICF is organized in two parts: 1) functioning and disability and 2) contextual factors. The first part, functioning and disability, consists of the body (body systems, body structures) and activities and participation (see Figure 2.4). Contextual factors consist of environmental factors (from immediate environment to general environment) and personal factors (although these are not classified in the ICF). This overview of the ICF shows the importance of *functioning* and the fact that the disability alone, if it exists, does not impair functioning. Furthermore, functioning is what happens in life—in activities and situations the person can participate in—not in artificial, service delivery, or clinical situations. How supportive and accessible the environment is has an impact on functioning. This environment can include family life, the home, the neighborhood, the community, child care or preschool, governmental policies, and societal attitudes and behaviors.

We were curious, therefore, to see how the MEISR matched up with the ICF. Conceptually, we could see the relationship, as shown in Figure 2.5. Our notion of goodness of fit is described as the interaction of 1) the demands of the routine with 2) the abilities and interests of the child. When those two dimensions match, we have good functioning. When they don't, we have poor functioning. We equate the demands of the routine to environmental factors, as shown in Figure 2.5. We equate child abilities to body functions and structures. We equate child interests to personal factors. Finally, we equate engagement, including independence and social relationships, to participation in activities. The interactions among these elements of the ICF with elements of the RBM show how the RBM has a functional framework consistent with that of the WHO. Because the MEISR is the child progress tool in the RBM, we crosswalked MEISR items with the classification system, as described in the next section.

### Crosswalking the MEISR and the ICF-CY
Because of the apparent congruence of the MEISR and the ICF, we crosswalked the two instruments. In the ICF literature, "crosswalking" is known as "linking." For each MEISR item, we found the most similar and specific ICF-CY "category" (i.e., code). ICF categories are organized under an alphanumeric system in which the letters stand for the different components: *b* for body functions, *s* for body structures, *d* for

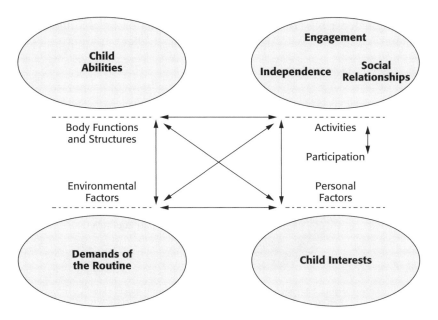

**Figure 2.5.** Congruence of the International Classification of Functioning, Disability and Health (ICF) and the MEISR and interactions among their components.

activities and participation, and *e* for environmental factors. These letters are followed by a numeric code corresponding to the chapter number (e.g., d7 for interpersonal interactions and relationships), followed by a second level with two digits, and a third or fourth level with one digit each (e.g., d710 for basic interpersonal interactions, d7104 for social cues in relationships, and d71040 for initiating social interactions).

Most of the MEISR items were linked to the Activities and Participation level (96.8%). A few items were linked to the Body Functions level (2.9%), and very few were linked to the Environmental level (0.3%).

### *How the MEISR Can Help Complete an ICF-CY Functional Profile*

A functional profile is a brief written description that provides information about someone's functioning in his or her natural environment. To write the functional profile based on the ICF-CY with the MEISR assessment, one should follow these steps:

1.  **Complete the MEISR.** The MEISR was developed for the family to complete or to complete in collaboration with a professional. Another possibility, however, is for a professional to complete it, following the RBI (McWilliam, 2010). A functional profile does not require full completion of all MEISR items. The RBI produces enough information to allow for scoring of enough MEISR items for the purpose of then completing a functional profile. Figure 2.6 shows this progression. The aim is to capture the information in the outer ring—the child's actual functioning in routines. The RBI captures much of that information, and the MEISR provides a method of documenting that information about child functioning from the RBI. The MEISR ratings then can help complete the ICF-CY functional profile.

2.  **Assign the relevant qualifier for each ICF-CY category checked in the MEISR.** For each item checked in the MEISR, the professional notes the ICF-CY category crosswalked with that item and assigns the appropriate qualifier. The qualifier describes the extent of problems in the respective domain, ranging from 0 (NO problem) to 4 (COMPLETE problem). To make a decision about the qualifier, professionals use the expected starting age and their knowledge of child development, comparing what is expected in typical development with what the child being assessed does.

3.  **Write the functional profile.** Based on MEISR scores for items within routines, write a short profile describing the child's significant functioning characteristics and indicate, for each characteristic, the ICF-CY category and qualifier in parentheses.

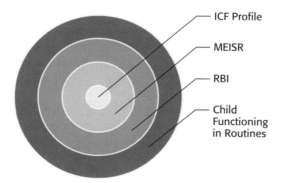

ICF Profile

MEISR

RBI

Child
Functioning
in Routines

**Figure 2.6.** Progression from child functioning, through needs assessment, to a functional profile. (*Key:* ICF, International Classification of Functioning; MEISR, Measure of Engagement, Independence, and Social Relationships; RBI, Routines-Based Interview.)

These three steps serve the triple purpose of conducting a functional assessment for intervention planning (RBI), acquiring information for progress monitoring and program evaluation (MEISR), and acquiring information for outcome measurement and classification (ICF-CY functional profile).

## Early Learning Standards

Early learning standards are documents listing expectations for what young children should know and be able to do. They were prompted by the passage of the Good Start, Grow Smart initiative in 2002, and as of 2014, all U.S. states and 4 U.S. territories had developed early learning standards for preschool children. Fifty-three of these states and territories have early learning standards for infants and toddlers (U.S. Department of Health and Human Services, 2014).

Research reviews from the early 2000s, such as "From Neurons to Neighborhoods: The Science of Early Childhood Development" (Shonkoff & Phillips, 2002) and *Eager to Learn: Educating Our Preschoolers* (Bowman, Donovan, & Burns, 2001), have contributed to the understanding of the importance of early education. Early learning standards were developed, to some extent, to define expectations for the knowledge, skills, and dispositions that parents and caregivers should seek to promote, so children can develop to their full potential. Furthermore, state administrators have used early learning standards as a tool to encourage high-quality programs. About half the statewide quality improvement rating systems (QRISs) for early childhood care refer to the state's early learning standards (Robbins, Smith, Stagman, & Kreader, 2012).

However, early learning standards do not come without risks. In 2002, the National Association for the Education of Young Children (NAEYC) and the National Association of Early Childhood Specialists in State Departments of Education (NAECS/SDE) issued a joint position statement that pointed out these risks and explored the essential features of developmentally effective early learning standards. Among the risks is the potential to label, retain, or deny services to children "failing" the standards, especially culturally and linguistically diverse children and children with disabilities (NAEYC & NAECS/SDE, 2002). NAEYC and NAECS/SDE addressed the need for tools to assess children's progress that 1) are clearly connected to important learning represented in the standards; 2) are technically, developmentally, and culturally valid; and 3) yield comprehensive, useful information.

### Tennessee Early Learning Developmental Standards
All states have early learning standards—the skills and knowledge the state expects early childhood programs to address. All the states' standards are quite similar. We took one state's standards, those of Tennessee, to determine what areas the MEISR addressed.

The *Tennessee Early Learning Developmental Standards: Birth–48 Months* (TN-ELDS), was revised in 2013 (Tennessee Department of Education, 2013). The TN-ELDS has 34 developmental categories operationalized into 60 standards, which in turn are organized into the following areas of development and learning:

- Approaches to learning (10 standards)
- Social-emotional development (9 standards)
- Language and early literacy (8 standards)
- Math (6 standards)
- Science (13 standards)

- Social studies (5 standards)

- Creative arts (6 standards)

- Physical development (3 standards)

Each standard is divided into four age groups (birth–12 months, 13 months–24 months, 25 months–36 months, and 37 months–48 months), and each age group has a description and examples of how a child might demonstrate that standard.

### Complementarity of the MEISR and TN-ELDS
The advantages of using the MEISR with the TN-ELDS are as follows. The MEISR is organized by routines, thereby making explicit how skills are functional. Having concrete observational skills sorted into functional areas is even more relevant for children with disabilities than for typically developing children. Finally, having the family complete, or at least be fully involved in its completion, the scale has all the advantages mentioned earlier.

### Crosswalking the MEISR and TN-ELDS
Each MEISR item was crosswalked with a TN-ELDS standard at three levels: the developmental category, the age group, and the number of the standard within the developmental category. The final exact agreement was 73% at the first level (when there was a disagreement at this level, interrater agreement at the next two levels was not calculated) with a mean kappa value of .67, 83% at the second level with a mean kappa of .73, and 82% at the third level with a mean kappa of .77.

All items from MEISR were crosswalked with at least one standard of the TN-ELDS. However, even though all TN-ELDS domains and strands were represented in the MEISR, only 57% of the TN-ELDS *standards* from 0 to 36 months matched MEISR items. Table 2.4 shows the number of TN-ELDS subdomains and the number of MEISR items crosswalked for each TN-ELDS domain.

The most frequently used TN-ELDS domains were strongly related to engagement, independence, and social relationships—obviously the core of the MEISR. The less frequently used TN-ELDS domains (less than 50%) are more specific to classroom routines, which can explain the results (for more information on this crosswalk, see Morales-Murillo, Garcia-Grau, Boavida, & McWilliam, 2017). The MEISR therefore captures much in the areas of physical development (100% of the subdomains), social-emotional development (81% of the subdomains), and approaches to learning (77%), but not so much in creative arts (22%), science (33%), or math (39%). Therefore, functional skills in home routines, as captured by the MEISR, are aligned with standards related to engagement (e.g., approaches to learning), independence (e.g., physical development), and social relationships (e.g., social-emotional development) but not so much with those related to preacademics.

**Table 2.4.** Number of TN-ELDS subdomains and of MEISR items for each domain

| TN-ELDS Domain | No. of Subdomains for Ages Birth–36 Months | No. of Subdomains Crosswalked | No. of MEISR Items Crosswalked |
|---|---|---|---|
| Creative arts | 18 | 4 | 4 |
| Science | 39 | 13 | 20 |
| Math | 18 | 7 | 12 |
| Language and early literacy | 24 | 14 | 86 |
| Social studies | 15 | 10 | 17 |
| Approaches to learning | 30 | 23 | 80 |
| Social-emotional development | 27 | 22 | 117 |
| Physical development | 9 | 9 | 111 |

Key: TN-ELDS, *Tennessee Early Learning Developmental Standards: Birth–48 Months.*

## Conclusion: MEISR, Functional Profiles, and Early Learning Standards

The crosswalking we conducted has shown the MEISR to be suitable for developing functional profiles and for addressing many areas of early childhood development. The ICF-CY has been painstakingly constructed with many experts from around the world (WHO, 2007), and the TN-ELDS reflects the early learning standards seen all across the United States (Robbins et al., 2012). The extent to which the MEISR is aligned with these frameworks shows its face validity.

## SUMMARY

In this chapter, we've presented the foundational framework of the MEISR and discussed how it aligns with the notable work of many researchers who have helped us understand how children learn. Embedded in this understanding is an acknowledgment of the powerful role family routines and activities play in children's learning. As children participate in day-to-day routines, they grow and learn. By understanding their individual levels of engagement, independence, and social relationships within the context of the family routines, we can partner with families to identify and enhance the natural learning opportunities that can help the child and family flourish. The MEISR, with its unique composition of functional abilities that are aligned with engagement, independence, and social relationships and organized around common family routines, provides a functional profile of children's abilities. It also fills an obvious void in the field of early intervention: that is, the need for a tool that is *not* organized by developmental domains (although it does provide a useful crosswalk of developmental domains). Rather, the MEISR provides a functional profile of children's routines-based functioning.

# CHAPTER 3

# The Routines-Based Interview

We described the purposes of assessment in Chapter 1 and made the case for an innovative method to determine a family's functional needs. Current standardized methods do not determine these needs. First, the field needs some method to identify functional goals or outcomes, otherwise known as target behaviors. One can think of the functionality of child outcomes as addressing participation or engagement needs, addressing independence needs, and addressing social relationship needs. Throughout this book, we stress the importance of these three domains. Second, family priorities need to be reflected in the IFSP. Third, outcomes should be broad enough to cover a variety of ways of displaying the target behavior yet narrow enough to know what is really being addressed. Fourth, the strategies or action steps should aim directly at the function problem. (Strategies should not be specified on initial IFSPs because strategies should be chosen by families and professionals together. On IFSP updates or annual reviews, they can be included, because the professional and the family will likely have talked about those strategies.) Strategies such as using oral-motor exercises might be employed to address an outcome related to eating and swallowing, but a more direct approach is to teach a child to chew and swallow. The rule is *teach first*. Fifth, the process for developing IFSPs needs to foster investment by caregivers other than the family, such as child care providers, in the outcomes. The RBI is a method that addresses these five needs. As such, the RBI is recommended (although not required) for professionals who are working with a family to complete the MEISR via interview (see Chapters 4 and 6).

This chapter discusses the RBI in depth: how it is used within two settings addressed by the RBM; what research supports the RBI; how routines are defined; and how the RBI is conducted, step by step. Recommended interview strategies and common professional concerns are addressed. Finally, the chapter discusses how the RBI can be implemented within intervention planning and where the MEISR fits into the process.

## CONFLUENCE OF TWO SETTINGS

The RBI is central to two settings addressed by the RBM: 1) home- and community-based service delivery and 2) managing inclusive classrooms. It was first described in *Family-Centered Intervention Planning: A Routines-Based Approach* (McWilliam, 1992), which was written primarily for helping classroom-based staff to be family friendly. The premise was that planning with families in a way that addressed families' true concerns for their children, both at home and in the classroom, would help overcome the barrier of not seeing families for as long a time each week and on their home turf, as happens in home visits. Many of the principles from the cooperatives where we tried out this and other practices evolved into the Individualizing Inclusion Model of classroom-based services (Wolery, 1997), which later became the

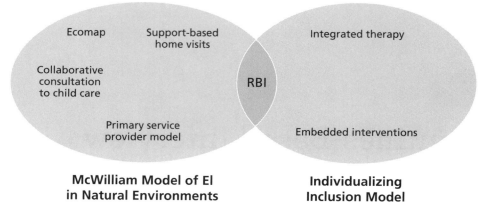

**Figure 3.1.** Confluence of two models: the McWilliam Model of Early Intervention (EI) in Natural Environments and the Individualizing Inclusion Model. (Reprinted from McWilliam, R. A. [2010]. *Routines-based early intervention: Supporting young children and their families* [p. 68]. Baltimore, MD: Paul. H. Brookes Publishing Co.)

Engagement Classroom Model (McWilliam & Casey, 2008). That model hinges on the RBI as an assessment of the ecological congruence between a child's abilities and the classroom environment. This assessment leads directly to the development of the IFSP or individualized education program (IEP). Once a list of functional behaviors is identified, all services are provided in the classroom to ensure teamwork between classroom staff and specialists such as speech-language pathologists, itinerant special educators, occupational therapists, and physical therapists. The specialists' responsibility is to make their intervention suggestions fit into classroom routines, and the teachers' responsibility is to embed those interventions into routines. These aspects of the RBI are illustrated in Figure 3.1. The model hinges on functional outcomes or goals, which come from the RBI.

By now, it is clear that the RBI is also central to the model of early intervention in homes and communities (e.g., child care, preschool). Again, the functionality of the child and family outcomes in situations where the family is receiving services in these natural environments makes the model of service delivery and the home and child care visits go more smoothly. In many ways, the RBI has proven to be a critical component within many other good features of early intervention services. Once you have functional child outcomes/goals (promoting engagement in routines) and family outcomes/goals, such as those generated through the RBI, the focus of services is clear. Professionals have 10 to 12 outcomes, enough that they do not need to supplement them, as they have done when they had only three (Jung & Baird, 2003). The nature of the visit also changes when you have RBI-generated outcomes/goals. Because the family chose these outcomes/goals, they are invested in them more than they are when professionals recommend them and families acquiesce. Furthermore, even the community caregivers, such as child care providers, are invested because the family considers their reports when deciding on outcomes/goals. A third influence the RBI has on services is the decision making about services. The RBI produces outcomes/goals related to engagement, independence, social relationships, and family needs. These domains do not belong to any discipline, yet all can contribute. The functionality and family-centeredness of the outcomes/goals make it more feasible to implement a PSP approach than a multidisciplinary approach.

## RESEARCH ON RBI

In the first study on the efficacy of using the RBI for IFSP development, 16 families were randomly assigned either to receive the RBI or to receive the business-as-usual IFSP development process (McWilliam et al., 2009). An RBI produced better outcomes than did the traditional approach to IFSP development. The families in the RBI group were more satisfied with the IFSP development process than were the families in the contrast group, and the contrast group had more variable responses. As expected, the number of outcomes was greater as a result of the RBI than as a result of the standard process. Finally, outcomes written as a result of the RBI were more functional than outcomes written as a result of the standard process.

In a study of a training program to improve IFSP/IEP goals and objectives through the RBI, 80 professionals received five face-to-face sessions and a follow-up session 3 months later (Boavida, Aguiar, & McWilliam, 2014). Quality ratings of goals and objectives increased by over three standard deviations. In research with 36 professionals who received training on the RBI, the quality of the outcomes/goals by the end of the study was correlated with the quality at the beginning of the study, the percentage of the professional's time allocated to working in early intervention as opposed to with older children, whether an RBI had been conducted (both at the beginning and the end of the study), and the quality of RBI at the end of the study (Boavida, Aguiar, McWilliam, & Correia, 2016). Functionality was not substantially related to prior training on the RBI, the professional's age, or the professional's experience. Goal quality scores were higher for those trained on the RBI than for those not trained.

We were interested in the psychometric properties of the RBI Implementation Checklist (Rasmussen & McWilliam, 2010), our measure of fidelity. (This has now been replaced by the RBI With Ecomap Checklist [McWilliam, 2016b].) We looked at the probability of correct responses on the items of 120 checklists, as a logistic function of the difference between the person and the item parameters (Boavida, Akers, McWilliam, & Jung, 2015). Rasch analysis indicated scores on the checklist were reliable. The RBI Checklist (With Ecomap) is provided in Appendix 3.1.

The RBI needs more research to match the extent to which it is used across the United States and around the world.

## CONDUCTING THE RBI

The previous chapter defined routines, which all families have. In the RBM, routines are not activities that the professional implements with the family. Instead, they are naturally occurring activities happening with some regularity, including caregiving events and simply hanging-out times. As reluctant as we might be to admit this, not everything happens in routines. Hence, at the beginning of the interview, we ask about major concerns first. In fact, conversations about routines do lead to many concerns beyond what happens in routines. Therefore, a routines-based interview is not as circumscribed as one might think. The interview has six stages, as shown in Figure 3.2. Some work happens before and after the interview.

### Preparation of Families and Staff

If the child spends more than about 12 hours a week in the care of someone other than the home caregivers (e.g., parents), the other caregiver (e.g., child care provider) should be included in the interview. It is ideal if this person can be present at the same meeting as the family. Often, however, outside caregivers and families are not free at the same time, in which case the second most ideal scenario is interviewing outside caregivers before the family. That allows the interviewer to convey what the outside caregiver has reported, so the family has all the information for making their decisions. In reality, however, because of the pressure of time to finish IFSP development, often the family is interviewed and we conduct the teacher (as an example of an outside caregiver) interview later. In that case, we still return to the parent with the teacher report, so the parent can change outcomes/goals.

In preparing for the interview, the main point to convey to families and classroom staff is to think about what routines (times of day, everyday events, and activities) they have and, in each one:

- What the expectations are
- What the child does
- How well that routine is working for the family or, for classroom routines, for the child

# RBI Outline

**I.  Beginning**
  a.  Who lives in the home with you and the child?
  b.  What are your main concerns?

**II.  Home Routines**
  a.  How does your day begin?
  b.  Start marking concerns with stars

  *In each routine . . .*
    1.  What is everyone else doing?
    2.  What does the child do?
    3.  Engagement (How well does the child participate in the activity? Stay involved?)
    4.  Independence
    5.  Social relationships (communication, getting along with others)
    6.  Rating 1–5 : How happy you are with this time of day? (*terrible* to *great*)
    7.  Transition to next routine: What happens next?

**III.  Classroom Routines**

  *In each routine . . .*
    1.  What is everyone else doing?
    2.  What does the child do?
    3.  Engagement (How well does the child participate in the activity? Stay involved?)
    4.  Independence
    5.  Social Relationships (communication, getting along with others)
    6.  Rating 1–5: How well does this activity work for the child?

**IV.  The Time, Worry, and Change Questions**
  a.  Do you have enough time for yourself or with another person?
  b.  When you lie awake at night worrying, what do you worry about?
  c.  If you could change anything about your life, what would it be?

**V.  Recap:** Review starred items (concerns). *This is just a reminder; it is not the list of outcomes/goals*

**VI.  Outcome/Goal Selection**
  a.  New sheet of paper: What would you like to work on—to have us help you with?
  b.  If necessary to get to minimum 8 outcomes/goals, hand notes to the family, showing them the starred items as a reminder.
  c.  If necessary, take back the notes and ask about starred items.
  d.  Once 10–12 outcomes/goals, ideally, are listed, ask for the priority order in terms of importance.

**Figure 3.2.**  Routines-Based Interview (RBI) outline. (Created by R. A. McWilliam, 2009.)

The Family Preparation Form (Harbin, 2005; McWilliam, 1992) is available in *Routines-Based Early Intervention* (McWilliam, 2010) to help families get ready for the interview. However, the form is not necessary.

The other preparation points are logistical: where, when, who, and so on. Families should be warned that the RBI lasts for 2 hours and that it is quite an intense conversation, so it works best if there are few distractions. This could include having someone else watch the child, if that is convenient for the family. This request is not made callously; the RBI is done only every 6 months and is quite different from a regular home visit. Some interviewers are self-conscious about making this request, but families appreciate being warned more than being surprised. Of course, some families are not able to arrange child care, which is fine.

## The Interview

The interview typically takes place in the family's home but can take place anywhere. It is easiest conducted at a table, such as a kitchen table, so the interviewer or notetaker has somewhere to place the pad of paper. Some interviewers and notetakers use computers, but not everyone finds them helpful when sharing notes with the family at the end.

The RBI can be done solo or with a notetaker. We typically train people with a notetaker because the interviewer has to think quickly and taking notes and coming up with good questions can be overwhelming until the interviewer is experienced. We recognize, however, that many interviewers will need to conduct RBIs solo. After they have had the help of a notetaker, they will need to practice interviewing and keeping notes. Readers can see numerous examples of solo interviewing on YouTube: Search for RBI McWilliam.

*Beginning*     The RBI may involve use of an ecomap. An ecomap is a picture of the family's informal, formal, and intermediate supports (Ray & Street, 2005). If an ecomap was developed before the RBI, the interviewer will know who lives in the home, which is relevant in the RBI. The interviewer will also know why the child is in early intervention, although that information can also come from other sources, such as the referral document and the evaluation report.

An important question to ask at the beginning is "What are your main concerns?" We need to know this, although some families enter early intervention with concerns and others enter because other people (e.g., doctors, child care providers) are concerned.

Traditionally, professionals asked about main concerns and then developed outcomes/goals to match those concerns. When families, understandably, had no idea about the level of detail they could invoke, they would often make general statements, perhaps related to walking and talking. Professionals, in good faith, would write down these two or three main concerns and write outcomes/goals for them.

Unfortunately, these well-meaning efforts to meet families' priorities were done with a method that did not capture families' true priorities, wishes, and aspirations for their child. We know this because, in the RBI, we ask families what their main concerns are. We then listen to the family for a further 2 hours and ask them what they want to work on. The list of goals at the end of the interview is much more specific than the initial main concerns. The child skills are more functional, and the family outcomes/goals are clear.

*Home Routines*     By asking the parent how his or her day begins, we introduce the idea that this interview is not only about the child—that we're interested in the primary caregiver and in other members of the family. Once we get into the routines of the day, typically waking up time, diaper change time, breakfast time, and so on, we get at six pieces of information, not necessarily in this order. First, we want to know what everyone else is doing and to understand how the routine goes and the help available to, or demands placed on, the primary caregiver at that time of day. Second, we want a description of the child's functioning in the routine—his or her engagement (third), independence (fourth), and social relationships (fifth).

We want details. Sixth, we want to know the family's satisfaction with this routine. The discussion of each routine takes 5 to 10 minutes. During this discussion, the notetaker places stars next to information that might be a concern for the family (e.g., the child is not doing something yet) or for the professionals (e.g., the parent seems to want more information on a topic). If all is going well in the routines, the professional asks the family what they would like the child to be doing 6 months hence that the child is not yet doing. Once the interview has enough information, often judged by whether sufficient stars have been marked, the next question is about the family's satisfaction with that time of day, on a scale of 1 to 5.

Once the parent has given that rating, the interviewer immediately asks what happens next. This allows the family to report routines in the order they happen in that family.

***Classroom Routines***    If the child attends a "classroom" program, the classroom caregiver, such as a teacher, is interviewed in much the same way. For each routine, the teacher is asked what everyone else does. The interviewer asks about the engagement, independence, and social relationships of the child. At the end, the question is different from satisfaction: The interviewer asks the teacher's opinion about the goodness of fit between the demands of the routine and the abilities and interests of the child.

We have discussed the timing of the classroom interview earlier. Sometimes it happens in the midst of the home interview, sometimes before, but most often, it happens afterward.

***The Time, Worry, and Change Questions***    Once all routines have been discussed or after an hour and a half has passed, the interviewer asks three important questions. These questions cannot be omitted for an interview conducted with fidelity, and they must be asked exactly as worded. Insistence on inclusion of the questions and the exact wording arose because some professionals, amazingly, were uncomfortable asking them. This led to the professionals' omitting the items or to their stumbling around them, making straightforward questions awkward. The questions, as seen in Figure 3.2, are as follows:

a.  Do you have enough time for yourself or with another person?

b.  When you lie awake at night worrying, what do you worry about?

c.  If you could change one thing in your life, what would it be?

These questions often provoke the most emotional answers, which might be why some early interventionists are afraid to ask them. Others are concerned that we might not be able to do anything about the answers. That does not matter. The mere act of asking the questions shows we care. In this model, we do not claim to fix or cure things: We claim to support and help.

***Recap***    Whoever took the notes—the interviewer or the notetaker—quickly goes over the concerns noted with stars in each routine to remind the parent of the conversation.

***Outcome/Goal Decisions***    Parents decide on outcomes/goals. We keep the notes to ourselves at the beginning, to help parents think about what is important, without simply choosing outcomes/goals from the first star onward. We then give them the notes as a prompt and, if necessary, discuss needs that seemed meaningful to them when they mentioned them. We usually end up with 10 to 12 outcomes/goals—a mixture of child and family outcomes/goals.

The RBI outline in Figure 3.2 shows the structure of the interview.

## Outcome Writing

Once outcomes have been identified, the service coordinator needs to put the outcomes onto the IFSP. (Note that in a blended service coordination model, which works best for the RBM, the service coordinator is also the family's PSP.) The service coordinator consults with other team members about the wording of outcomes, although the parent's words are often enough. In the RBM, child outcomes/goals are written as participation-based goals, in which the purpose of the skill the family chose is framed as participation in the routines where the skill was needed. For example, the family might choose standing independently as an outcome because, in the conversation about outside time, inside hanging-out time, and dressing time, the parent had said that if Charlie could stand independently, he would be able to participate better. Therefore, the first part of the participation-based goal would read, *Charlie will participate in outside time, inside hanging-out time, and dressing time by standing independently.*

The model stipulates that outcomes/goals should be measurable with acquisition, generalization, and maintenance criteria. Therefore, this example outcome/goal might continue, *We will know he can do this when he stands without assistance for 1 minute* (i.e., the acquisition criterion) *during outside time, one hanging-out time, and dressing time in 1 day* (i.e., the generalization criterion) *for 5 consecutive days* (i.e., the maintenance criterion).

## INTERVIEW STRATEGIES

Conducting a good interview requires knowing child development, knowing family functioning, and having good people skills. The following interview behaviors are critical for the success of an RBI:

- Be natural and as informal as is appropriate.

- Put the parent at ease with this naturalness and informality.

- Look the parent in the eye when he or she is talking.

- Avoid the use of jargon; if the parent uses jargon, ask what he or she means.

- Nod and in other ways affirm what the parent is saying.

- From time to time, express admiration for what the parent does with his or her family.

- Express understanding about how the parent might feel (e.g., "I bet you feel really good about that," or "I bet that's really frustrating"); more safely, ask the parent how he or she feels.

- Place papers being written on flat, so the parent can see what is being written—distance notwithstanding.

- Find a point of personal contact and very briefly use "self-disclosure" or "therapeutic use of self."

- If the parent cries, offer to stop the conversation.

- If the parent becomes emotional, either move on to another topic or ask if he or she would like to talk about something else.

- As much as possible, refrain from engaging in judgmental talk about the other parent, if only interviewing one parent.

- Ask about later, specific routines to move the interview along if it is taking a long time; the goal is to reach the recap in 90 minutes.

- Ask detailed questions at the beginning of the interview to show the parent the level of detail required.

- Keep the structure of the six questions *per routine*:

  - What's everyone doing?

  - What's this child doing?

- What's this child's engagement like?

- What's this child's independence like?

- What are this child's social relationships like?

- How satisfactory is this time of day (home), or how good a fit are this routine and the child (classroom)?

## THE MOST COMMON CONCERN AMONG PROFESSIONALS

Many professionals are concerned that families will not choose "relevant" things to work on or that they will have "wrong" priorities. For example, the family might be concerned about a child's inability to put puzzles together, when the professional is more concerned that the child is not using words. First, this concern sometimes is related to a mismatch between what was found on the evaluation for eligibility and the outcomes or goals resulting from the RBI. Such a mismatch would perhaps reveal the different purposes of these assessments. The former is for determining status relative to normalcy. The latter is for determining needs for functioning in routines. Assessments conducted for different purposes can be expected to produce different ideas about what to work on. The model described here clearly puts more weight on routines-based needs than on test-based deficits.

Second, confusion between eligibility for services and necessity of services is rampant in our field. Just because a child qualifies for speech-language pathology services, for example, does not mean that he or she needs them. In fact, there is no criterion for determining "need" for services in early intervention. It is all a matter of clinical judgment. Professionals should refrain as much as possible from using the term "needing services." The alternative is to say that services would be helpful to meet needs, goals, or outcomes. Understandably, this is not a popular notion because of the fear that payers for services will adopt the notion to say that early intervention services are "unneeded" and therefore should not be paid for. But the specific point being made here is that qualification for a service should not be translated as "necessity" for a service.

Third, just because a family does not identify a skill as a priority and an outcome or goal does not mean that no one will address it. Many learning opportunities are afforded to children beyond what is on their IFSPs or IEPs. If, in the earlier example in which the child was not using words, the family did not choose a language outcome/goal, that does not mean no one is going to work on the child's learning to communicate. All parents work on that, as do child care providers and other caregivers. What could be complicated is that, in some systems, if the PSP needed the help of a speech-language pathologist, such help might not be available without a speech or language outcome/goal. Restricting consultation because of no associated outcome/goal is an unfortunate and common policy.

Fourth, as families obtain more information, they might add skills that, at the time of the RBI, were not important. Early interventionists who worry about "critical periods" for intervening early can relax, to some extent, because the idea of critical periods has largely been replaced by the more forgiving idea of "windows of opportunity" (Bailey, 2002). A critical period implies that, if you do not intervene by a certain age, you have lost the opportunity to teach a child that skill. That does not happen, but if you intervene before a certain age, the child is more likely to learn more easily.

Fifth, professionals do have the ethical obligation to provide families with any information they have, but when a child is first entering services, they have not had a chance to convey that information. As time passes, families might learn about the importance of a skill they did not originally choose. Professionals need to be very careful about what concerns they try to raise with parents, which leads to the sixth point: It is the parents' child, not the professional's child. Altogether, therefore, the list a family produces at the end of the RBI will be a functional, meaty one that will enhance family's quality of life and the child's learning.

## IMPLEMENTATION WITHIN INTERVENTION PLANNING

When should the RBI be done in the intervention planning process? Options include conducting the RBI during the intake visit, during evaluation, between the evaluation and the IFSP meeting, at the IFSP meeting, or after the IFSP meeting. There are advantages and disadvantages to each, and where to fit in the RBI is a local decision; that is, programs and communities are best at deciding this for themselves. We discuss some of the pros and cons of each option in the following sections.

### At Intake

The RBI is an effective tool for getting to know the family, which is often a goal of an intake visit. However, so much official business needs to be done at intake, such as explaining rights to families, describing early intervention, and obtaining consents for evaluation, that the meeting would be awfully long. This could be especially problematic for programs with high false-positive referrals (i.e., too many children referred—e.g., > 10% tested for delay are found to be ineligible for services). The RBI is too time consuming to be used on an inordinate number of ineligible families. In most cases, therefore, the intake visit is not going to be an ideal option for implementation of the RBI.

### At Evaluation

If the evaluation can be done quickly enough, it might be possible to conduct an RBI too. But, it generally will make this visit too long.

Increasingly, communities are scoring instruments from the information provided during the RBI. Thus, much of the testing is obviated by the interview. A few items might need to be administered after the interview, but this is an efficient way to kill two birds with one stone. Better still, it allows the emphasis of the assessment period to be the needs-based, functional interview, rather than the decontextualized testing. This adaptation is only efficient for children who are highly likely to be eligible. Otherwise, as mentioned earlier, the interview is expensive for an ineligible child. If a program finds that more than 10% of the children they test for eligibility are ineligible, it should either do the evaluation first or institute screening at intake. For programs that find most children referred for delay to be delayed, scoring instruments during the RBI is increasingly popular.

### Between Evaluation and IFSP

For programs that want to keep their evaluation intact, one option is to schedule another meeting between the evaluation and the IFSP meeting. Because of the 45-day limit between referral and the IFSP meeting, this can be challenging. But it is better to separate formal testing in this way than to do testing and the interview on the same day. Doing them on the same day means starting with the testing, which conveys at the beginning that professionals with their tools have valuable information about the child. It can affect the family's confidence in the value of their descriptions of the child.

### At the IFSP Meeting

Some programs do the RBI as part of the IFSP meeting, which creates the same challenge as other options that involve doing more than one thing in the meeting: It can make for an excessively long meeting. The advantage of combining these two functions is that the RBI produces the outcomes, so one might as well proceed with the IFSP. Many professionals find it helpful, however, to do some work between the outcome selection and the IFSP meeting. Some professionals work with the family anyway, to establish the criteria for participation-based goals. Of course, any of this pre-IFSP work is subject to review by the family. Professionals should not worry about doing some of this work apart from the family, because there is no question that the outcomes belong to the family. Furthermore, the RBI provides the context and functional need, so the service coordinator is likely to propose rewording and strategies consistent with the family's wishes.

---

### A Friendly Warning

Some early interventionists have used information about routines to try to establish the times of day when outcomes that were produced from tests would be applicable. That is, they test the child, suggest outcomes, and then look for routines in which to teach the skills. This is the wrong way around. The outcomes should come from needs during the routines, not from tests. Routines are not an afterthought or just an application context. They are at the forefront of identifying needs.

---

## After the IFSP Meeting

Occasionally, programs have opted to do the RBI after the IFSP meeting, which is fraught with problems. The most obvious problem is that the outcomes come from the RBI, so the team has to revise the outcomes as soon as the RBI is done. Sometimes programs work with an interim IFSP, with the outcomes developed at the IFSP meeting essentially ignored and replaced with outcomes developed at the RBI.

Why would early interventionists do this? If they work in a system where they have no control over the IFSP process and that refuses to use the RBI, they have little option. Another reason might be a situation in which the ongoing service provider is not decided upon until the IFSP meeting, and other people are involved in the evaluation, assessment, and IFSP development—and thus the service provider wants to hear all the information that is generated at the RBI. In that case, it is an issue of wanting to be the person who does the interview.

When to do the RBI is a local decision. The two most successful methods, by and large, are fitting in an extra meeting for the RBI, between the evaluation and the IFSP meeting, and combining the evaluation and the RBI, scoring the instrument during the RBI.

Numerous people can be at the RBI. The family decides which family members will be present. The child does not have to be there. When scheduling the RBI, it is suggested that professionals ask families to provide as distraction free a setting as possible, with minimal interruptions. Families should also be reassured that if they can't find someone to watch the child or handle other interruptions, it is fine. One would never ask families to find someone to watch their child during regular home visits, but the RBI only takes place once or twice a year. It is acceptable to ask families to reduce the likelihood of disruptions.

In terms of professionals' involvement, ideally, two would be present, although one is manageable. If the RBI is being used as part of the multidisciplinary evaluation (i.e., the information is going to appear in the present level of functioning section of the IFSP), two or more professionals representing different disciplines might need to be there anyway. The second person can do the following:

- Help ask questions (although one person should take the lead)
- Take notes
- Handle interruptions
- Perhaps score a developmental test

To review implementation issues for children entering the program for different reasons, first consider those with established conditions (sometimes known as "medical diagnoses"). They, like all children entering Part C, need to be offered a multidisciplinary evaluation (MDE). This is a quirk of the law because usually all that is needed for eligibility is a medical report stating the child's diagnosis related to developmental disabilities. Although children with established conditions need an MDE (*assessment* of present level of functioning in five domains), they do not need to be *tested*, unless the state requires it. Scores are unnecessary for these children's eligibility, so the RBI is a relevant way to get descriptions of present level of functioning.

## WHERE DOES THE MEISR FIT IN?

The RBI is the preferred method of obtaining the family's outcomes/goals. Unlike the MEISR, it deals with information about any functioning that might occur in a routine (versus the limitation of predetermined skills). For example, suppose an issue in a family, during meals, is that Theo (the sibling of Danny, who has disabilities) often hits and pushes Danny. On the MEISR, no items in the meal times routine address a sibling's aggression. Furthermore, Danny reacts to the mildest of shoves with excessive screaming. That also is not on the MEISR. But these two behaviors, one from Theo and the other from Danny, are ruining the family's meal times. The RBI would capture this.

A second advantage of the RBI is also illustrated in this example: It includes family needs, which the MEISR does not. The RBI even captures family-level needs not directly related to the child. For example, the mother might say she has no time for herself and then chooses that as an outcome/goal. Again, the MEISR provides no opportunity for family outcomes/goals.

A third advantage of the RBI is that it provides an opportunity to establish a positive relationship with the family, whereas the MEISR does not require interaction between the professional and the family; the family can complete it without the professional being present. Robin McWilliam and Cami Stevenson have provided workshops on "Falling in Love Through the RBI," explaining how professionals and families form a strong bond simply through the experience of the interview.

The MEISR can help professionals' completion of the RBI in four ways.

## Preparation for the Interview

Because the MEISR has many functional skills organized by routines, interviewers can examine it in advance of conducting an interview. This might be especially important for professionals with little experience in thinking about child functioning in routines. Families can benefit from reviewing the MEISR before the RBI, to help them think about their child's functioning in routines. In addition, giving the MEISR to the family prior to the RBI can help them prepare too.

## Assistance During the Interview

This second way the MEISR can help is a variation on the first. An interviewer or, more practically, a notetaker can have a copy of the MEISR at the interview as a prompt for questions to ask. When we train people at our RBI Certification Institute, the MEISR is one of the tools available to the interview pair.

## Triangulation of Interview Data

A professional can complete the MEISR during or after the RBI to quantify the information the family has provided. Because the notes taken during the RBI are cryptic—we do not want long notes or they ruin the recap—the completed MEISR might be attractive to professionals who like numbers and documentation.

## Child Outcomes Summary Ratings

As described in Chapter 5, the MEISR is useful for determining children's age-anchored progress on federal child outcomes. If an RBI is used for outcome/goal decisions on the IFSP, completing the MEISR, as described in the previous section on triangulation, can then be part of the information for Child Outcomes Summary (COS) ratings.

In conclusion, the RBI and the MEISR are highly compatible but serve mostly different purposes, which is why we have both. Use the RBI to help families decide on outcomes/goals, and use the MEISR to monitor progress, aid with the RBI, and inform the COS process.

## SUMMARY

This chapter has explained the process of conducting the RBI. The RBI is central to home- and community-based service delivery and to managing inclusive classrooms, settings addressed by the RBM. This chapter discussed research on the efficacy of using the RBI for IFSP development; use of the RBI has produced better outcomes and higher family satisfaction than traditional approaches to IFSP development that do not use the RBI.

The RBI has six stages, described in this chapter. Before conducting the RBI, the intervention professional needs to prepare the child's caregivers—the family and, in some cases, caregivers outside the home. This preparation should address what the expectations are for each of the child's everyday routines, what the child does during each routine, and how well that routine is working for the family or, for classroom routines, for the child. Next, during the first stage of the RBI, the professional asks the family about who lives in the home, why the child received special services, and what the caregiver's main concerns are. The second stage of the RBI addresses home routines; the third addresses any classroom routines; and the fourth stage addresses the time, worry, and change questions with the caregiver. The fifth stage is a recap of the interview so far, and the sixth stage focuses on outcome/goal selection.

This chapter summarized common concerns among intervention professionals and discussed how the RBI can be implemented at any of various points during the IFSP process. Finally, we concluded by discussing four ways the MEISR can help professionals in completing the RBI: as a means of preparing for the interview; as a prompt for questions to ask during the interview; as an aid in triangulating interview data; and as a means of determining children's age-anchored progress on federal child outcomes.

# Routines-Based Interview Checklist (With Ecomap)

*With Cami M. Stevenson*

# Routines-Based Interview Checklist (With Ecomap)

Interviewer(s): _____

| | |
|---|---|
| Observer: _____ | Date: _____ |
| Notetaker: _____ | Items Correct: _____ Scored: _____ %: _____ |
| Met Criteria for Fidelity:    YES    NO | Bold Items Correct: _____ Scored: _____ %: _____ |
| | EISR Items Correct: _____ %: _____ |

**Fidelity.** When training professionals to use the RBI with fidelity, we now recommend (a) 80% of all scored items correct, (b) 80% of the bold items, and (c) at least 6 of the engagement, independence, and social relationships items.

**Exact wording.** In a few places, the exact wording must be used. We have *italicized* those scripted statements or questions.

**Bold items.** Points of emphasis are in **bold**. Trainers should focus on these items when giving feedback. They can also <u>not</u> approve a person's fidelity achievement, if that person missed too many bold items. In the RBI Certification Institute, we no longer fail someone on the basis of missing one bold item.

| Scoring | + | +/− | − |
|---|---|---|---|
| | Observed as described | Partially observed | Not observed or observed to be incorrect |

| Did the interviewers . . . | Score | | | Comments |
|---|---|---|---|---|
| **Ecomap** | | | | |
| 1. Greet the family and make introductions, including what each person was going to do (e.g., take notes)? | + | | | |
| 2. **Tell the family the purpose of the ecomap: to get a picture of who the family has as resources, including friends and family, and to help meet needs?** | | | | |
| 3. Tell the family they don't have to say anything they don't want to say? | | | | |
| 4. Ask the family who lived in the home with the child and draw a box in the middle of the paper to show these people? Can include pets. | | | | |

*Measure of Engagement, Independence, and Social Relationships (MEISR™), Research Edition,*
by R. A. McWilliam and Naomi Younggren.

| Did the interviewers . . . | Score | Comments |
|---|---|---|
| **Ecomap** (*continued*) | | |
| 5. Ask about which child is receiving specialized services and why? | | |
| 6. Ask other children's ages? | | |
| 7. Ask about the extended family on the side of the person providing information? | | |
| 8. Draw informal supports above the nuclear family box? | | |
| 9. **For each informal support, ask follow-up question to estimate level of support (e.g., how often respondent talks to or sees the support person)?** | | |
| 10. **For each support, draw support-level lines (i.e., strong, moderate, just present, stressful)?** | | |
| 11. Ask about the extended family on the side of an adult partner (e.g., spouse)? | | |
| 12. Ask about friends, including the BFF of the person providing information? | | |
| 13. Ask about neighbors? | | |

| Did the interviewers . . . | Score | Comments |
|---|---|---|
| **Ecomap** *(continued)* | | |
| 14. Ask about spiritual supports (e.g., church, synagogue, mosque)? | | |
| 15. Ask about work, including how much the adults like their work and how well it pays, such as, "Does it pay big bucks?" | | |
| 16. Ask about any recreational activities family members do? | | |
| 17. **Ask about services anyone in the family receives, especially the child in early intervention/early childhood special education (EI/ECSE)?** | | |
| 18. **For each formal support, ask follow-up question to estimate level of support (e.g., how much the respondent liked the support provider)?** | | |
| 19. Ask about child care, preschool, school, or other care the children in the house attend? | | |
| 20. Ask about medical professionals involved with the child? | | |
| 21. Ask about financial supports (i.e., agencies paying for things)? Include insurance. | | |
| 22. Once the family said no more supports were present, ask them what they thought of the picture? | | |

| Did the interviewers . . . | Score | Comments |
|---|---|---|
| **Ecomap (continued)** | | |
| 23. Repeat that this information will be used to help meet the goals the family will decide on at the end of the RBI? | | |
| 24. Tell the family what would happen with the ecomap (e.g., copy made for the family, put in file)? | | |
| 25. If continuing onto the RBI, tell the family that, next, they would be asked about their day-to-day life, to help them decide on early intervention priorities? | | |
| **Beginning of RBI** | | |
| 26. Arrange seating so lead interviewer is next to parent and notetaker, if there is one, is next to the lead? | | |
| 27. If no ecomap preceded the RBI, include the purpose of the RBI (i.e., to get to know the family and help them decide what they want to get out of EI/ECSE)? | | |
| 28. **Ask the parents their main concerns for their child or family?** | | |
| **Routines** | | |
| 29. Stay focused on routines rather than developmental domains? | | |
| 30. Use "time of day" instead of "routine"? | | |
| 31. Use open-ended questions, initially, to gain an understanding of the routine and functioning (followed by closed-ended questions if necessary)? | | |

| Did the interviewers . . . | Score | Comments |
|---|---|---|
| **EISR (Items 32–42)** | | |
| 32. For each routine, find out what people in the family or classroom other than the child are doing? | | |
| 33. **Ask questions about how the child participates in each routine (engagement)?** | | |
| 34. **Ask questions about whether the child is engaged with adults, other children, or objects?** | | |
| 35. **Ask questions about the sophistication of the child's engagement (e.g., repetitive, differentiated, problem solving, constructive)?** | | |
| 36. **Ask questions related to independence in each routine?** | | |
| 37. **Ask questions about the child's asking for and receiving help?** | | |
| 38. **Ask questions about how independent the caregiver wants the child to be during this routine?** | | |
| 39. **Ask questions related to the child's receptive communication in each routine (social relationships)?** | | |
| 40. **Ask questions about the child's expressive communication (words, signs, pictures/symbols, augmentative communication)?** | | |
| 41. **Ask questions about the child's getting along with others?** | | |

| Did the interviewers . . . | Score | Comments |
|---|---|---|
| **EISR (Items 32–42)** *(continued)* | | |
| 42. **Ask developmentally appropriate questions?** | | |
| 43. Ask for the interviewee's perspective on behaviors (why he or she thinks the child does what he or she does)? | | |
| 44. **Ask what the interviewee would like to see happen 6 months hence, if and only if there were no problems in the routine?** | | |
| 45. **At the end of the interviewee's description of each routine, ask for a 1–5 rating of the parent's satisfaction or of the teacher's perception of the goodness of fit? To parent:** *"On a scale of 1 to 5, with 1 being terrible and 5 being great, how would you rate this time of day?"* **To teacher:** *"On a scale of 1 to 5, how well does this time of day work for [the child]?"* **(With both, use exact words "terrible" and "great.")** | | |
| 46. Include routines apart from the home where the child spends > 15 hours a week (e.g., child care, preschool)? This can be with those caregivers present or by report from a previous RBI with them. | | |
| 47. To transition between routines, ask, *"What happens next?"* | | |
| **Family Issues** | | |
| 48. Ask the family, *"Do you have enough time for yourself or with another person?"* (ask only if this information was not obtained previously)? | | |
| 49. Ask the family, *"When you lie awake at night worrying, what do you worry about?"* | | |

| Did the interviewers . . . | Score | Comments |
|---|---|---|
| **Family Issues** (*continued*) | | |
| 50. **Ask the family, "If you could change anything about your life, what would it be?"** | | |
| 51. Explain the next step in the process: the recap? | | |
| **Style** | | |
| 52. Use good affect (e.g., facial expressions, tone of voice, responsiveness)? | | |
| 53. **Maintain a good flow (conversational, not a lot of time spent writing, no dead time)?** | | |
| 54. Maintain focus throughout the session? Attention should be on the interview—not the child or others; use eye contact. | | |
| 55. Affirm what the interviewee reported doing (nodding, positive comments)? | | |
| 56. **Use active listening (rephrasing, clarifying, summarizing)?** | | |
| 57. Avoid giving advice? | | |
| 58. Maintain a nonjudgmental stance? | | |

*Measure of Engagement, Independence, and Social Relationships (MEISR™), Research Edition,*
by R. A. McWilliam and Naomi Younggren.

50

| Did the interviewers . . . | Score | Comments |
|---|---|---|
| **Style** *(continued)* | | |
| 59. Return easily to the interview after an interruption? | | |
| 60. **Allow the family to state their own opinions, concerns, etc. (i.e., avoid leading the family toward what the interviewer thinks is important or guiding the family on goals or things to work on before outcome selection)?** | | |
| 61. Acknowledge feelings before facts, especially with sensitive information such as the time, worry, and change questions? | | |
| **Note Taking (scored separately if notetaker was used)** | | |
| 62. If a dedicated notetaker is used, discuss how much the lead interviewer wants help with questions? | | |
| 63. Organize notes by routine, with a clear heading for each? | | |
| 64. Write down concerns and other significant information (not details)? | | |
| 65. Aim for about three stars for most routines? | | |
| 66. Place the stars in the left-hand margin? | | |
| 67. Check with the dedicated notetaker, if being used, to ensure he or she has noted concerns? | | |

| Did the interviewers . . . | Score | Comments |
|---|---|---|
| **Note Taking (scored separately if notetaker was used)** *(continued)* | | |
| 68. Dedicated notetaker: Ask clarifying questions, for repetition, or for additional information? | | |
| 69. Include the 1–5 rating for each routine? | | |
| 70. Dedicated notetaker: Prompt the lead to ask for the rating, if necessary? | | |
| 71. Dedicated notetaker: Help the lead if any difficulties arose (e.g., dead time, family doesn't understand the question, lead doesn't understand the answer) but stay within the agreed-upon role? | | |
| 72. Dedicated notetaker: Move next to a parent (recap occurs only with families, not teachers) and recap (i.e., summarize) the starred concerns? | | |
| 73. **Recap in 5–7 minutes, mentioning all concerns and organized by routines?** | | |
| 74. During the recap, check the parent's understanding, from time to time, but not elicit or reinforce additional discussion, unless necessary for clarification? | | |
| **Outcome/Goal Decisions** | | |
| 75. If necessary, lead interviewer resume place next to parent? | | |
| 76. **Take out a clean sheet of paper and ask the family what they wanted to work on (i.e., a new list)?** | | |

| Did the interviewers . . . | Score | Comments |
|---|---|---|
| **Outcome/Goal Decisions** *(continued)* | | |
| 77. Give the family plenty of time to think about what they might want? | | |
| 78. If the family decided on < 10 outcomes/goals, hand them the notes? | | |
| 79. If the family still hasn't decided on 10 outcomes/goals, look at the notes together with the family? | | |
| 80. Stop encouraging when 12 outcomes/goals have been decided upon? | | |
| 81. Clarify any child outcomes/goals the family mentions that are not functional (i.e., not relevant to the child's routines)? | | |
| 82. Write down relevant routines for every child outcome/goal? | | |
| 83. Ensure at least one family goal is included, by prompting the family, if necessary? | | |
| 84. **Ask the family to prioritize the outcomes/goals based on the order of importance to them?** | | |
| 85. Tell the family what will happen next with this information (e.g., outcomes/goals written in behavioral, measurable terms; services decided upon [e.g., the outcomes/goals will be written on the individualized plan and services to address them will be decided, with the family])? | | |

| Did the interviewers . . . | Score | Comments |
|---|---|---|
| **Optional: Writing Participation-Based and Family Outcomes/Goals With Family** | | |
| 86. Ask the family if they'd like to take a break before the goal-writing portion starts? | | |
| 87. Proceed through the outcomes/goals in the family's priority order? | | |
| 88. For child outcomes/goals, write what [child's name] will participate in? | | |
| 89. Write the routines in which the skill is desired? | | |
| 90. Write *by* and the present participle of the verb with any qualifier (e.g., eating with a spoon, sitting with minimal support, completing puzzles, using two-word combinations, playing nicely with another child)? | | |
| 91. Discuss with the family how we will know the child can do this (i.e., acquisition criterion), if necessary, giving them suggestions of types of criteria (e.g., "For example, you could aim for him eating a certain number of spoonfuls in a meal")? Usually frequency, duration, distance, or volume. | | |
| 92. Discuss with the family during how many of the target routines the skill should be displayed (only one, all, two of three, etc.) in 1 day? | | |
| 93. Discuss with the family over what amount of time the skill should be displayed (3 consecutive days, a full week, 4 days in 1 week, etc.)? | | |
| 94. For family outcomes/goals, discuss with the family one criterion, which can be a target date (e.g., by August 1), or more, as appropriate? | | |

Add all +s, and put total on front page. Add all items scored, ignoring –s or blanks, and put this number on front page. Divide the first number (i.e., all +s) by second number (i.e., all items scored) and multiply by 100 to obtain the percentage steps correct. Put this number on the front page. Do the same for bold items and for EISR items.

SECTION II

# Ways to Use the MEISR

# Purpose, Organization, Uses, and Misuses

In this chapter, we describe the assessment process and the intended purpose of the MEISR within that process. We also explain the organization of the MEISR and discuss its many uses before providing an overview of how to complete it. We conclude by calling attention to potential misuses of the MEISR.

## THE ASSESSMENT PROCESS

Assessment can be thought of as the process for gathering information to answer questions and make decisions (Squires, 2015). In the process of assessing young children, it is important to think about how children learn. They learn in the context of everyday routines and activities. For this reason, to understand a child's functioning, it makes sense to assess it only in the authentic context of familiar routines and in partnership with their loving and knowing caregivers. Neisworth and Bagnato define authentic assessment as the "systematic recording of information about the naturally occurring behaviors of young children and families in their daily routines" (2004, p. 204). In authentic assessment, observation and interview are natural methods of inquiry. Observation includes intently watching a child and taking note of what the child does freely within the context of naturally occurring antecedents and consequences. Through observation, we can understand the child's typical functioning in his or her natural developmental ecology, within daily routines that organically elicit functional skills and behaviors (Bagnato, 2007). Interviewing parents and caregivers, who are familiar with the child, is another naturalistic means of gathering authentic assessment information. By acknowledging these primary caregivers' natural opportunities to interact with and observe their children and by inquiring about their observations, professionals can most easily facilitate completion of the MEISR. Moreover, because MEISR skills are functional, most caregivers will be able to rate every skill on the MEISR.

### The Purpose of Assessment: How and Why It Begins

In the field of early childhood development, we engage in assessment for a variety of purposes to answer varied questions. For example, our purpose might be screening, and the question we are trying to answer might be whether further testing is needed. If the purpose were to determine if the child and family are eligible for early intervention, then the questions would be different, and the methods and tools used would differ as well. The same is true if the assessment purpose was to obtain information for program planning or progress monitoring. We need to know the purpose and questions we hope to answer to choose effectively the best methods and tools needed to collect the data and then to analyze those data in light of the purpose and questions.

If the question is not clearly understood by the team, the information gathered might not answer the question. Worse yet, the information gathered might be misused. Examples of misusing assessment results include using standardized evaluation testing results to define individualized outcomes for intervention (i.e., the child missed these items on the test and those items mechanically become the IFSP outcomes) or using testing results alone to determine services (e.g., the child has delays in communication and therefore needs speech therapy). As Shepard, Kagan, and Wurtz stated, "The intended use of an assessment—its purpose—determines every other aspect of how the assessment is conducted" (1998, p. 6).

The MEISR, like any other early childhood assessment tool, cannot answer all of the questions teams will need to answer as they support the family through the early intervention journey. Nor can the MEISR, or any other single assessment tool or test, definitely answer any one question. Some tools are more robust than others, but the tools alone do not determine decisions. Assessment is the process of getting to know the child and family, and it requires more than the mere completion of a single tool. Assessment requires input from the people who know the child best—parents and other primary caregivers—and from professionals with expertise in child development.

## Key Players in Assessment

Families know their children best and love their children most. For practitioners, this is an ever-critical point to fully trust and remember. In early intervention, it is the family and primary caregivers who spend the most time with the child. They see, guide, and support the child throughout a myriad of actions, interactions, and reactions that occur day in and day out. Accordingly, parents and other primary caregivers must be part of the assessment process. Regardless of the questions the team is trying to answer (i.e., the purpose of the assessment), family and caregiver input is critical.

Although professionals acknowledge the importance of parent/caregiver input in assessment, it is also common for professionals to question their input: Are they over- or underestimating their child's abilities? Children behave differently in different settings and situations with familiar and less familiar adults and peers. When professional observations differ from what caregivers report, it does not mean that the caregiver is over- or under-reporting the child's abilities. Bruckner, McLean, and Snyder (2011) pointed out that, when discrepancies occur, parents and other caregivers should not be regarded as being inaccurate; rather, these instances should be acknowledged as opportunities for further discussion to guide team decisions based upon the assessment purpose. Suppose you ask a parent how his or her child plays with other children, and the parent responds, "Oh, she is great playing with other kids. She is with her cousins all the time." Meanwhile, you might recall your observations of the child and how she mostly wandered about, not showing any interest in peers. Possibly, the parent interpreted the question differently: She heard, *Does your child play in the company of other children?* while you may have been thinking, *How does the child interact with peers during play times?* Although both you and the parent are accurate reporters, your recollections of the child's behaviors are essentially in response to differently interpreted questions. This is why thoughtful discussions between practitioners and family members are essential. There is no shortcut when it comes to including families in the assessment process.

## OVERVIEW: CONTENT AND STRUCTURE OF THE MEISR

The MEISR is a list of skills young children (birth–36 months) might use to participate in their everyday home activities. In this section, we describe its organization around these everyday routines and the items. (The current MEISR was revised from the 2007 version, by adding a transition section, including clarification and examples for items early intervention providers interpreted differently, clarifying starting ages, and restating the items to be participation based. For details about how the MEISR was first developed in 2007 and its psychometric and usability properties, see the Appendix at the end of this book.) We also provide a brief introduction to scoring items within a routine; for in-depth scoring guidelines, see Chapter 7.

Essential to the MEISR is the assessment of children's participation in the everyday routines of their homes. These routines have been selected on the basis of 25 years of experience in asking families about their daily lives. Each routine is discussed with reference to the kinds of skills needed for EISR in it. Routines are times of day. They are not skill areas. For example, *getting dressed* is the time of day when the child gets dressed, during which many skills are displayed—not only dressing skills, but also making choices, communicating, and following directions. One can talk about a *dressing time*, so we know it is a routine. However, we would not have a *making choices routine*. This is a skill area, not a time of day. Eating is a skill area; meals are the routine. *Going potty* (eliminating in the potty) is the skill area; *toileting/diaper* is the routine. The MEISR is organized around 14 commonly reported family routines:

1. Waking Up

2. Toileting/Diapering

3. Meal Times

4. Dressing Time

5. Hangout – TV – Books

6. Play With Others

7. Nap Time

8. Outside Time

9. Play by Him- or Herself

10. Bath Time

11. Bedtime

12. Going Out

13. Grocery Shopping

14. Transition Time

Within each routine are items reflecting the skills a child may demonstrate during completion of that routine. (The number of items varies across different routines.) Each of the routines is described in further detail in the following sections.

***Waking Up***    This routine is about the child's waking up, which might be later than the parents' and rarely is before it. Although the first routines-based question in the RBI is *How does your day begin?*, in the MEISR, the first routine is the child's waking up. As families read this, they can see the level of detail with which the tool deals, as shown in Figure 4.1. The waking up routine has many skills beginning in the first 12 months of life and only five beginning after that.

| 1. Waking Up   Participates in waking up time by . . . | Typical starting age in months | Not yet | Sometimes | Often or Beyond this | Func | Dev | Diff |
|---|---|---|---|---|---|---|---|
| 1.01  Making vocal sounds | 0 | 1 | 2 | 3 | S | CM | K |
| 1.02  Showing enjoyment when held, rocked, touched by caregiver | 0 | 1 | 2 | 3 | S | S | S |
| 1.03  Looking at caregiver and making eye contact | 0 | 1 | 2 | 3 | S | S | S |
| 1.04  Easily turning head to both sides | 1 | 1 | 2 | 3 | I | M | A |
| 1.05  Acting happy to see or hear caregiver | 1 | 1 | 2 | 3 | S | S | S |
| 1.06  Showing interest in crib toys (e.g., watching mobile) | 2 | 1 | 2 | 3 | E | CG | K |
| 1.07  Turning over from side to tummy or side to back | 2 | 1 | 2 | 3 | I | M | A |
| 1.08  Smiling, kicking, moving arms excitedly when sees caregiver | 2 | 1 | 2 | 3 | S | S, M | S |
| 1.09  Reaching out for or batting at toys, repeating action with enjoyment | 3 | 1 | 2 | 3 | E | CG, M | K |
| 1.10  Playing with hands and feet, touching and watching movements | 3 | 1 | 2 | 3 | E | CG | K |
| 1.11  Turning toward the sound of caregiver's voice | 3 | 1 | 2 | 3 | S | S | S |
| 1.12  Maintaining sitting at least briefly | 5 | 1 | 2 | 3 | I | M | A |
| 1.13  Raising arms to be picked up when caregiver reaches for child | 5 | 1 | 2 | 3 | S | CM, S | S |
| 1.14  Sitting when placed in sitting | 6 | 1 | 2 | 3 | I | M | A |
| 1.15  Moving up and down by bending knees when supported in standing | 6 | 1 | 2 | 3 | I | M | A |
| 1.16  Calling out for caregivers (e.g., shouting, vocalizing) | 7 | 1 | 2 | 3 | S | CM, S | A |
| 1.17  Waking up without crying immediately (calming self) | 8 | 1 | 2 | 3 | E | S | S |
| 1.18  Standing and cruising around crib | 10 | 1 | 2 | 3 | I | M | A |
| 1.19  Saying "mama" or "dada" when sees Mama or Dada | 12 | 1 | 2 | 3 | S | CM, S | S |
| 1.20  Standing for several seconds without support | 12 | 1 | 2 | 3 | I | M | A |
| 1.21  Playing with toys momentarily until caregiver comes (i.e., coping) | 18 | 1 | 2 | 3 | E | S | S |
| 1.22  Responding to caregiver's greeting with a sign or word | 18 | 1 | 2 | 3 | S | CM | S |
| 1.23  Leaving room to find caregiver | 24 | 1 | 2 | 3 | I | S | A |
| 1.24  Letting caregiver know how he/she is feeling (e.g., happy) by saying so or responding to a question | 30 | 1 | 2 | 3 | S | S | S |
| 1.25  Following directions involving descriptions (e.g., get the *big* pillow; be *quiet*, Sissy is still sleeping) | 33 | 1 | 2 | 3 | S | CG, CM | K |

A.  Total items scored 3 (Often or Beyond this): _____

B1.  Total items scored for child's age: _____

B2.  Percentage of items mastered by age (A / B1 * 100): _____%

C1.  Total items scored for full routine: _____

C2.  Percentage of items mastered by routine (A / C1 * 100): _____%
*Add scores to the MEISR Scoring Summary page*

**Figure 4.1.**   MEISR items within the Waking Up routine.

***Toileting/Diapering***      This routine, shown in Figure 4.2, usually occurs as needed, although a few times might be predictable, such as after a bath and after waking up. While children are in diapers (British: nappies), the skills involved are mostly centered around attentional engagement and participation during diaper change. Starting around age 12 months but often much later, children indicate that they need to eliminate. Preceding that, parents can often tell *when* the child is eliminating, although, if the child is not communicating overtly, that is not exactly a child skill.

***Meal Times***      This time of day is the richest for opportunities to show EISR. With 47 items, as shown in Figure 4.3, it covers positioning, eating, drinking, communicating, and getting along with others—functional skills essential for participation in meal time. We know from conducting RBIs that breakfast, lunch, supper/dinner, and snacks can vary for an individual child and family, so parents have to complete this section in terms of what the child most commonly does. If a child uses a feeding tube and takes nothing by mouth, the items related to oral eating or drinking should be marked as *not yet.* Meal times require skills that emerge across the age span of birth to 36 months, making them a particularly useful routine for determining needs.

***Dressing Time***      Many of these skills start after the child's first birthday. Each routine has EISR skills, so even though getting dressed obviously has independent self-help skills, it has social and social communication items, as well as engagement items. See Figure 4.4.

***Hangout – TV – Books***      This routine is the unstructured time that happens in most homes, often in a living room, den, or other room. Although books are excellent for children's development and TV/video watching is not, the reality of family life is that the TV might be on. To deny that would be to miss asking about family functioning as it actually happens, which is the purpose of this tool. As shown in Figure 4.5, this routine includes positioning (e.g., sitting),

| 2. Toileting/Diapering  Participates in toileting/diapering time by . . . | Typical starting age in months | Not yet | Sometimes | Often or Beyond this | Func | Dev | Soc |
|---|---|---|---|---|---|---|---|
| 2.01  Quieting when picked up by caregiver | 0 | 1 | 2 | 3 | E | S | S |
| 2.02  Cooperating with diaper change without being inconsolably fussy | 1 | 1 | 2 | 3 | S | S | S |
| 2.03  Paying attention to surroundings, including caregiver's face | 1 | 1 | 2 | 3 | E | CG | K |
| 2.04  Vocalizing frequently with apparent intent (short, loud, different pitches) | 9 | 1 | 2 | 3 | S | CM | K |
| 2.05  Indicating when he or she needs to be changed by vocalizing | 12 | 1 | 2 | 3 | S | CM | A |
| 2.06  Following routine directions with a prompt with items in sight (e.g., *put diaper in bin*) | 15 | 1 | 2 | 3 | S | CM | K |
| 2.07  Using a sign or word about toilet/diapering (e.g., to comment or respond) | 18 | 1 | 2 | 3 | S | CM | K |
| 2.08  Washing hands, completing the steps with prompting (might need help reaching things and rinsing off soap) | 24 | 1 | 2 | 3 | I | A | A |
| 2.09  Using the toilet (or potty chair) with assistance | 24 | 1 | 2 | 3 | I | A | A |
| 2.10  Lowering pants (may need help with fasteners or getting over diaper) | 24 | 1 | 2 | 3 | I | A | A |
| 2.11  Using two-word phrases to express self (e.g., *me potty, go potty, me poop*) | 24 | 1 | 2 | 3 | S | CM | K |
| 2.12  Staying dry for 3 hours | 25 | 1 | 2 | 3 | I | A | A |
| 2.13  Indicating a need to go to the bathroom and actually going, most of the time | 30 | 1 | 2 | 3 | I | A | A |
| 2.14  Indicating need to go in enough time to get to the bathroom, usually | 30 | 1 | 2 | 3 | I | A | A |
| 2.15  Responding to questions about bowel movement/urination (poop and pee—knows the difference) | 30 | 1 | 2 | 3 | S | CG | K |
| 2.16  Lasting the whole night without wetting | 33 | 1 | 2 | 3 | I | A | A |
| 2.17  Attempting to wipe self | 33 | 1 | 2 | 3 | I | A | A |
| 2.18  Talking about the toilet | 33 | 1 | 2 | 3 | S | CM | K |
| 2.19  Managing toileting mostly by self, may need reminders and help with wiping | 33 | 1 | 2 | 3 | I | A | A |
| 2.20  Doing several steps in toilet routine without being prompted (e.g., goes to potty, pulls pants down, sits on potty) | 33 | 1 | 2 | 3 | E | CG | K |

A.  Total items scored 3 (Often or Beyond this): _____

B1.  Total items scored for child's age: _____

B2.  Percentage of items mastered by age (A / B1 * 100): _____%

C1.  Total items scored for full routine: _____

C2.  Percentage of items mastered by routine (A / C1 * 100): _____%

*Add scores to the MEISR Scoring Summary page*

4

**Figure 4.2.**  MEISR items within the Toileting/Diapering routine.

| 3. Meal Times  Participates in meal times by . . . | Typical starting age in months | Not yet | Sometimes | Often or Beyond this | Func | Dev | Soc |
|---|---|---|---|---|---|---|---|
| 3.01  Opening mouth when caregiver gives bottle or breast for nursing | 0 | 1 | 2 | 3 | I | A | A |
| 3.02  Sucking strongly enough when nursing or bottle feeding | 0 | 1 | 2 | 3 | I | A | A |
| 3.03  Drinking appropriate amount from bottle or when nursing | 0 | 1 | 2 | 3 | I | A | A |
| 3.04  Swallowing following a few sucks | 0 | 1 | 2 | 3 | I | A | A |
| 3.05  Feeding on a fairly consistent schedule (e.g., every 3–4 hours) | 3 | 1 | 2 | 3 | I | A | A |
| 3.06  Sitting in a high chair upright without slumping over | 5 | 1 | 2 | 3 | I | M | A |
| 3.07  Remaining calm (at least briefly) while waiting for feeding when hungry | 6 | 1 | 2 | 3 | E | S | S |
| 3.08  Holding own bottle (if bottle fed) | 6 | 1 | 2 | 3 | I | A | A |
| 3.09  Beginning to eat solid food (e.g., teething cracker) | 6 | 1 | 2 | 3 | I | A | A |
| 3.10  Raking foods with fingers to pick up and eat | 7 | 1 | 2 | 3 | I | A, M | A |
| 3.11  Eating with little or no drooling (except for teething) | 7 | 1 | 2 | 3 | I | A | A |
| 3.12  Feeding self with fingers (half or more of meal) | 9 | 1 | 2 | 3 | I | A | A |
| 3.13  Chewing food (e.g., cracker, cookie) | 9 | 1 | 2 | 3 | I | A | A |
| 3.14  Using thumb and forefinger to pick up small pieces of food (like pinching) | 10 | 1 | 2 | 3 | I | A, M | A |
| 3.15  Following simple requests (e.g., eat more, drink your water) | 12 | 1 | 2 | 3 | S | CM | K |
| 3.16  Following pointing by looking to person and object | 12 | 1 | 2 | 3 | S | CM | K |
| 3.17  Drinking from a cup with a lid by him- or herself (e.g., trainer cup) | 12 | 1 | 2 | 3 | I | A | A |
| 3.18  Bringing spoon to mouth, eating some of the food from it | 12 | 1 | 2 | 3 | I | A | A |
| 3.19  Using pointing to communicate (e.g., as if to say "look" or "I want") | 12 | 1 | 2 | 3 | S | CM | K |
| 3.20  Saying "no" with meaning | 13 | 1 | 2 | 3 | S | CM | K |
| 3.21  Using a spoon to eat sticky foods (e.g., mashed potatoes) (might include some spilling) | 15 | 1 | 2 | 3 | I | A | A |
| 3.22  Indicating when hungry or thirsty with a sign or word | 15 | 1 | 2 | 3 | S | CM | A |
| 3.23  Pointing or vocalizing clearly to indicate food preference | 16 | 1 | 2 | 3 | S | CM | A |
| 3.24  Using a spoon independently for most of the meal | 18 | 1 | 2 | 3 | I | A | A |
| 3.25  Drinking appropriate amount from open cup at one time (with each sip) | 18 | 1 | 2 | 3 | I | A | A |
| 3.26  Staying seated for meal while he or she is eating with others | 18 | 1 | 2 | 3 | E | S | S |
| 3.27  Using signs or words to ask for at least one *specific* food or drink | 18 | 1 | 2 | 3 | S | CM | A |
| 3.28  Communicating "more" with signs or words | 18 | 1 | 2 | 3 | S | CM | A |
| 3.29  Communicating "finished" with signs or words | 18 | 1 | 2 | 3 | S | CM | A |
| 3.30  Putting an appropriate amount of food in mouth at a time | 18 | 1 | 2 | 3 | I | A | A |
| 3.31  Climbing forward onto adult-sized chair or backing into a child-sized chair | 18 | 1 | 2 | 3 | I | M | A |
| 3.32  Eating a variety of foods | 23 | 1 | 2 | 3 | I | A | A |

*(continued)*

5

**Figure 4.3.**  MEISR items within the Meal Times routine.

(continued)

| 3. Meal Times   Participates in meal times by . . . | Typical starting age in months | Not yet | Sometimes | Often or Beyond this | Func | Dev | Dis |
|---|---|---|---|---|---|---|---|
| 3.33  Removing easy wrappers or peels before eating (e.g., sliced orange peel) | 23 | 1 | 2 | 3 | I | A | A |
| 3.34  Waiting for food for a few minutes, without fussing | 24 | 1 | 2 | 3 | E | S | S |
| 3.35  Handling fragile items carefully (e.g., drinking glass) | 24 | 1 | 2 | 3 | E | S, A | A |
| 3.36  Using words to ask for help (e.g., when opening drink box) | 24 | 1 | 2 | 3 | S | CM | A |
| 3.37  Following a two-part command (e.g., give me the plate and put cup in sink) | 25 | 1 | 2 | 3 | S | CM | K |
| 3.38  Using words (pronouns) "I," "me" to refer to self (e.g., I did it) | 27 | 1 | 2 | 3 | S | CM | K |
| 3.39  Biting off pieces of hard foods (e.g., apple slices, carrot stick) | 30 | 1 | 2 | 3 | I | A | A |
| 3.40  Using a napkin to clean mouth and hands | 30 | 1 | 2 | 3 | I | A | A |
| 3.41  Spreading with a knife with supervision and help | 30 | 1 | 2 | 3 | I | A | A |
| 3.42  Using a fork to stab food and eat it | 30 | 1 | 2 | 3 | I | A | A |
| 3.43  Serving him- or herself (e.g., sandwich from plate, scooping from bowl) | 33 | 1 | 2 | 3 | I | A, M | A |
| 3.44  Making choices about food (e.g., saying what's wanted, choosing desired food from menu pictures) | 33 | 1 | 2 | 3 | S | CG, CM | A |
| 3.45  Cooperating with caregivers' requests, most of the time | 33 | 1 | 2 | 3 | S | S | S |
| 3.46  Engaging in conversation using short sentences | 34 | 1 | 2 | 3 | S | CM | S |
| 3.47  Having the fork control to stab, dip in sauce, and get to mouth | 36 | 1 | 2 | 3 | I | A | A |

A.  Total items scored 3 (Often or Beyond this): _____

B1.  Total items scored for child's age: _____

C1.  Total items scored for full routine: _____

B2.  Percentage of items mastered by age (A / B1 * 100): _____%

C2.  Percentage of items mastered by routine (A / C1 * 100): _____%

*Add scores to the MEISR Scoring Summary page*

6

**Figure 4.3.**   MEISR items within the Meal Times routine.

| 4. Dressing Time   Participates in dressing time by . . . | Typical starting age in months | Not yet | Sometimes | Often or Beyond this | Func | Dev | Dis |
|---|---|---|---|---|---|---|---|
| 4.01  Attending to sound of caregiver's voice | 0 | 1 | 2 | 3 | S | S | S |
| 4.02  Allowing caregiver to dress him or her without getting overly upset or showing strong discomfort for clothing or touch | 0 | 1 | 2 | 3 | E | S | S |
| 4.03  Responding positively to physical contact and holding | 0 | 1 | 2 | 3 | E | S | S |
| 4.04  Inspecting his or her hands | 2 | 1 | 2 | 3 | E | CG | K |
| 4.05  Communicating with vocal sounds | 2 | 1 | 2 | 3 | S | CM | K |
| 4.06  Responding to own name when called (e.g., pausing, alerting, vocalizing) | 6 | 1 | 2 | 3 | S | CM | S |
| 4.07  Babbling with adult-like inflection (e.g., baba, mama, or different syllables together, mado, bada) | 8 | 1 | 2 | 3 | S | CM | K |
| 4.08  Assisting by extending an arm or leg for a sleeve or pants leg | 11 | 1 | 2 | 3 | I | A | A |
| 4.09  Pointing correctly to one body part on self when asked | 15 | 1 | 2 | 3 | S | CM, CG | K |
| 4.10  Removing an article of clothing by him- or herself (e.g., socks, hat) | 15 | 1 | 2 | 3 | I | A | A |
| 4.11  Indicating he or she understands the name of an article of clothing (e.g., looking at or otherwise acknowledging when caregiver says shoes, shirt) | 15 | 1 | 2 | 3 | S | CM | K |
| 4.12  Recognizing self in mirror (e.g., pointing at self) | 15 | 1 | 2 | 3 | E | CG, S | K |
| 4.13  Indicating what he or she wants to wear (gesturing/verbalizing when given choice) | 18 | 1 | 2 | 3 | S | CM | A |
| 4.14  Undoing fasteners (e.g., unzipping large zipper, snaps) | 18 | 1 | 2 | 3 | I | A | A |
| 4.15  Helping undress self (e.g., removing shoes) | 18 | 1 | 2 | 3 | I | A | A |
| 4.16  Using gestures or words to identify two or more body parts | 18 | 1 | 2 | 3 | S | CM | K |
| 4.17  Using some signs or words to comment or respond | 18 | 1 | 2 | 3 | S | CM | K |
| 4.18  Following directions to fetch something (e.g., go get your shoes) | 18 | 1 | 2 | 3 | S | CM | K |
| 4.19  Persisting with trying to put on/take off some clothes (might still need help to complete task) | 24 | 1 | 2 | 3 | I | A | A |
| 4.20  Identifying five or more body parts (e.g., pointing at oneself, others, or doll) | 24 | 1 | 2 | 3 | E | CG | K |
| 4.21  Following two-step directions (e.g., first shoes on, then outside) | 25 | 1 | 2 | 3 | E | CM | K |
| 4.22  Dressing him- or herself with assistance (i.e., helping) | 28 | 1 | 2 | 3 | I | A | A |
| 4.23  Putting shoes on (maybe on wrong feet and not tied) | 30 | 1 | 2 | 3 | I | A | A |
| 4.24  Putting on coat with assistance | 30 | 1 | 2 | 3 | I | A | A |
| 4.25  Describing clothing preference (e.g., want dinosaur jammies, princess skirt) | 30 | 1 | 2 | 3 | S | CM | A |

(continued)

7

**Figure 4.4.**   MEISR items within the Dressing Time routine.

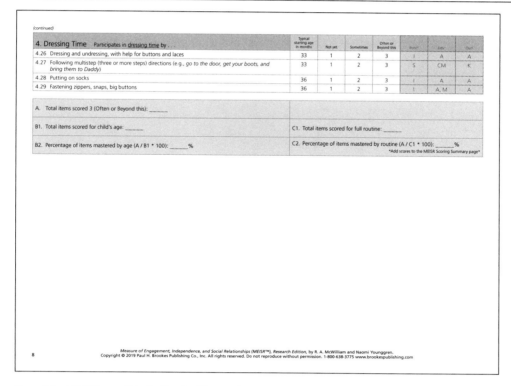

*(continued)*

| 4. Dressing Time  Participates in <u>dressing time</u> by . . . | Typical starting age in months | Not yet | Sometimes | Often or Beyond this | Eng* | Dev* | Out* |
|---|---|---|---|---|---|---|---|
| 4.26  Dressing and undressing, with help for buttons and laces | 33 | 1 | 2 | 3 | I | A | A |
| 4.27  Following multistep (three or more steps) directions (e.g., *go to the door, get your boots, and bring them to Daddy*) | 33 | 1 | 2 | 3 | S | CM | K |
| 4.28  Putting on socks | 36 | 1 | 2 | 3 | I | A | A |
| 4.29  Fastening zippers, snaps, big buttons | 36 | 1 | 2 | 3 | I | A, M | A |

A.  Total items scored 3 (Often or Beyond this): _____

B1.  Total items scored for child's age: _____                    C1.  Total items scored for full routine: _____

B2.  Percentage of items mastered by age (A / B1 * 100): _____%        C2.  Percentage of items mastered by routine (A / C1 * 100): _____%

*Add scores to the MEISR Scoring Summary page*

**Figure 4.4.**   MEISR items within the Dressing Time routine.

| 5. Hangout – TV – Books  Participates in <u>hanging-out time</u> by . . . | Typical starting age in months | Not yet | Sometimes | Often or Beyond this | Eng* | Dev* | Out* |
|---|---|---|---|---|---|---|---|
| 5.01  Responding positively to being held and cuddled | 0 | 1 | 2 | 3 | S | S | S |
| 5.02  Responding differently to the voice of a stranger from that of caregiver | 3 | 1 | 2 | 3 | S | S | S |
| 5.03  Looking at an object and watching it move in different directions (up, down, left, right) | 3 | 1 | 2 | 3 | E | CG | K |
| 5.04  Pushing up on hands when lying on tummy | 5 | 1 | 2 | 3 | I | M | A |
| 5.05  Reaching forward to get toys when supported in sitting | 5 | 1 | 2 | 3 | I | M | A |
| 5.06  Having fun pointing to and pulling on facial features of caregivers | 5 | 1 | 2 | 3 | S | S | S |
| 5.07  Rolling back to tummy and tummy to back both directions | 7 | 1 | 2 | 3 | I | M | A |
| 5.08  Pulling up to stand on furniture | 8 | 1 | 2 | 3 | I | M | A |
| 5.09  Playing with books (e.g., looking at, touching, mouthing) | 8 | 1 | 2 | 3 | E | CG | K |
| 5.10  Attending to objects mentioned during conversation (e.g., looking at dog when mentioned, looking at ball) | 10 | 1 | 2 | 3 | E | CG | K |
| 5.11  Moving about to explore, looking back to caregiver | 12 | 1 | 2 | 3 | S | S | S |
| 5.12  Showing interest looking at pictures in a book | 12 | 1 | 2 | 3 | E | CG | K |
| 5.13  Staying with caregiver looking at a book at least a few minutes | 12 | 1 | 2 | 3 | E | S | S |
| 5.14  Vocalizing to get caregiver attention to start or change activity | 12 | 1 | 2 | 3 | S | CM | A |
| 5.15  Exploring drawers and cabinets | 13 | 1 | 2 | 3 | E | CG, M | K |
| 5.16  Turning pages in books (might be several at a time) | 14 | 1 | 2 | 3 | I | M | K |
| 5.17  Figuring out how to activate/get a toy (e.g., turning toy on, climbing to get toy) | 18 | 1 | 2 | 3 | I | CG | K |
| 5.18  Showing clear preference for picture/book/show | 18 | 1 | 2 | 3 | E | CG | K |
| 5.19  Recognizing him- or herself in a picture by pointing or looking | 19 | 1 | 2 | 3 | E | CG | K |
| 5.20  Naming a character when seen in a book/show | 24 | 1 | 2 | 3 | E | CG, CM | K |
| 5.21  Pointing to and naming pictures in a book/show (three or more pictures) | 24 | 1 | 2 | 3 | S | CM, CG | K |
| 5.22  Talking about books/shows when they are being read/watched | 24 | 1 | 2 | 3 | S | CM | K |
| 5.23  Responding to emotions of others, sometimes with prompting (e.g., laughing at another's laugh, approaching crying child) | 24 | 1 | 2 | 3 | S | S | S |
| 5.24  Using a word like "big" or "little" to describe things | 25 | 1 | 2 | 3 | E | CG, CM | K |
| 5.25  Understanding and naming actions of things in books/shows (e.g., running, eating, crying) | 30 | 1 | 2 | 3 | S | CM | K |
| 5.26  Attending while watching or listening to a show or book with caregiver | 30 | 1 | 2 | 3 | E | S | S |
| 5.27  Pretending to read | 30 | 1 | 2 | 3 | E | CG | K |
| 5.28  Talking about book/show characters when not visible | 30 | 1 | 2 | 3 | S | CM | K |
| 5.29  Naming what book/show he or she would like to read/watch | 33 | 1 | 2 | 3 | S | CM | A |

*(continued)*

**Figure 4.5.**   MEISR items within the Hangout – TV – Books routine.

| 5. Hangout – TV – Books  Participates in hanging-out time by . . . | Typical starting age in months | Not yet | Sometimes | Often or Beyond this | Func* | Dev* | Dur* |
|---|---|---|---|---|---|---|---|
| 5.30  Understanding "two" (e.g., *you can pick two books/shows*) | 33 | 1 | 2 | 3 | E | CG | K |
| 5.31  Responding to others' feelings with caring behavior, without adult prompting (e.g., patting crying baby, kissing hurt finger) | 33 | 1 | 2 | 3 | S | S | S |
| 5.32  Helping tell story by commenting/gesturing about what's happening | 33 | 1 | 2 | 3 | E | CM, CG | K |
| 5.33  Behaving appropriately when watching a show alone (~20 minutes) | 33 | 1 | 2 | 3 | E | S | S |
| 5.34  Responding to characters on a show (e.g., when character asks audience a question or directs audience to imitate) | 36 | 1 | 2 | 3 | E | CM | K |
| 5.35  Asking "wh" questions (what, when, why) | 36 | 1 | 2 | 3 | S | CM | S |
| 5.36  Cooperating when his/her show/game/program is changed | 36 | 1 | 2 | 3 | S | S | S |
| 5.37  Recognizing own name or a letter from own name when written | 36 | 1 | 2 | 3 | E | CG | K |
| 5.38  Saying what will happen next in the story | 36 | 1 | 2 | 3 | E | CG | K |

A.  Total items scored 3 (Often or Beyond this): _____

B1.  Total items scored for child's age: _____

B2.  Percentage of items mastered by age (A / B1 * 100): _____%

C1.  Total items scored for full routine: _____

C2.  Percentage of items mastered by routine (A / C1 * 100): _____%
*Add scores to the MEISR Scoring Summary page*

**Figure 4.5.**  MEISR items within the Hangout – TV – Books routine.

playing with books, staying with adult reading a book, talking about TV shows or videos, and social awareness (e.g., empathy).

***Play With Others***     Play time can be completely unstructured or can be organized by an adult. In the MEISR, play time with others, shown in Figure 4.6, is treated as separate from play time alone. It includes social skills, communication, and concepts such as ownership of toys or items.

***Nap Time***     A time of day expressly designed for nonengagement might seem like a peculiar routine to include, but the ritual around the daytime rest is common and, frankly, has the potential for problems. It includes such skills as attending to repetitive sounds or movements to get to sleep, reducing the number of naps in the day, and sleeping in a bed. See Figure 4.7.

***Outside Time***     Perhaps no time is as underrated today, in America, for its fun and learning opportunities as spending time outdoors, the routine shown in Figure 4.8. This routine includes such skills as protracted engagement (e.g., staying outside for 30 minutes—at younger ages, with an adult), moving about (e.g., regaining balance and walking upstairs), and using "playground" equipment such as a swing.

***Play by Him- or Herself***     American children spend little time playing alone, compared to other children and compared to yesteryear. Yet this time is important for their development and for family functioning. Having this section on the MEISR might encourage families to consider this routine. It includes such skills as using motor skills to get and to manipulate toys, making independent choices, and playing with toys appropriately. It also reaches the higher levels of engagement, with symbolic play. See Figure 4.9.

| 6. Play With Others  Participates in play time with others by . . . | Typical starting age in months | Not yet | Sometimes | Often or Beyond this | | | |
|---|---|---|---|---|---|---|---|
| 6.01 Reacting to sounds (e.g., startling) | 0 | 1 | 2 | 3 | E | CG | K |
| 6.02 Following caregiver with his or her eyes | 3 | 1 | 2 | 3 | E | S | S |
| 6.03 Getting excited as caregiver approaches/starts playful game (e.g., squealing) | 3 | 1 | 2 | 3 | S | S | S |
| 6.04 Wiggling or vocalizing to continue social play (e.g., bouncing) with caregiver | 4 | 1 | 2 | 3 | S | S, CG | S |
| 6.05 Playing with others, without fussing or getting upset | 6 | 1 | 2 | 3 | S | S | S |
| 6.06 Rolling back to tummy | 6 | 1 | 2 | 3 | I | M | A |
| 6.07 Playing simple games with caregiver or older child (e.g., peek-a-boo) | 6 | 1 | 2 | 3 | S | CG, S | S |
| 6.08 Imitating others (e.g., patting, banging) | 6 | 1 | 2 | 3 | S | CG | K |
| 6.09 Showing interest in children (e.g., looking at, vocalizing, gesturing) | 9 | 1 | 2 | 3 | S | S | S |
| 6.10 Indicating he or she understands what "no" means | 9 | 1 | 2 | 3 | S | CM, S | K |
| 6.11 Talking or babbling back and forth in a sort of conversation with caregiver | 11 | 1 | 2 | 3 | S | CM, S | S |
| 6.12 Attempting to climb on things (e.g., onto furniture, in boxes) | 11 | 1 | 2 | 3 | I | M | A |
| 6.13 Repeating things (e.g., sounds, actions) when laughed at by others | 11 | 1 | 2 | 3 | S | CM, S | S |
| 6.14 Indicating understanding of simple request with clear gestures (e.g., *come here, give me*) | 12 | 1 | 2 | 3 | S | CM | K |
| 6.15 Playing a back-and-forth game (e.g., pushing ball, moving to get toy back) | 12 | 1 | 2 | 3 | S | S, CG | S |
| 6.16 Imitating actions using toys/objects (e.g., banging a drum, stirring with a spoon) | 12 | 1 | 2 | 3 | S | CG | K |
| 6.17 Playing apart from familiar caregiver (5 minutes or longer) | 15 | 1 | 2 | 3 | S | S | S |
| 6.18 Playing with a variety of toys in their intended manner (e.g., scribbling on paper, stacking rings on ring stacker toy) | 15 | 1 | 2 | 3 | E | CG | K |
| 6.19 Playing back-and-forth (early turn taking) game with another child (with caregiver assistance) | 18 | 1 | 2 | 3 | S | S | S |
| 6.20 Playing side by side with other children, interacting with gestures | 18 | 1 | 2 | 3 | S | S, CM | S |
| 6.21 Cleaning up toys, as part of routine, when asked (e.g., putting toy in box) | 22 | 1 | 2 | 3 | S | CM, S | S |
| 6.22 Indicating ownership over toys or items with peers (e.g., might grab toy) | 23 | 1 | 2 | 3 | S | S | S |
| 6.23 Singing some words in familiar songs (e.g., "Happy Birthday," "Twinkle Twinkle") | 24 | 1 | 2 | 3 | E | CM | K |
| 6.24 Maintaining motor control over his or her body in relationship to others (e.g., walks well, moves around others) | 24 | 1 | 2 | 3 | I | M | A |
| 6.25 Showing interest in playing with other children (e.g., going to where they are) | 24 | 1 | 2 | 3 | S | S | S |
| 6.26 Playing simple make-believe with another (e.g., shopping, putting things in toy grocery cart, going to peer/adult to get more) | 24 | 1 | 2 | 3 | E | CG, S | S |
| 6.27 Protecting own territory/toys/objects by saying "mine" | 24 | 1 | 2 | 3 | I | CM | S |
| 6.28 Sustaining (~15 minutes) play with children, might need caregiver to help with disputes | 30 | 1 | 2 | 3 | E | S | S |

*(continued)*

11

**Figure 4.6.**   MEISR items within the Play With Others routine.

---

*(continued)*

| 6. Play With Others  Participates in play time with others by . . . | Typical starting age in months | Not yet | Sometimes | Often or Beyond this | | | |
|---|---|---|---|---|---|---|---|
| 6.29 Being bossy with other children (e.g., has ideas, might try to be in charge) | 30 | 1 | 2 | 3 | S | S | S |
| 6.30 Separating from parent without acting anxious, in familiar settings | 30 | 1 | 2 | 3 | S | S | S |
| 6.31 Playing with others but might have preferred play partners | 30 | 1 | 2 | 3 | S | S | S |
| 6.32 Initiating play with other children and talking to others with words | 30 | 1 | 2 | 3 | S | S, CM | S |
| 6.33 Playing group games with adult help (e.g., Ring Around the Rosie) | 30 | 1 | 2 | 3 | S | S | S |
| 6.34 Seeking caregiver help with conflicts (e.g., going to caregiver when peer grabs his or her toy) | 30 | 1 | 2 | 3 | S | S | S |
| 6.35 Playing without messing up others' creations (e.g., blocks, painting) | 36 | 1 | 2 | 3 | E | S | S |
| 6.36 Asking another child for a turn with a toy | 36 | 1 | 2 | 3 | S | S | S |
| 6.37 Using loud (including rough and tumble) and quiet play at appropriate times/in appropriate contexts | 36 | 1 | 2 | 3 | E | S | S |
| 6.38 Staying quiet when playing hide-and-seek with others | 36 | 1 | 2 | 3 | E | CG | S |

A.  Total items scored 3 (Often or Beyond this): _____

B1. Total items scored for child's age: _____

B2. Percentage of items mastered by age (A / B1 * 100): _____%

C1. Total items scored for full routine: _____

C2. Percentage of items mastered by routine (A / C1 * 100): _____%
*Add scores to the MEISR Scoring Summary page*

**Figure 4.6.**   MEISR items within the Play With Others routine.

| 7. Nap Time  Participates in nap time by . . . | Typical starting age in months | Not yet | Sometimes | Often or Beyond this | Func* | Dev* | Out* |
|---|---|---|---|---|---|---|---|
| 7.01 Falling asleep in response to caregiver's actions (e.g., nursing, rocking) | 0 | 1 | 2 | 3 | E | S | S |
| 7.02 Taking frequent naps (30 minutes to 4 hours at a time) | 0 | 1 | 2 | 3 | I | A | A |
| 7.03 Staying awake for periods during the day (e.g., 2–3 hours) | 3 | 1 | 2 | 3 | I | A | A |
| 7.04 Waking up, perhaps by rolling over (back to side), without crying immediately | 4 | 1 | 2 | 3 | E | S, M | S |
| 7.05 Napping at predictable times (establishing nap schedule) | 6 | 1 | 2 | 3 | I | A | A |
| 7.06 Playing with toys, beyond mouthing or banging | 9 | 1 | 2 | 3 | E | CG | K |
| 7.07 Using objects (e.g., blanket, stuffed toy) to self-soothe/regulate emotions | 12 | 1 | 2 | 3 | E | S | S |
| 7.08 Giving up one nap | 12 | 1 | 2 | 3 | I | A | A |
| 7.09 Giving hugs or kisses as part of sleep/nap routine | 14 | 1 | 2 | 3 | S | S | S |
| 7.10 Taking one nap a day, which is typically enough | 18 | 1 | 2 | 3 | I | A | A |
| 7.11 Understanding directions, such as "Finish this (be specific), then it's nap time" | 24 | 1 | 2 | 3 | S | CM, CG | K |
| 7.12 Resting/playing quietly by self for a while (20+ minutes) | 30 | 1 | 2 | 3 | E | A | S |
| 7.13 Getting through the day without a nap | 33 | 1 | 2 | 3 | I | A | A |
| 7.14 Sleeping through the night and not taking a daytime nap | 36 | 1 | 2 | 3 | I | A | A |

A. Total items scored 3 (Often or Beyond this): _____

B1. Total items scored for child's age: _____

B2. Percentage of items mastered by age (A / B1 * 100): _____ %

C1. Total items scored for full routine: _____

C2. Percentage of items mastered by routine (A / C1 * 100): _____ %
*Add scores to the MEISR Scoring Summary page*

13

**Figure 4.7.** MEISR items within the Nap Time routine.

| 8. Outside Time  Participates in outside time by . . . | Typical starting age in months | Not yet | Sometimes | Often or Beyond this | Func* | Dev* | Out* |
|---|---|---|---|---|---|---|---|
| 8.01 Looking at object 8–10 inches away | 0 | 1 | 2 | 3 | E | CG | K |
| 8.02 Holding object placed in his or her hand | 2 | 1 | 2 | 3 | I | M | A |
| 8.03 Holding one and reaching for a second toy or object | 6 | 1 | 2 | 3 | I | M | A |
| 8.04 Walking independently at least a few steps | 13 | 1 | 2 | 3 | I | M | A |
| 8.05 Running (might look like fast walk) | 16 | 1 | 2 | 3 | I | M | A |
| 8.06 Moving ride-on wheeled toys (no pedals) with feet | 20 | 1 | 2 | 3 | I | M | A |
| 8.07 Jumping up so that both feet are off the ground | 24 | 1 | 2 | 3 | I | M | A |
| 8.08 Going up the ladder and down small slide | 24 | 1 | 2 | 3 | I | M | A |
| 8.09 Using sandbox toys appropriately (e.g., not throwing or eating sand) | 24 | 1 | 2 | 3 | E | CG | K |
| 8.10 Playing purposefully with playground toys (figuring out their best use) | 24 | 1 | 2 | 3 | E | CG | K |
| 8.11 Playing outside without fussing (with supervision for ~30 minutes) | 24 | 1 | 2 | 3 | E | S | S |
| 8.12 Showing interest in the playground (might have favorite toy/activity) | 24 | 1 | 2 | 3 | E | CG | K |
| 8.13 Catching a large ball (e.g., beach ball) | 24 | 1 | 2 | 3 | I | M | A |
| 8.14 Walking upstairs alone (both feet on each step), using rail if needed | 24 | 1 | 2 | 3 | I | M | A |
| 8.15 Walking downstairs alone (both feet on each step), using rail if needed | 26 | 1 | 2 | 3 | I | M | A |
| 8.16 Jumping off small step or bottom of slide with both feet together | 27 | 1 | 2 | 3 | I | M | A |
| 8.17 Walking forward and backward with balance while playing | 28 | 1 | 2 | 3 | I | M | A |
| 8.18 Walking upstairs alone (alternating feet—one foot on each step) | 30 | 1 | 2 | 3 | I | M | A |
| 8.19 Understanding descriptions such as hot, cold, dirty, wet (e.g., the ball is dirty, the sand is wet) | 30 | 1 | 2 | 3 | S | CM, CG | K |
| 8.20 Riding on toy with pedals at least a short distance | 33 | 1 | 2 | 3 | I | M | A |
| 8.21 Climbing on jungle gyms with hands and feet | 33 | 1 | 2 | 3 | I | M | A |
| 8.22 Engaging with others in a game with turn taking (e.g., jumping over rope, chalk line; might need caregiver guidance) | 34 | 1 | 2 | 3 | S | S | S |
| 8.23 Understanding simple rules (but might still test limits) | 34 | 1 | 2 | 3 | E | S | S |
| 8.24 Following caregiver's directions given from a distance | 36 | 1 | 2 | 3 | S | CM | K |
| 8.25 Using big slides (about 6 feet/2 meters high) | 36 | 1 | 2 | 3 | I | M | A |
| 8.26 Swinging on regular swing (might still not pump feet effectively) | 36 | 1 | 2 | 3 | I | M | A |

A. Total items scored 3 (Often or Beyond this): _____

B1. Total items scored for child's age: _____

B2. Percentage of items mastered by age (A / B1 * 100): _____ %

C1. Total items scored for full routine: _____

C2. Percentage of items mastered by routine (A / C1 * 100): _____ %
*Add scores to the MEISR Scoring Summary page*

14

**Figure 4.8.** MEISR items within the Outside Time routine.

| 9. Play by Him- or Herself   Participates in play time by him- or herself by . . . | Typical starting age in months | Not yet | Sometimes | Often or Beyond this | Func | Dev | Dnf |
|---|---|---|---|---|---|---|---|
| 9.01  Lying on back turning head (might prefer one side but can do both) | 0 | 1 | 2 | 3 | I | M | A |
| 9.02  Repeating actions with toys (e.g., banging at toys, kicking legs to move toy) | 3 | 1 | 2 | 3 | E | CG | K |
| 9.03  Exploring objects with hands and mouth | 3 | 1 | 2 | 3 | E | CG | K |
| 9.04  Grasping own foot and taking it to mouth to explore | 5 | 1 | 2 | 3 | E | CG, M | K |
| 9.05  Lying on tummy and reaching for toys with one hand | 6 | 1 | 2 | 3 | I | M | A |
| 9.06  Seeking partly hidden items, such as pacifier or bottle or favored toy | 6 | 1 | 2 | 3 | E | CG | K |
| 9.07  Working to get out-of-reach toy by pivoting, rolling, stretching | 7 | 1 | 2 | 3 | E | M | A |
| 9.08  Sitting independently (not propped with hands) | 8 | 1 | 2 | 3 | I | M | A |
| 9.09  Making toys work by self (e.g., pushing to reactivate action) | 9 | 1 | 2 | 3 | E | CG | K |
| 9.10  Dropping or throwing objects while exploring objects | 9 | 1 | 2 | 3 | E | M, CG | K |
| 9.11  Moving from sitting to hands and knees to crawl on hands and knees | 9 | 1 | 2 | 3 | I | M | A |
| 9.12  Crawling on hands and knees to get toys or objects of interest | 9 | 1 | 2 | 3 | I | M | A |
| 9.13  Picking up small objects effectively, with tip of index finger and thumb | 10 | 1 | 2 | 3 | I | M | A |
| 9.14  Putting toys in and out of containers (e.g., dumping and filling) | 12 | 1 | 2 | 3 | E | CG | K |
| 9.15  Watching where toy moves out of sight and going to get it (e.g., ball, car) | 12 | 1 | 2 | 3 | E | M, CG | K |
| 9.16  Using both hands equally well in play to explore | 12 | 1 | 2 | 3 | I | M | A |
| 9.17  Playing with toys, showing awareness of toy functions (e.g., banging on drum, drinking from cup) | 12 | 1 | 2 | 3 | E | CG | K |
| 9.18  Using nonwords to express emotion (e.g., uh-oh, oops, ah) | 12 | 1 | 2 | 3 | S | CM | S |
| 9.19  Patting at pictures in books, turning one or more pages at a time | 15 | 1 | 2 | 3 | E | M, CG | K |
| 9.20  Picking up toys/objects from floor while standing | 15 | 1 | 2 | 3 | I | M | A |
| 9.21  Selecting favorite toy or object and going to get it by him- or herself | 15 | 1 | 2 | 3 | I | CG | A |
| 9.22  Sustaining play by self for a few minutes without caregiver in clear sight | 18 | 1 | 2 | 3 | E | S | S |
| 9.23  Constructing things during play (e.g., build or stacks blocks) | 19 | 1 | 2 | 3 | E | CG, M | K |
| 9.24  Indicating understanding of where toys or other things belong (e.g., goes to shelf to find specific toy, puts toy away) | 21 | 1 | 2 | 3 | E | CG | K |
| 9.25  Holding crayon with three fingers to color | 23 | 1 | 2 | 3 | I | M | A |
| 9.26  Jabbering and saying true words too during play | 24 | 1 | 2 | 3 | E | CM | K |
| 9.27  Pretending by linking two or more actions (e.g., feeding, burping, and putting doll down for nap) | 24 | 1 | 2 | 3 | E | CG | K |
| 9.28  Pretending objects are something else (e.g., block to represent food) | 24 | 1 | 2 | 3 | E | CG | K |
| 9.29  Matching two or more identical shapes or colors (e.g., putting round blocks together, picking out same-colored cars) | 24 | 1 | 2 | 3 | E | CG | K |

*(continued)*

15

**Figure 4.9.**   MEISR items within the Play by Him- or Herself routine.

---

*(continued)*

| 9. Play by Him- or Herself   Participates in play time by him- or herself by . . . | Typical starting age in months | Not yet | Sometimes | Often or Beyond this | Func | Dev | Dnf |
|---|---|---|---|---|---|---|---|
| 9.30  Pretending with elaborate make-believe (e.g., dress up, pretending to be a mommy, firefighter, or teacher) | 30 | 1 | 2 | 3 | E | CG | K |
| 9.31  Showing pride in accomplishments (e.g., clapping, saying "I did it," or otherwise drawing attention to task he or she did) | 30 | 1 | 2 | 3 | S | S | S |
| 9.32  Persisting when something is difficult, trying different ways | 30 | 1 | 2 | 3 | E | CG | K |
| 9.33  Maintaining safety while playing independently (e.g., doesn't play with stove) | 30 | 1 | 2 | 3 | I | A, CG | A |
| 9.34  Scribbling, making lines or zig zags (i.e., more than just marks on paper) | 33 | 1 | 2 | 3 | E | M, CG | K |
| 9.35  Playing within safe boundaries (e.g., driveway versus street) | 36 | 1 | 2 | 3 | I | CG | A |

A.   Total items scored 3 (Often or Beyond this): _____

B1.  Total items scored for child's age: _____

B2.  Percentage of items mastered by age (A / B1 * 100): _____%

C1.  Total items scored for full routine: _____

C2.  Percentage of items mastered by routine (A / C1 * 100): _____%
*Add scores to the MEISR Scoring Summary page*

**Figure 4.9.**   MEISR items within the Play by Him- or Herself routine.

***Bath Time*** Bath time is rich with opportunities for fun and learning. It can also present challenges. It includes such skills as splashing in the water, retrieving dropped toys, and washing body parts on request, as shown in Figure 4.10. The MEISR lists child skills, but in many routines, the adult's role is critical—none more so than bath time because of safety, getting the child in and out of the bath, and attending to the child the whole time.

***Bedtime*** Bedtime can be a beautiful time of the day in a family, or it can be a nightmare. In many families, it just is, which is rather unfortunate, because of its potential for fun and learning. It includes such skills as staying in a near-dark room, going through the steps of the bedtime routine, and cooperating with adults' requests to go to bed. See Figure 4.11.

***Going Out*** This routine, shown in Figure 4.12, addresses all outings from the house except grocery shopping, which is treated as a separate routine. Outings begin with the transition from the home and end with the transition back to home. The demands of this routine often involve being in strange places, having somewhat narrow bands of acceptable behavior, and encountering unfamiliar adults. The routine is important as a context for child skills, such as making transitions, and the important adult opportunity to get out of the house.

***Grocery Shopping*** Going to the grocery store is well known in the disability literature as a rich context for various skills and for possible problems. It is also an essential routine for parents, many of whom take along their infant or toddler. It includes such skills as acknowledging others, sitting in the cart, identifying items, and walking, as shown in Figure 4.13.

| 10. Bath Time   Participates in bath time by . . . | Typical starting age in months | Not yet | Sometimes | Often or Beyond this | | | |
|---|---|---|---|---|---|---|---|
| 10.01 Engaging with caregiver without fussing or getting upset | 0 | 1 | 2 | 3 | E | S | S |
| 10.02 Sitting up propped with arms at least briefly and with head upright | 5 | 1 | 2 | 3 | I | M | A |
| 10.03 Smiling at and playing with own image in mirror | 5 | 1 | 2 | 3 | E | S | S |
| 10.04 Making eye contact, babbling (baba, dada), or otherwise interacting with caregiver | 6 | 1 | 2 | 3 | S | S, CM | S |
| 10.05 Splashing in the water | 6 | 1 | 2 | 3 | E | CG | K |
| 10.06 Reaching for and grasping toy, if sitting securely with support | 6 | 1 | 2 | 3 | I | M | A |
| 10.07 Holding washcloth and imitating caregiver's washing actions | 9 | 1 | 2 | 3 | I | CG | K |
| 10.08 Showing toy to caregiver but not necessarily releasing it | 9 | 1 | 2 | 3 | S | S | S |
| 10.09 Retrieving toys that have fallen into the water | 9 | 1 | 2 | 3 | E | CG | K |
| 10.10 Responding with gestures when asked "want up," "all done" | 9 | 1 | 2 | 3 | S | CM | K |
| 10.11 Holding out arm to be washed | 11 | 1 | 2 | 3 | E | A | A |
| 10.12 Walking with one or both hands held | 12 | 1 | 2 | 3 | I | M | A |
| 10.13 Indicating understanding of a familiar word about bath (e.g., *up, splash*) | 12 | 1 | 2 | 3 | S | CM | K |
| 10.14 Playing with objects in the tub using caregiver to help repeat enjoyable action (e.g., giving caregiver toy to pour, blow bubbles) | 12 | 1 | 2 | 3 | E | CG | K |
| 10.15 Understanding directions and names of things (e.g., *wash feet, get cup*) | 18 | 1 | 2 | 3 | S | CG, CM | K |
| 10.16 Letting caregiver brush his or her teeth (may hold or chew on brush) | 18 | 1 | 2 | 3 | E | A | A |
| 10.17 Standing on one foot, with help (e.g., for drying, putting on pajama bottoms) | 18 | 1 | 2 | 3 | I | M | A |
| 10.18 Cooperating (no fussing) with hair washing | 19 | 1 | 2 | 3 | S | S | S |
| 10.19 Identifying him- or herself in mirrors (e.g., saying name or nickname) | 20 | 1 | 2 | 3 | E | CG | K |
| 10.20 Indicating if the water temperature is uncomfortable (words or gestures) | 20 | 1 | 2 | 3 | S | CM | A |
| 10.21 Putting away bath toys, as part of bath routine, on request with prompting | 22 | 1 | 2 | 3 | E | CM, S | S |
| 10.22 Washing body parts independently (e.g., feet, hands, legs) | 24 | 1 | 2 | 3 | I | A | A |
| 10.23 Cooperating with caregiver for hair brushing | 24 | 1 | 2 | 3 | S | S | S |
| 10.24 Talking during bath time with caregiver understanding half or more of the words he or she says | 24 | 1 | 2 | 3 | S | CM | K |
| 10.25 Brushing teeth with some help | 25 | 1 | 2 | 3 | I | A | A |
| 10.26 Using towel to dry, making drying actions, but still needing help to get dry | 30 | 1 | 2 | 3 | I | A | A |

*(continued)*

17

**Figure 4.10.** MEISR items within the Bath Time routine.

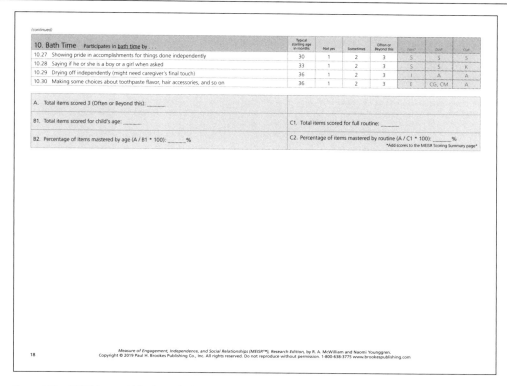

(continued)

| 10. Bath Time   Participates in <u>bath time</u> by . . . | Typical starting age in months | Not yet | Sometimes | Often or Beyond this | Pres* | Dist* | Out* |
|---|---|---|---|---|---|---|---|
| 10.27  Showing pride in accomplishments for things done independently | 30 | 1 | 2 | 3 | S | S | S |
| 10.28  Saying if he or she is a boy or a girl when asked | 33 | 1 | 2 | 3 | S | S | K |
| 10.29  Drying off independently (might need caregiver's final touch) | 36 | 1 | 2 | 3 | I | A | A |
| 10.30  Making some choices about toothpaste flavor, hair accessories, and so on | 36 | 1 | 2 | 3 | E | CG, CM | A |

A.  Total items scored 3 (Often or Beyond this): _____

B1.  Total items scored for child's age: _____

B2.  Percentage of items mastered by age (A / B1 * 100): _____%

C1.  Total items scored for full routine: _____

C2.  Percentage of items mastered by routine (A / C1 * 100): _____%

*Add scores to the MEISR Scoring Summary page*

18

**Figure 4.10.**   MEISR items within the Bath Time routine.

| 11. Bedtime   Participates in <u>bedtime</u> by . . . | Typical starting age in months | Not yet | Sometimes | Often or Beyond this | Pres* | Dist* | Out* |
|---|---|---|---|---|---|---|---|
| 11.01  Falling asleep in response to caregiver (e.g., nursing, rocking) | 0 | 1 | 2 | 3 | S | S | S |
| 11.02  Sleeping for a 4-hour interval at night | 2 | 1 | 2 | 3 | I | A | A |
| 11.03  Sleeping in his or her own crib or bed (i.e., able to do so) | 3 | 1 | 2 | 3 | I | A | A |
| 11.04  Sleeping for 6+ hours (might awaken and fall back to sleep) | 6 | 1 | 2 | 3 | I | A | A |
| 11.05  Comforting self to fall asleep (might use blanket, pacifier to self-regulate) | 6 | 1 | 2 | 3 | E | S | S |
| 11.06  Sleeping for 8–12 hours at night | 12 | 1 | 2 | 3 | I | A | A |
| 11.07  Indicating what he or she wants at bedtime (e.g., pointing, gesturing) | 12 | 1 | 2 | 3 | S | CM | A |
| 11.08  Indicating understanding a word during bedtime routine (e.g., bed) | 12 | 1 | 2 | 3 | S | CM | K |
| 11.09  Using a sign or word to indicate he or she wants to or does not want to sleep | 18 | 1 | 2 | 3 | S | CM | A |
| 11.10  Picking up and carrying larger toy (e.g., stuffed toy, big blanket) | 18 | 1 | 2 | 3 | I | M | A |
| 11.11  Going through the steps in the bedtime routine with caregiver assistance (might even remind caregiver if a step is missed) | 24 | 1 | 2 | 3 | I | S | S |
| 11.12  Joining in to sing a song or say a rhyme (repeating part of it) | 24 | 1 | 2 | 3 | E | CG | K |
| 11.13  Staying in bed throughout the night once put to bed (if expected to) | 30 | 1 | 2 | 3 | I | A | A |
| 11.14  Cooperating with caregivers' request to go to sleep | 30 | 1 | 2 | 3 | S | S | S |
| 11.15  Going to bed fairly quickly (little dawdling) | 33 | 1 | 2 | 3 | E | S | S |
| 11.16  Talking about his or her day or what will happen tomorrow | 36 | 1 | 2 | 3 | S | CM | K |

A.  Total items scored 3 (Often or Beyond this): _____

B1.  Total items scored for child's age: _____

B2.  Percentage of items mastered by age (A / B1 * 100): _____%

C1.  Total items scored for full routine: _____

C2.  Percentage of items mastered by routine (A / C1 * 100): _____%

*Add scores to the MEISR Scoring Summary page*

19

**Figure 4.11.**   MEISR items within the Bedtime routine.

| 12. Going Out  Participates in going out by . . . | Typical starting age in months | Not yet | Sometimes | Often or Beyond this | | | |
|---|---|---|---|---|---|---|---|
| 12.01 Calming when picked up | 0 | 1 | 2 | 3 | E | S | S |
| 12.02 Settling and being relaxed when held or nestled in carrier | 0 | 1 | 2 | 3 | E | S | S |
| 12.03 Crying to indicate discomfort | 0 | 1 | 2 | 3 | S | CM | A |
| 12.04 Smiling purposefully in response to caregiver | 2 | 1 | 2 | 3 | S | S | S |
| 12.05 Making cooing sounds | 2 | 1 | 2 | 3 | S | CM | K |
| 12.06 Looking at or watching caregiver move | 3 | 1 | 2 | 3 | E | CG | K |
| 12.07 Turning head toward a voice (i.e., searching environment for speaker) | 3 | 1 | 2 | 3 | E | CG | K |
| 12.08 Comforting self with pacifier, thumb, or object | 4 | 1 | 2 | 3 | E | S | S |
| 12.09 Lifting head when pulled to sitting (e.g., to be placed in stroller) | 5 | 1 | 2 | 3 | I | M | A |
| 12.10 Responding differently to familiar caregiver versus strangers | 6 | 1 | 2 | 3 | S | S | S |
| 12.11 Waving or gesturing in response to bye-bye | 9 | 1 | 2 | 3 | S | CM | S |
| 12.12 Walking with or without help when given the opportunity | 12 | 1 | 2 | 3 | I | M | A |
| 12.13 Showing understanding of simple questions (e.g., child looks at Mama when asked, "Where's Mama?") | 12 | 1 | 2 | 3 | S | CM | K |
| 12.14 Letting others help (a little stranger anxiety) but still liking constant sight of caregiver | 12 | 1 | 2 | 3 | S | S | S |
| 12.15 Moving from sitting to standing independently, may use support to pull up | 12 | 1 | 2 | 3 | I | M | A |
| 12.16 Pointing to show or drawing caregiver's attention to something | 14 | 1 | 2 | 3 | S | CM | S |
| 12.17 Pointing to something in the distance (e.g., outside) to show caregiver | 18 | 1 | 2 | 3 | S | CM | S |
| 12.18 Using a sign or word to say what he or she wants (e.g., cup, bunny) | 18 | 1 | 2 | 3 | S | CM | A |
| 12.19 Finding a way to occupy self for a few minutes while the caregiver is busy | 18 | 1 | 2 | 3 | E | A | A |
| 12.20 Imitating sounds heard (e.g., animals, vehicles) with or without prompt | 18 | 1 | 2 | 3 | S | CM | K |
| 12.21 Imitating two-word phrase related to going out (e.g., go park, ride car) | 18 | 1 | 2 | 3 | S | CM | K |
| 12.22 Showing affection toward others (e.g., hugging, patting, using affectionate words) | 18 | 1 | 2 | 3 | S | S | S |
| 12.23 Sitting in car seat, leaving the seatbelt fastened for safety | 24 | 1 | 2 | 3 | E | S | A |
| 12.24 Holding caregiver hand, knowing the social rule to do that | 24 | 1 | 2 | 3 | E | S | S |
| 12.25 Saying "mine" to show ownership of his or her things with others | 24 | 1 | 2 | 3 | S | S | S |
| 12.26 Climbing into the car or car seat independently | 24 | 1 | 2 | 3 | I | M | A |
| 12.27 Responding to simple questions (e.g., What's that?) with words | 27 | 1 | 2 | 3 | S | CM | K |
| 12.28 Taking just one of something when told he or she can have only one | 27 | 1 | 2 | 3 | E | CG | K |
| 12.29 Staying with a caregiver when walking (may need frequent reminders) | 30 | 1 | 2 | 3 | E | S | S |

*(continued)*

20

**Figure 4.12.**   MEISR items within the Going Out routine.

*(continued)*

| 12. Going Out  Participates in going out by . . . | Typical starting age in months | Not yet | Sometimes | Often or Beyond this | | | |
|---|---|---|---|---|---|---|---|
| 12.30 Responding to "no" or redirection without a tantrum (e.g., *no, we can't have ice cream now; you can play here but not there*) | 30 | 1 | 2 | 3 | S | CG, S | S |
| 12.31 Saying first and last name when asked | 30 | 1 | 2 | 3 | S | CG | K |
| 12.32 Naming familiar people or animals (e.g., *Papa* for grandpa, *kitty* for cat or familiar cat's name) | 30 | 1 | 2 | 3 | S | CM, CG | K |
| 12.33 Experimenting with balance, taking a few steps on curb edge (if safe to do so) | 33 | 1 | 2 | 3 | I | M | A |
| 12.34 Telling others about things not present (e.g., *Mommy goed work*) | 36 | 1 | 2 | 3 | S | S, CM | S |
| 12.35 Waiting during errands (e.g., at cash register) | 36 | 1 | 2 | 3 | E | S | S |

| | |
|---|---|
| A.  Total items scored 3 (Often or Beyond this): _____ | |
| B1. Total items scored for child's age: _____ | C1. Total items scored for full routine: _____ |
| B2. Percentage of items mastered by age (A / B1 * 100): _____ % | C2. Percentage of items mastered by routine (A / C1 * 100): _____ %  *Add scores to the MEISR Scoring Summary page* |

21

**Figure 4.12.**   MEISR items within the Going Out routine.

| 13. Grocery Shopping  Participates in grocery shopping by... | Typical starting age in months | Not yet | Sometimes | Often or Beyond this | | | |
|---|---|---|---|---|---|---|---|
| 13.01 Attending to sound of caregiver's voice | 0 | 1 | 2 | 3 | S | S | S |
| 13.02 Looking at caregiver's mouth and eyes when face to face | 2 | 1 | 2 | 3 | E | S | S |
| 13.03 Reaching for items/toys that are given (with an open hand or open hands) | 5 | 1 | 2 | 3 | E | M | A |
| 13.04 Responding to *bye-bye* by looking and might try waving | 7 | 1 | 2 | 3 | S | CM | S |
| 13.05 Sitting independently in the cart | 9 | 1 | 2 | 3 | I | M | A |
| 13.06 Pointing or reaching for named item (e.g., "get apple" when shown two items) | 9 | 1 | 2 | 3 | S | CM | K |
| 13.07 Understanding rule to sit in the cart and only occasionally fussing (up to 30 minutes) | 12 | 1 | 2 | 3 | E | S | S |
| 13.08 Indicating what he or she wants (e.g., pointing, gesturing) | 12 | 1 | 2 | 3 | S | CM | A |
| 13.09 Imitating saying a new word (e.g., *cake, banana, eggs*) | 14 | 1 | 2 | 3 | S | CM | K |
| 13.10 Carrying items while walking (e.g., small bag) | 18 | 1 | 2 | 3 | E | M | A |
| 13.11 Recognizing and labeling grocery items (three or more) | 18 | 1 | 2 | 3 | E | CM | K |
| 13.12 Understanding yours and mine (e.g., *this is your drink and this is mine*) | 21 | 1 | 2 | 3 | S | CM | K |
| 13.13 Pushing a stroller or pretend shopping cart | 24 | 1 | 2 | 3 | I | M | A |
| 13.14 Getting items parents have requested off shelf | 30 | 1 | 2 | 3 | S | CM | K |
| 13.15 Showing interest in other children | 30 | 1 | 2 | 3 | S | S | S |
| 13.16 Responding appropriately to unknown adults in the grocery store | 33 | 1 | 2 | 3 | S | S | S |
| 13.17 Walking around things (small and large), moving, and stepping over | 33 | 1 | 2 | 3 | I | M | A |
| 13.18 Walking alongside the cart (staying in safe proximity) | 36 | 1 | 2 | 3 | I | A | A |

A. Total items scored 3 (Often or Beyond this): _____

B1. Total items scored for child's age: _____

B2. Percentage of items mastered by age (A / B1 * 100): _____%

C1. Total items scored for full routine: _____

C2. Percentage of items mastered by routine (A / C1 * 100): _____%
*Add scores to the MEISR Scoring Summary page*

**Figure 4.13.** MEISR items within the Grocery Shopping routine.

***Transition Time***    A section on transitions between routines is included, in part because we know that transition times can be particularly challenging for young children and their families. Family routines occur in different sequences, so it would be inappropriate to assume that children typically transition from bath time to bedtime, for example. The transition section of the MEISR, as shown in Figure 4.14, encourages the family to consider transitions that are typical in their family. These may include transitions from one routine to another as well as transitions that may occur within a routine, for example, getting in and out of the tub at bath time.

Not all the routines in the MEISR will be equally meaningful to any one family perhaps, and other routines, not included here, might be more meaningful. Nevertheless, these 14 common family routines should provide enough information to be able to develop a functional profile of the child in his or her home environment.

## Items Within the 14 Routines

The items within the 14 routines were drawn from consideration of what engagement with adults, peers, and materials in each routine would entail. Items also address independence and social relationships. This information came from experience with hundreds of RBIs and from looking at curriculum-based tools that appeared to have plenty of functional items. Domains were not the organizing framework, because that framework does not lend itself to salience in context. For example, although using single-word labels could be considered functional, in fact it's only functional if it helps a child be engaged in daily routines. The ability to label flash cards with a speech-language pathologist is considered an irrelevant skill in routines-based early intervention.

Some items are repeated because the skills they describe are essential for participation in different routines. For example, children need to be able to walk or otherwise move

| 14. Transition Time  Participates in transition times by . . . | Typical starting age in months | Not yet | Sometimes | Often or Beyond this | Rtne* | Uhm* | Ours* |
|---|---|---|---|---|---|---|---|
| 14.01  Making at least one transition from one routine/activity to another without getting upset or overly fussy | 0 | 1 | 2 | 3 | I | S | S |
| 14.02  Showing awareness of new, strange, different situations by changing behavior (e.g., quieting, looking around more, crying, clinging to caregiver) | 6 | 1 | 2 | 3 | S | S | S |
| 14.03  Listening or attending to caregiver talking without getting distracted | 10 | 1 | 2 | 3 | S | CM | S |
| 14.04  Giving toy or object to caregiver upon request | 12 | 1 | 2 | 3 | S | CM | K |
| 14.05  Showing an emotional response that fits the situation (e.g., resisting unwanted change, obvious pleasure with desired transitions) | 15 | 1 | 2 | 3 | S | S | S |
| 14.06  Recognizing funny transitions and laughs (e.g., putting shoes on hands, giving cup upside down, no water in tub) | 15 | 1 | 2 | 3 | E | CG, S | K |
| 14.07  Trying to do things on own and possibly resisting transitions by fussing | 18 | 1 | 2 | 3 | I | A | A |
| 14.08  Showing awareness of familiar routines and proceeding when prompted | 24 | 1 | 2 | 3 | E | S | S |
| 14.09  Showing shyness or caution in new situations | 24 | 1 | 2 | 3 | S | S | S |
| 14.10  Complying, with prompts/support, despite clear reluctance to change | 30 | 1 | 2 | 3 | S | S | S |
| 14.11  Obeying some consistent and familiar rules related to moving from one activity/routine to another | 30 | 1 | 2 | 3 | S | CM, S | S |
| 14.12  Cooperating with if–then rules, such as first we do _____ , then we'll _____ (might protest anyway) | 33 | 1 | 2 | 3 | S | CM, CG | K |
| 14.13  Stating desires about transitions or changes without a tantrum | 33 | 1 | 2 | 3 | S | CM, S | A |
| 14.14  Talking about some feelings about transitions (e.g., I like Grandma's, I hate going to bed) | 36 | 1 | 2 | 3 | S | CM, S | S |
| 14.15  Following a number of rules and might remind others of rules (e.g., you have to wear smock to paint) | 36 | 1 | 2 | 3 | E | S | S |

A.  Total items scored 3 (Often or Beyond this): _____

B1.  Total items scored for child's age: _____

B2.  Percentage of items mastered by age (A / B1 * 100): _____%

C1.  Total items scored for full routine: _____

C2.  Percentage of items mastered by routine (A / C1 * 100): _____%
*Add scores to the MEISR Scoring Summary page*

**Figure 4.14.**  MEISR items within the Transition Time routine.

independently in a number of routines, so the skill appears in a number of routines. Furthermore, a child's performing the skill in one routine is not a guarantee that he or she performs it in another routine. If we had restricted skills to one routine only, we would have fallen into the trap of ignoring context. In items including the word "independently," this means with no physical assistance.

Figure 4.15 shows the distribution of items across the 14 routines.

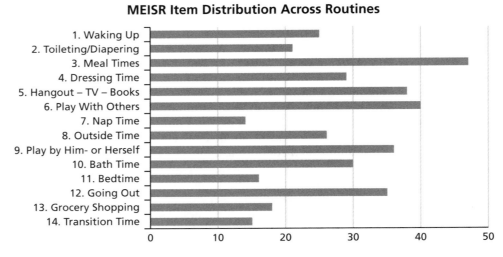

**Figure 4.15.**  MEISR item distribution across the 14 routines.

## How Items Are Scored

To score the items within each routine, the person or people completing the MEISR rate each functional skill, using a 1 to 3 rating scale included in the MEISR. A rating of 1 indicates "not yet," meaning the child does not yet perform the skill described by this item. A rating of 2 indicates "sometimes," meaning the child performs the skill, but inconsistently. A rating of 3 indicates "often or beyond this." "Often" means the child performs the skill consistently. "Beyond this" means the child has mastered the skill and replaced it with one that is more advanced. For detailed guidance on how to complete the MEISR with families and how to score the results, see Chapters 6 and 7.

## REASONS FOR USING THE MEISR

Although the MEISR cannot do everything, it is a robust, multifaceted tool that can be useful at each juncture in the IFSP process. Depending upon the team's assessment purpose, the MEISR is uniquely designed to provide a profile of a child's functioning. For example, it can provide information about the child's functioning organized around routines; items are also linked with typical starting age, with developmental domains, with the three nationally measured child outcomes, and with EISR.

Considering the amount of detail in the MEISR and the useful cross-referencing, the MEISR has multiple benefits. Within the context of early intervention, the MEISR can be used to do the following:

1. Provide informational support to families about their child's development, about the value of routines, and about the value of embedded interventions.

2. Depending upon assessment purpose, provide a profile of the child's functioning in the context of family routines as well as information about functioning within the context of functional areas, developmental domains, and the nationally measured child outcomes.

3. Help the family decide upon functional outcomes they want to address as part of their IFSP.

4. Assist the early intervention team (which always includes the family) to determine the COS ratings as part of measuring the national child outcomes; this use of the MEISR is discussed in detail in Chapter 5.

5. Facilitate a routines-based approach to intervention.

6. Monitor the child's functional progress.

7. As described in Chapter 6, help prepare the family and early intervention professionals for the RBI.

Let's explore each of these uses a bit further.

## Provide Informational Support to Families

Providing informational support, along with emotional support and material support, is one of the core responsibilities of early intervention (McWilliam & Scott, 2001). The MEISR has the potential to be a powerful source of information to families. It provides an opportunity to assess child functioning across the day, which might not happen otherwise. From the MEISR, families can obtain information about child development, about the value of routines, and about the value of embedded interventions.

*Child Development*     The MEISR can help families understand the different types of functional skills occurring in common family routines. Because it includes starting ages for each skill, families also learn about different age expectations, including what is developmentally appropriate. Families can also identify a child's strengths. They might see, for example, that the child is strong in independence in many routines. Although early intervention professionals might highlight the child's inabilities, his or her strengths are important for families to notice and build upon to promote participation and learning in day-to-day routines.

***The Value of Routines***     The MEISR reinforces for families the value of everyday routines that provide many learning opportunities. Research has shown that, across families, 11 categories of family and home activities and 11 categories of community activities are potential learning times (Dunst, Hamby, Trivette, Raab, & Bruder, 2000). In the same way that people might not realize that play is actually when learning occurs, they might not realize that, in early childhood, learning occurs in every chunk of the day. By the time children are older, many of their daily routines are not teaching them anything new. However, in early childhood, so many skills and concepts are emerging that every routine is minimally an opportunity for engagement and maximally an opportunity for learning. Consider diaper changing time, for example: As the baby participates in this time of the day, he is using his muscles and learning how to lift his legs, he is reaching to get the toy that his caregiver offers him, he is figuring out how to activate the toy or touch his mom's nose as they engage in a playful exchange, and so on. Endless learning opportunities are embedded in each routine. Routines are what makes up the fabric of family day-to-day life. They are where family life is played out, where relationships are tested and strengthened, and how life at home is chunked into segments. Sometimes, the segments are defined more by location than by the clock. For example, families will talk about routines when they are hanging out in the living room or when they are outside. The time of day is not as salient as the place. On the MEISR, they are all routines. The MEISR reminds families that routines are where intervention happens—where caregivers interact with the child. Because it is organized around common family routines, the MEISR also makes sense to families.

***The Value of Embedded Interventions***     The MEISR reinforces in families how important and feasible it is to "intervene" with children in the context of everyday routines. Intervene is in quotation marks here to acknowledge that, usually, intervention is accomplished through purposeful parenting during the routine. Such embedded interventions make use of the natural stimuli in routines, happen anyway, and are relevant to the child and the adult. (Interventions that emerge from needs identified in routines and are then implemented in those routines are properly embedded, compared to a process in which the practitioner decides on interventions through a non–routines-based assessment and then looks for routines into which to embed the interventions [Shelden & Rush, 2013].) Routines have natural antecedents for desired behaviors and natural consequences. For example, when the child is riding in the car and a truck passes, the parent can say, "It's a truck," or, "Beep-beep," prompting the child to vocalize (a desired behavior). The antecedent was the presence of the truck. The consequence of the child's vocalization could be the parent's repeating the child's vocalization or praising the child. If they are at the grocery store, and the child says, "Cereal," upon seeing his or her usual breakfast cereal, the parent might give the child the cereal box to hold.

One of the natural features of home and community routines is that the parent or other adult caregiver is with the child: Little kids aren't left alone much for safety reasons. Therefore, if the parent is talking to and playing with the child, some inadvertent teaching is going on. As Mark Wolery (2012) has said, children learn from their parents whether you want them to or not. When teaching and learning happen in routines, the topic is relevant to the child and to the adult. Consider how teaching and learning differ when they occur outside of a family routine, rather than within one. When a parent is told to do speech exercises with a child, the adult might not see how the exercises are going to help, and he or she might forget to do them. The child might also not understand the purpose of saying sounds over and over. If, however, the child has not been speaking during one or more routines and the parent has targeted helping the child use his words to communicate as a goal, the routines provide topics about which to talk, and, for the child, the parent-desired communication makes sense. Therefore, the MEISR helps remind the family that everyday routines are the context for teaching and for embedding interventions.

## Profile a Child's Functioning

Unlike any other assessment tool in early intervention, the MEISR is uniquely designed to provide a profile of a child's functioning that can be used for different purposes. Most importantly, it is organized around common family routines, providing a summary of a child's functional skills. As noted earlier, this is critical for informing families about the value of embedded intervention, as well as the multiple natural learning opportunities that can occur within the context of the things a family does naturally. This embedding negates the "need" for isolated therapy focused on discrete skills that are unlikely to be meaningful to the child or family.

Aside from family routines, the MEISR can also provide information about child routines-based skills in different functional areas. By examining how items are linked with EISR, the team can understand a child's strengths and needs in light of these functional areas. For example, examining the MEISR in this way, the team might learn that, although the child struggles with independence, he is easily engaged and quite socially connected across a variety of family routines. Knowing this can help the team explore ways to build upon the child's strengths to enhance his independence in routines most useful to the family.

The MEISR can also provide information about child routines-based skills in different developmental domains: adaptive, cognitive, communication, motor, and social. This can be helpful when a team is considering eligibility, but it is important to note that using the MEISR for eligibility determination would be a misuse, as the tool was not designed for that purpose. Nevertheless, a team can use the MEISR to augment other information to determine a child's early intervention eligibility based on state-determined eligibility criteria. Furthermore, if the child's current functioning is to be reported by domains, as is required in the United States, the MEISR can provide meaningful information for that report.

A third crosswalk option embedded in the MEISR is the possibility of exploring a child's routines-based skills organized by the three national early childhood outcomes: 1) positive social-emotional skills, 2) acquisition and use of knowledge and skills, and 3) use of appropriate behaviors to meet their needs. As with eligibility determination, neither the MEISR nor any other single tool is designed to generate high-quality COS ratings automatically. Yet, the MEISR is a valuable tool that does what no other known early intervention assessment tool does: It provides a rich profile of a child's functioning organized by each of the three national child outcomes and by age expectations. This profile yields helpful information that teams can pair with other information about a child's functioning to generate highly reliable COS ratings for each outcome. The next chapter elaborates on this use of the MEISR, as does the following section.

## Help Determine IFSP Outcomes

As previously mentioned, the RBI is better than the MEISR for helping families choose goals. This is because the RBI captures many more nuances of a family's day-to-day routines than does the MEISR, is interactive between the parent and professional, and captures family needs beyond the child's. However, if the RBI is not done, the MEISR provides a functional assessment of the goodness of fit between the demands of routines and the child's abilities and interests. This is perhaps the most functional assessment of all. We don't advocate for a deficit approach, but families can see what skills children are missing in different routines and decide whether to target those for intervention. Not all skills are important for all families, so families still need to think about what it is that they want, regardless of what skills are included on a tool. Using information from the MEISR, the team can explore the goodness of fit and identify functional outcomes the family wants included on their IFSP. Identifying outcomes, via exploration of a child's functional participation in routines and family satisfaction with routines, generates more meaningful outcomes than doing so based upon domain-specific deficits or missed items from conventional tests alone.

## Help Teams Determine COS Ratings

Measuring the results of early intervention for children is a U.S. federal reporting requirement of all state early intervention programs. Specifically, states are required to report on the percentage of infants and toddlers with IFSPs who demonstrated improved 1) positive social-emotional skills, 2) acquisition and use of knowledge and skills, and 3) use of appropriate behaviors to meet their needs. These three child outcomes represent the integrated nature of how children develop, and they cross the five domains of development. They also help us shift our focus from discrete, domain-specific skills to children's functional skills and behaviors in the context of day-to-day life. The MEISR is crosswalked with the three nationally reported child outcomes and can provide information about a child's functional abilities by age and within the context of each of the three outcomes. This information is useful when teams convene to determine where the child is functioning relative to same-age peers in each of the three outcomes. Further explanation of how the MEISR can assist the COS process is provided in Chapter 5.

## Facilitate a Routines-Based Approach to Intervention

Because the MEISR is organized around routines, it naturally facilitates a focus on routines rather than an emphasis on deficits in domains or on professional disciplines. It might be tempting to use the MEISR as a curriculum, but as stated earlier, it was not developed for families or professionals to choose isolated skills the child is not performing as outcomes. This attention to children's weaknesses is common in our field, and we do not condone it. Rather, the MEISR can help teams consider the child's functional participation in routines and help the family identify and enhance their child's natural learning opportunities within the mix of things they do naturally. Because the MEISR is organized around routines, it can help teams maintain a focus on routines-based interventions when used effectively.

## Progress Monitoring

The MEISR shows families the progress their children make on meaningful behaviors, which are those supporting children's participation in normal life. It can also be used to keep track of a child's gains in competence in routines as well as in the functional areas of EISR, the five developmental domains, and the three national outcomes. Ultimately, a child's mean ratings and the percentage of skills mastered should increase. In addition, it is useful if an assessment tool can show a child's progress visually. For this reason, we have always liked the original Hawaii Early Learning Profile (Parks et al., 1992), which had scoring sheets to be completed with different colors at different assessment points. The MEISR can also be used in this way to present an understandable visual depiction of a child's functional progress over time. The scoring method is addressed in Chapter 7.

## Assist in Conducting the RBI

With its primary organization by routines, the MEISR is a natural complement to the RBI. MEISR items, at least those around the child's age, would typically be asked about during an RBI. The MEISR can be used ahead of the RBI, to prepare the interviewer with questions that could be asked; during the interview, again to help interviewers with questions or to have a second person capture child-functioning information that emerges from the interview; or after the interview, again to capture information (especially if the interview was video recorded). Using the MEISR in conjunction with the RBI also helps ensure understanding of some skills that might be overlooked in an RBI.

## COMPLETING THE MEISR

As we have discussed, the MEISR is a multifaceted tool designed to suit a variety of purposes. Next, we will present an overview of how it is implemented, including who can complete it, where it is completed, how it is completed, and when in the early intervention process it might be completed. For a more detailed discussion of implementation, see Section III of this book.

### Who Can Complete the MEISR?

The MEISR was designed to be completed by adults living with the child. It can be completed independently by parents or other caregivers in the family, meaning without professional assistance. Alternatively, the family could complete it, collaboratively, with early intervention professionals. Regardless, caregiver input is essential; it cannot be completed independently by professionals. In fact, it would be impossible for a professional to complete the MEISR without parent or caregiver input, because these adults know the answers (i.e., if and how their child demonstrates the different contextually based items on the MEISR).

*Independent Completion by Caregivers*    A parent or other caregiver may complete the MEISR independently or work with the other parent or other adults to decide on the ratings (1, 2, or 3). Only one completed MEISR per child is needed. Most programs will not want two separate MEISRs completed at the same time for the same child. However, if the child is in the custody of two parents, the family and professionals can decide on the value of separate MEISRs.

To complete the MEISR, caregivers can begin at the beginning or start at any desired routine, although starting at the beginning may be the easiest to manage. As will be discussed in Chapter 6, the caregiver should complete all items on the tool. By inviting the caregiver to complete all items, you have the ability to calculate mastery by age *and* by total items in routine.

*Collaborative Completion by Caregivers and Professionals*    Some families don't complete the MEISR independently. They might not have time, might not read, or might not speak English or any of the other languages into which the MEISR might be translated. Given that some families might not complete the MEISR, it is possible to complete all or part of it collaboratively. When doing so, work through the items with the family using discussion, interview, observation, or reading and completing the protocol together. As noted earlier, the MEISR cannot be completed independently by a professional or professionals; it must have the input from those living with the child. In some circumstances, the professional can make assumptions about earlier developmental skills and just score them as "Often or Beyond this" (3). For example, a child who *participates* in the *Waking Up* routine by *Standing for several seconds without support* (1.20) is beyond the prior item (1.14) *Sitting when placed in sitting*. Care should be taken, though, not to make too many assumptions. Instructions for using basals and ceilings are provided in Chapter 7 (the scoring chapter).

### Where Is the MEISR Completed?

The MEISR can be completed just about anywhere. The MEISR consists of a paper protocol, so a caregiver could potentially complete it at his or her leisure in a variety of locations, such as in the comfort of the home, while waiting for an appointment, on a drive to visit relatives (as a passenger!), or while watching the child at the playground. If professionals are working with the family to complete the MEISR, the location will be best determined by the adults' availability. If it is completed in a public place, such as the park, professionals must be mindful about confidentiality.

## How Is the MEISR Completed?

The MEISR can be partly or entirely completed by the family, as noted earlier. It might also be partly or entirely completed via family interview. We, of course, advocate for its use with the RBI. The MEISR can also be completed using a combination of authentic assessment interviewing and observation. The following sections describe how a practitioner can complete the MEISR during a family interview or an observation.

### Completion via Family Interview 
The MEISR, with its unique organization around common family routines, is a natural tool to use when interviewing families about their day-to-day routines and activities. Many early intervention programs embed discussions and data collection about family routines at some point in their process. Rather than just asking, "What does a typical day look like?" or, a little more specifically, "Tell me about meal time," "Tell me about dressing," "How do outings go?" and so on, the professional can use the MEISR for guidance in capturing more detail about the child's functional abilities within family routines. The professional can review the MEISR before the discussion with the family, share a copy with the family to prepare them as well, use it during the discussion, and even use it after the discussion to identify missed items the team needs to revisit. Although a professional can complete the MEISR during any family interview, ideally, he or she would do so during the RBI.

Of course, when conversing with families about their day, you wouldn't ask each question on the MEISR in a mechanical way. Rather, use the MEISR as a tool to predetermine the details to inquire about and to guide you during the conversation. For example, a professional might ask questions, such as the following, to invite the family to share more about their different routines. By starting with open-ended questions, the professional can encourage the family to share rich detail and then ask more specific follow-up questions as needed, as illustrated below:

> *Tell me about waking up time.* [Time to listen.] *How do you know she is awake?* [Time to listen.] *What does she do when she sees you?* [Time to listen.] *What kind of mood is she in when she wakes up?* [Time to listen.] *What position is she in, or is she moving about?* [Time to listen.] *How is she moving?* [Time to listen.] *What is she saying?* [Time to listen.] *How does she respond to you?* [Time to listen.] *What kind of things are nearby her?* [Time to listen.] *What is she doing with those things?* [Time to listen.] Depending upon the parent's response, the professional might ask more specific questions to complete the MEISR, such as, *When she is moving, do you see her playing with her hands and feet, touching them, and watching them move* (1.10)*? When you go to get her, is she raising her arms to be picked up* (1.13)*?*

Programs using the RBI will also find the MEISR a prized tool. It can be given to or reviewed with the family to prepare them for the RBI. It can help the interviewer understand how functional skills align with EISR and what kind of questions the interviewer can ask to capture the rich detail that is part of the RBI. It can guide the interviewer to ask developmentally appropriate follow-up questions. It can also be completed by a second interviewer during the RBI, or the notetaker can use it as a resource to add questions.

Completing the MEISR in part or in full via family interview, ideally the RBI, is an effective use of team time. It also ensures collection of rich information about child functioning beyond simply knowing what time a child wakes or that the child wakes up, eats breakfast, gets dressed, and so on. It is the rich detail that the MEISR includes that truly helps a team benefit from discussions around family routines. This in turn helps the team know the family priorities and identify and enhance children's natural learning opportunities.

## Breakfast (Lucas, 24 Months)

- Breakfast is in the kitchen. He eats with the rest of us. He and the girls usually have cereal. If it's on the run, the girls will give him a Pop-Tart. He can't get the wrapper off. If he needs help, he doesn't ask, he just tries to bite through the wrapper. He doesn't have much patience to wait, even for less than 5 minutes, if he wants something. Rather, he fusses until someone helps.

- Fortunately, most breakfasts are not on the run, and Lucas follows directions to sit at the table initially. But he does not stay at the table. He follows other simple requests, like "eat more" or "finish your drink."

- He gets into and sits in a regular chair at first, but squirms, up on knees and down on bum and up again. He comes and goes from the table. We often have to chase him back to the table.

- When eating, he eats by himself and no longer needs to be fed. He chews his food well—no stuffing or drooling.

- He uses a spoon well and by himself; he spills some. He can take little bites. He'll pick up (pinch) small bits and eat them one at a time.

- At meals, he can be picky—he mostly likes carb foods. A favorite is chicken nuggets. He says "no" when I give him something he doesn't like. Veggies always get a no.

- He drinks from a sippy cup. But not a regular cup; he dumps that and doesn't know how much to tip the cup. And I can only give him plastic cups—he has broken the glass ones.

- When he's done eating, he pushes the bowl away or just leaves the table without returning.

- If he wants more, he'll reach or point for things, even climb on the table; I don't like that. He can say "eat and drink," but doesn't always say that but goes to get what he wants. "More" and "finished" are not yet part of his vocabulary.

- After breakfast, if he played more than ate and the things are put away, he sometimes asks for drink by saying "juice." He'll sometimes say "waf" for waffles—he loves waffles.

- He knows "cookie" too and where they are kept on top of the fridge. He'll point to and ask for cookie. He knows when I point to cookie that means it's cookie time.

**Figure 4.16a.** Example of interview responses that can be used to assess functioning during meal times.

Figure 4.16a includes an excerpt of the information Lucas's mom provided during a discussion about breakfast. The interviewer used the MEISR to guide her in gathering rich information about what Lucas does during breakfast. The sections in gray are actual statements that can be scored on the MEISR. Through this rich discussion, the team was able to complete the MEISR form for the Meal Times routine. Items completed based on this discussion are shown in Figure 4.16b.

***Completion via Authentic Assessment Observation With the Family***     The MEISR also lends itself to completion, in part, by observing the child with the family. The family and the professional can observe the child and watch for the varied routines-based abilities included in the MEISR. It is possible for professionals to assist families with this process by engaging in authentic assessment observations of the child doing what he or she typically does and reviewing that information with the family to complete the MEISR. Family input is important in this process to verify if the observed actions are in fact typical for the child—and only the family knows that best.

Figure 4.17a shows authentic assessment observation notes taken during an observation of Lucas at the park. The professional took these notes while she and his mom were watching

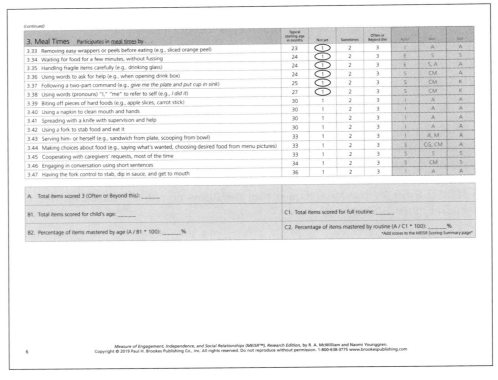

| 3. Meal Times  Participates in meal times by . . . | Typical starting age in months | Not yet | Sometimes | Often or Beyond this | Func | Dev | Use |
|---|---|---|---|---|---|---|---|
| 3.01 Opening mouth when caregiver gives bottle or breast for nursing | 0 | 1 | 2 | 3 | I | A | A |
| 3.02 Sucking strongly enough when nursing or bottle feeding | 0 | 1 | 2 | 3 | I | A | A |
| 3.03 Drinking appropriate amount from bottle or when nursing | 0 | 1 | 2 | 3 | I | A | A |
| 3.04 Swallowing following a few sucks | 0 | 1 | 2 | 3 | I | A | A |
| 3.05 Feeding on a fairly consistent schedule (e.g., every 3–4 hours) | 3 | 1 | 2 | 3 | I | M | A |
| 3.06 Sitting in a high chair upright without slumping over | 5 | 1 | 2 | 3 | I | A | A |
| 3.07 Remaining calm (at least briefly) while waiting for feeding when hungry | 6 | 1 | 2 | 3 | E | S | S |
| 3.08 Holding own bottle (if bottle fed) | 6 | 1 | 2 | 3 | I | A | A |
| 3.09 Beginning to eat solid food (e.g., teething cracker) | 6 | 1 | 2 | 3 | I | A | A |
| 3.10 Raking foods with fingers to pick up and eat | 7 | 1 | 2 | 3 | I | A, M | A |
| 3.11 Eating with little or no drooling (except for teething) | 7 | 1 | 2 | ③ | I | A | A |
| 3.12 Feeding self with fingers (half or more of meal) | 9 | 1 | 2 | ③ | I | A | A |
| 3.13 Chewing food (e.g., cracker, cookie) | 9 | 1 | 2 | ③ | I | A | A |
| 3.14 Using thumb and forefinger to pick up small pieces of food (like pinching) | 10 | 1 | 2 | ③ | I | A, M | A |
| 3.15 Following simple requests (e.g., eat more, drink your water) | 12 | 1 | 2 | ③ | S | CM | K |
| 3.16 Following pointing by looking to person and object | 12 | 1 | 2 | ③ | S | CM | K |
| 3.17 Drinking from a cup with a lid by him- or herself (e.g., trainer cup) | 12 | 1 | 2 | ③ | I | A | A |
| 3.18 Bringing spoon to mouth, eating some of the food from it | 12 | 1 | 2 | ③ | I | A | A |
| 3.19 Using pointing to communicate (e.g., as if to say "look" or "I want") | 12 | 1 | 2 | ③ | S | CM | K |
| 3.20 Saying "no" with meaning | 13 | 1 | 2 | ③ | S | CM | K |
| 3.21 Using a spoon to eat sticky foods (e.g., mashed potatoes) (might include some spilling) | 15 | 1 | 2 | ③ | I | A | A |
| 3.22 Indicating when hungry or thirsty with a sign or word | 15 | 1 | ② | 3 | S | CM | A |
| 3.23 Pointing or vocalizing clearly to indicate food preference | 16 | 1 | 2 | ③ | S | CM | A |
| 3.24 Using a spoon independently for most of the meal | 18 | 1 | 2 | ③ | I | A | A |
| 3.25 Drinking appropriate amount from open cup at one time (with each sip) | 18 | ① | 2 | 3 | I | A | A |
| 3.26 Staying seated for meal while he or she is eating with others | 18 | ① | 2 | 3 | E | S | S |
| 3.27 Using signs or words to ask for at least one *specific* food or drink | 18 | 1 | ② | 3 | S | CM | A |
| 3.28 Communicating "more" with signs or words | 18 | ① | 2 | 3 | S | CM | A |
| 3.29 Communicating "finished" with signs or words | 18 | ① | 2 | 3 | S | CM | A |
| 3.30 Putting an appropriate amount of food in mouth at a time | 18 | 1 | 2 | ③ | I | A | A |
| 3.31 Climbing forward onto adult-sized chair or backing into a child-sized chair | 18 | 1 | 2 | ③ | I | M | A |
| 3.32 Eating a variety of foods | 23 | 1 | ② | 3 | I | A | A |

*(continued)*

5

**Figure 4.16b.**  Example of how functioning during the Meal Times routine could be assessed based on the responses shown in Figure 4.16a.

*(continued)*

| 3. Meal Times  Participates in meal times by . . . | Typical starting age in months | Not yet | Sometimes | Often or Beyond this | Func | Dev | Use |
|---|---|---|---|---|---|---|---|
| 3.33 Removing easy wrappers or peels before eating (e.g., sliced orange peel) | 23 | ① | 2 | 3 | I | A | A |
| 3.34 Waiting for food for a few minutes, without fussing | 24 | ① | 2 | 3 | E | S | S |
| 3.35 Handling fragile items carefully (e.g., drinking glass) | 24 | ① | 2 | 3 | E | S, A | A |
| 3.36 Using words to ask for help (e.g., when opening drink box) | 24 | ① | 2 | 3 | S | CM | A |
| 3.37 Following a two-part command (e.g., *give me the plate and put cup in sink*) | 25 | ① | 2 | 3 | S | CM | K |
| 3.38 Using words (pronouns) "I," "me" to refer to self (e.g., *I did it*) | 27 | ① | 2 | 3 | S | CM | K |
| 3.39 Biting off pieces of hard foods (e.g., apple slices, carrot stick) | 30 | 1 | 2 | 3 | I | A | A |
| 3.40 Using a napkin to clean mouth and hands | 30 | 1 | 2 | 3 | I | A | A |
| 3.41 Spreading with a knife with supervision and help | 30 | 1 | 2 | 3 | I | A | A |
| 3.42 Using a fork to stab food and eat it | 30 | 1 | 2 | 3 | I | A | A |
| 3.43 Serving him- or herself (e.g., sandwich from plate, scooping from bowl) | 33 | 1 | 2 | 3 | I | A, M | A |
| 3.44 Making choices about food (e.g., saying what's wanted, choosing desired food from menu pictures) | 33 | 1 | 2 | 3 | S | CG, CM | A |
| 3.45 Cooperating with caregivers' requests, most of the time | 33 | 1 | 2 | 3 | S | S | S |
| 3.46 Engaging in conversation using short sentences | 34 | 1 | 2 | 3 | S | CM | S |
| 3.47 Having the fork control to stab, dip in sauce, and get to mouth | 36 | 1 | 2 | 3 | I | A | A |

A.  Total items scored 3 (Often or Beyond this): _____

B1.  Total items scored for child's age: _____

B2.  Percentage of items mastered by age (A / B1 * 100): _____%

C1.  Total items scored for full routine: _____

C2.  Percentage of items mastered by routine (A / C1 * 100): _____%
*Add scores to the MEISR Scoring Summary page*

6

**Figure 4.16b.**  Example of how functioning during the Meal Times routine could be assessed based on the responses shown in Figure 4.16a.

---

## Authentic Assessment Observations (Outdoors) (Lucas, 24 Months)

- Climbs up slide, using feet and hands, gets almost to the top
- Goes down slide backward on feet holding on, then turns around and goes down on bum
- Does again on the parallel slide, getting closer, but not to the top
- Slides down backward on belly, turns around, stands on end of slide
- Jumps off slide from standing position with both feet
- Walks up slide steps, one foot on a step and using handrail; on hands and knees at first landing, then walks up remaining steps
- Sits down at top of slide and slides down
- Runs across playground across grass and sidewalk
- Follows after ball, picks it up, tosses it up and forward with both hands
- Throws ball upward underhanded at small basket hoop
- Runs after ball when it rolls away, goes toward road

---

**Figure 4.17a.** Example of authentic observations that could be used to assess functioning during outside time.

him play. Together, the professional and family discussed the observations and collaboratively completed several MEISR items in the Outside Time routine. The comments in gray are actual statements that the family and professional discussed as the parent scored the items on the MEISR. Through this focused authentic assessment, the team was able to complete several of the items for the MEISR Outside Time routine, as shown in Figure 4.17b.

| 8. Outside Time  Participates in outside time by . . . | Typical starting age in months | Not yet | Sometimes | Often or Beyond this | | | |
|---|---|---|---|---|---|---|---|
| 8.01 Looking at object 8–10 inches away | 0 | 1 | 2 | (3) | E | CG | K |
| 8.02 Holding object placed in his or her hand | 2 | 1 | 2 | (3) | I | M | A |
| 8.03 Holding one and reaching for a second toy or object | 6 | 1 | 2 | (3) | I | M | A |
| 8.04 Walking independently at least a few steps | 13 | 1 | 2 | (3) | I | M | A |
| 8.05 Running (might look like fast walk) | 16 | 1 | 2 | (3) | I | M | A |
| 8.06 Moving ride-on wheeled toys (no pedals) with feet | 20 | 1 | 2 | 3 | I | M | A |
| 8.07 Jumping up so that both feet are off the ground | 24 | 1 | 2 | (3) | I | M | A |
| 8.08 Going up the ladder and down small slide | 24 | 1 | 2 | (3) | I | M | A |
| 8.09 Using sandbox toys appropriately (e.g., not throwing or eating sand) | 24 | 1 | 2 | 3 | E | CG | K |
| 8.10 Playing purposefully with playground toys (figuring out their best use) | 24 | 1 | 2 | (3) | E | CG | K |
| 8.11 Playing outside without fussing (with supervision for ~30 minutes) | 24 | 1 | 2 | (3) | E | S | S |
| 8.12 Showing interest in the playground (might have favorite toy/activity) | 24 | 1 | 2 | (3) | E | CG | K |
| 8.13 Catching a large ball (e.g., beach ball) | 24 | 1 | 2 | 3 | I | M | A |
| 8.14 Walking upstairs alone (both feet on each step), using rail if needed | 24 | 1 | 2 | (3) | I | M | A |
| 8.15 Walking downstairs alone (both feet on each step), using rail if needed | 26 | 1 | 2 | 3 | I | M | A |
| 8.16 Jumping off small step or bottom of slide with both feet together | 27 | 1 | 2 | (3) | I | M | A |
| 8.17 Walking forward and backward with balance while playing | 28 | 1 | 2 | 3 | I | M | A |
| 8.18 Walking upstairs alone (alternating feet—one foot on each step) | 30 | 1 | 2 | (3) | I | M | A |
| 8.19 Understanding descriptions such as hot, cold, dirty, wet (e.g., *the ball is dirty, the sand is wet*) | 30 | 1 | 2 | 3 | S | CM, CG | K |
| 8.20 Riding on toy with pedals at least a short distance | 33 | 1 | 2 | 3 | I | M | A |
| 8.21 Climbing on jungle gyms with hands and feet | 33 | 1 | 2 | 3 | I | M | A |
| 8.22 Engaging with others in a game with turn taking (e.g., jumping over rope, chalk line; might need caregiver guidance) | 34 | 1 | 2 | 3 | S | S | S |
| 8.23 Understanding simple rules (but might still test limits) | 34 | 1 | 2 | 3 | E | S | S |
| 8.24 Following caregiver's directions given from a distance | 36 | 1 | 2 | 3 | S | CM | K |
| 8.25 Using big slides (about 6 feet/2 meters high) | 36 | 1 | 2 | 3 | I | M | A |
| 8.26 Swinging on regular swing (might still not pump feet effectively) | 36 | 1 | 2 | 3 | I | M | A |

A. Total items scored 3 (Often or Beyond this): _____

B1. Total items scored for child's age: _____

C1. Total items scored for full routine: _____

B2. Percentage of items mastered by age (A / B1 * 100): _____ %

C2. Percentage of items mastered by routine (A / C1 * 100): _____ %
*Add scores to the MEISR Scoring Summary page*

**Figure 4.17b.** Example of how functioning during the Outside Time routine could be assessed based on the responses shown in Figure 4.17a.

***Completion via a Combination of Approaches***    How the MEISR is completed will depend in part on family and child circumstances and the early intervention professionals. In some instances, the family might complete the MEISR entirely. It might be completed via family interview or the RBI or with the inclusion of shared observations.

## USING THE MEISR IN THE IFSP PROCESS

The MEISR has value at many steps in early intervention. In this section, we'll explore how it might be used at different entry-to-exit processes to help answer different assessment questions and purposes. It alone, however, does not answer all the questions. Rather, information from the MEISR can assist teams with answering processes-related questions and can provide informational support to families. Recognizing that each state and early intervention program works through the early intervention process a bit differently, it will be important to examine the local process to see how the MEISR can ultimately enhance practice. Table 4.1 provides an overview or "roadmap" of ways the MEISR can be useful at different points in the IFSP process. Each is discussed further in the following sections.

### Intake

The intake process begins the family's early intervention journey. It includes learning about what brought the family to early intervention, providing information about the program, beginning the family–professional relationship, and helping the family understand their essential participation and decision-making roles. The intake process, which could take one or more visits, varies across states and among programs. It should also be guided by each child's and family's unique circumstances.

**Table 4.1.**    Roadmap for using the MEISR in the individualized family service plan (IFSP) process

| Process | Questions the MEISR Can Help Answer | How the MEISR Can Help Inform Families | What the MEISR Does Not Do |
|---|---|---|---|
| Intake/Screening | What are some of the child's routines-based skills? | Provides information about child development and routines-based learning. | The MEISR is not a screening tool, and it is not recommended that it be completed in its entirety at intake/screening. |
| Evaluation for Eligibility | What are the child's routines-based skills within the five developmental domains? | Provides information about child development and routines-based learning. | The MEISR does not yield age-equivalency or standard scores that might be needed for eligibility determination. |
| Routines-Based Interview (RBI) | What are the child's functional skills within common family routines? What skills might the interviewer ask about during the RBI? | Prepares the family for the type of information that will be gathered during the RBI. | It is not a protocol for the RBI. |
| IFSP Development | What are the child's routines-based strengths and needs? | Helps the family identify priorities for intervention. | The MEISR does not identify family-level outcomes. |
| Ongoing Intervention | What is the child doing/not doing? | Helps inform the family of functional skills. | It is not intended as a strict curriculum. |
| Progress Monitoring | How is the child progressing in terms of routines-based skills? | Helps the family see child's routines-based progress. | It does not inform progress in routines not included in the MEISR (e.g., classroom routines). |
| Program Accountability (Child Outcomes Summary [COS]) Rating | What is the mix of functional skills a child demonstrates by each of the three child outcomes? | Helps the family see the child's skills in relation to the three outcomes. | It does not generate a COS rating. |

If the team's intake process includes gathering information about the child's participation in family routines, the MEISR can be helpful. If this is not a goal of the intake process, however, the MEISR would be too detailed to include during intake. State intake processes are increasingly including discussion about family routines, but they should not include detailed discussions about routines if the RBI will occur later. Families often have to tell the same story over and over, so we have to avoid this repetition. To best determine if the MEISR would enhance the intake process, think first about the goals and purpose of the local intake process.

## Evaluation and Eligibility

Evaluation and eligibility are processes that help teams understand a child's developmental levels in light of the state's eligibility criteria. When determining eligibility, under the category of developmental delay, the team needs information to conclude if the child exhibits a significant delay in one or more of the five domains of development that meets state eligibility criteria.

The MEISR was not developed as a single tool for determining a child's eligibility for early intervention. Yet there is a growing body of research exploring the use of authentic assessment for eligibility determination (Bagnato, Macy, Salaway, & Lehman, 2007). It can be argued that authentic assessment is a better fit for understanding the developmental realities of a child's participation in day-to-day routines and activities. Furthermore, use of authentic assessments, rather than conventional standardized tools, can expedite the process (Macy & Bricker, 2006). This is because conventional tests alone are ill-suited for identifying family intervention priorities. Yet many states require standardized norm-referenced assessments as part of the eligibility process. So, how can the MEISR be used in the evaluation and eligibility process?

Although the MEISR does not include precise scores for the five domains of development, it can provide information about child functioning in each domain. It is this information that teams might find useful in determining evaluation and eligibility determination. For example, if a team questions the standardized evaluation results, they could examine the child's scores for the MEISR items linked with the domain or domains in question. Not only does the MEISR include truly functional skills, but it also includes notable item density that can help teams discern a child's functioning beyond single standardized evaluation scores. For example, the MEISR includes 13 cognitive items at the 24-month level, far more than what is typically found on a conventional evaluation. The additional items on the MEISR help profile the child's abilities with richer detail than would a conventional test. It is this detail, in the context of family routines, that can help the team truly understand the child's functional abilities.

Information from the MEISR can also be useful to guide a team's informed-opinion process for determining whether a child exhibits a significant delay in development according to the state's eligibility criteria. Informed opinion "refers to the knowledgeable perceptions of caregivers and professionals about the elusive and subtle capabilities of children in different settings that must be defined and quantified so that individuals or teams are able to reach accurate decisions about eligibility for early intervention" (Bagnato et al., 2006, p. 1). Because the MEISR can provide information about child functioning in relation to developmental domains, it can help teams comprehend the mix of abilities a child demonstrates. Depending upon state policies and the questions a team hopes to answer during the evaluation and eligibility determination, the MEISR may be a useful addition or a useful tool to augment the process as needed.

## IFSP Development

IFSP development includes the process of identifying what the family wants to include as intervention outcomes on their IFSP. Traditionally, this involved asking families questions such as, "What would you like your child to be able to do?" "In 6 months to a year from now, what

**Table 4.2.** Two types of individualized family service plan outcomes

| Specific and Contextual Outcomes | Vague and Decontextualized Outcomes |
|---|---|
| Teddy will participate in meal times by saying "all done" rather than pushing his plate on the floor. | Teddy will increase his communication skills. |
| When Teddy says "all done" at 1 meal time a day for 2 consecutive weeks. | When Teddy says 50 words. |
| Teddy will participate in meal times by sitting in a regular chair. | Teddy will stop climbing and wiggling in chairs. |
| When Teddy sits on his bottom in the regular chair for 10 minutes in 1 meal time a day for 2 consecutive weeks. | When Teddy is better behaved when sitting. |
| Teddy will participate in meal times by eating a variety of food beyond chicken nuggets and chips. | Teddy will tolerate eating different food. |
| When Teddy eats 2 different foods at 1 meal time a day for 2 consecutive weeks. | Teddy tolerates 5 new foods. |

do you hope your child is doing?" or "What do you want to work on?" It is no surprise that responses to these questions often resulted in broad statements about improving developmental domains or achieving general milestones resembling sitting up, talking, and so forth; or the response might have been, "I don't know." This is because decontextualized questions are too broad for the team to identify the specific functional priorities a family has for their child and for the family. This is where the MEISR and, of course, the RBI are discernably useful.

It is through the process of completing the MEISR that the family is able to understand the child's goodness of fit with family routines, identify challenging times, and pinpoint the specific child- and family-level actions that would enhance the child's functioning and, ultimately, improve the family's quality of life. The MEISR can help the team ask meaningful questions about family priorities rather than those that result in a "deer in the headlights" response.

Drawing upon the results of the MEISR, the professional can inquire about routines and functional abilities. For example, "As you completed the MEISR and we talked about meal time, you said Teddy is pushing his plate on the floor rather than saying all done or finished (3.29). He still needs to be picked up and put in the highchair and is not yet getting on a regular chair or child-sized chair (3.31), and he has become very fussy, eating only chicken nuggets and chips and not a variety of foods (3.32). Knowing that meal time is currently a challenge, do you want to include any of these skills as intervention outcomes?"

When IFSP outcomes are specific and contextual, they are more understandable and relevant, meaning the entire team understands what the family wants to happen and how they will know when those priorities are achieved. Consider the contrast between the two columns of items shown in Table 4.2.

## USING THE MEISR TO SUPPORT COS MEETINGS

COS meetings are those convened to measure the three early childhood outcomes, as part of the federal reporting requirements for U.S. early intervention services to infants and toddlers with disabilities and their families. The majority of states use the COS process and the 7-point COS scale to rate how close or far a child is from age-expected functioning. Many states and programs also embed COS into their IFSP process. For states and programs using the COS process, the MEISR may be an ideal tool. The MEISR does not generate the end rating on the COS scale. It does, however, provide useful information about child functional performance in relation to each of the three early childhood outcomes.

To discuss the multifaceted components of the COS process, including how the MEISR is useful, we direct you to Chapter 5, in which we define the COS process and illustrate how the MEISR can help teams generate high-quality COS ratings.

## USING THE MEISR TO SUPPORT SERVICE DELIVERY AND PROGRESS MONITORING

Within the context of ongoing intervention support, the MEISR encourages a routines-based focus. Again, the MEISR is not intended as a curriculum. Rather, it is a tool for keeping track of a child's functionally relevant skills within family routines. As children get older, obviously they acquire more skills in routines. The compendium of skills that constitutes the MEISR can therefore be used to monitor progress.

Many people have become accustomed to using developmental-age measures of developmental growth. This reflects, in part, our cultural obsession with knowing how children stack up against their peers. To some degree, this comparison has a place in early intervention eligibility determination and measuring child outcomes. An overemphasis on age and particularly age alone, however, discounts the critical elements of how children learn and progress.

Children learn through repetition of meaningful activities with familiar and trusting caregivers. Children need meaningful opportunities to practice things repeatedly, which happens in family routines. Think about how many times and in how many different ways a child explores a new toy before mastering and then expanding upon its playful use. Although it is possible to conduct drills with children to encourage their learning of specific information, such approaches do *not* promote children's real understanding of the information or facilitate their applying it in meaningful contexts. Rather, the focus of young children's learning should be on promoting their EISR in family and community routines. Conceptualized in this way, it becomes obvious why the MEISR is a useful tool for inspiring a routines-based concentration and monitoring functional child progress in the context of family routines: "The content of intervention is based on the needs of the child, but the feasibility of intervention is related to the daily routines of the family" (Bernheimer & Keogh, 1995, p. 425).

Reviewing the child's progress can happen in the following order, which will be meaningful for most families.

## Progress in Routines

Review the new skills since the previous assessment, which would typically have been 6 months earlier, and discuss with the family how they feel about the child's competence at each time of day. Discuss those items scored 2 or even 1 so the family can consider whether they want to work on those skills. In the course of this conversation, be certain the context of the routine is not lost. Doing so would create a decontextualized, deficit-oriented discussion. Rather, discussing the missed and emerging items within the context of the routine can help the family figure out how they can help their child participate better in the routines of the day versus focusing only on "missed items."

## Progress in EISR

Pay attention to the newly mastered EISR items. Discuss with the family the child's functioning in routines by these functional areas. For example, the interventionist might point out that the child has gained a number of social relationship skills during dressing. This might help the family focus on what social relationship skills to address next. Another example of discussing functioning by EISR might be to point out to the family functional areas in which the child has not gained skills, such as independence.

## Progress in Developmental Domains

Reviewing progress by domains is a less functional focus than progress by routines. Yet teams might find this useful when discussing progress and considering continued eligibility.

## Progress in Early Childhood Outcomes

Reviewing progress in each of the three child outcomes can be particularly useful for programs that measure these outcomes annually. It will also prove useful as the family prepares to exit early intervention and the team completes the COS rating process.

## Progress With Other Tools

Programs and states might use other tools for monitoring progress with standardized scores. The MEISR could be a supplement used to provide examples of functional behaviors in routines. Further exploration of the MEISR with other tools is addressed in Chapter 2 and in the Appendix.

## MISUSES

Just as we address uses of the MEISR, it is important to highlight how the MEISR should not be used. This section is needed for two reasons. First, people have misused other assessment instruments, and the same could happen with this one. Second, the MEISR can be used for many purposes, as we just highlighted. But, as we describe next, it cannot be used to achieve every assessment purpose.

## For Diagnosis

It's unlikely that people would consider the MEISR an appropriate tool for determining what's "wrong" with a child, which is often the purpose of a diagnostic tool. As stated earlier, the MEISR is intended to provide a profile of a child's functioning. It is not a diagnostic tool. Information gained from the MEISR might, however, be a useful augmentation to the diagnostic process, especially when information about a child's routines-based functioning is needed.

## For Determining Eligibility

The age anchors on the MEISR could be used to help teams determine a delay and therefore to make a child eligible for services, but it was not designed for this purpose. The age anchors are to help families understand that not all skills are expected at all ages and to help with measurement of the national child outcomes, for which the team has to know the child's performance compared to age expectations. Furthermore, the ages on the instrument are the ages when the skill emerges; we don't give the range of time over which that typically occurs. Nor is the age provided as a cutoff point after which a caregiver's response of "not yet" would constitute a child's delay in acquiring that skill. Again, it is the starting age. Although the MEISR alone is not intended for determining a child's percentage of delay in the five domains of development, in light of state eligibility criteria, it can augment information from other tools. It can provide a rich understanding of a child's functioning that may assist a team with making an eligibility decision, especially when applying an informed-opinion process. Yet, it is important to know that the MEISR was not designed to be used as a standalone tool for eligibility determination.

## As a Deficit-Oriented Curriculum

We walk a fine line between advocating for the MEISR not to be used to identify deficits and understanding that, in some regard, it will be considered a tool that could help families identify targets for intervention. The MEISR, however, is not intended as a curriculum, meaning professionals aim for every skill to be worked on. Some skills might not be relevant or important to a family. Even if a child is delayed in a particular skill, we might not address it directly, because it's unimportant to the family, it is unimportant relative to other priorities, or it was a battle the family didn't pick. Teachers treat curriculum items, however, as necessary items to teach.

## SUMMARY

The MEISR is not a tool simply to be dragged out at assessment time. It is a tool that, in addition to profiling a child's functional abilities, can empower families by ensuring that they have their voice heard in the team's understanding about what the child can and cannot do. The authenticity of their viewpoint, as the people who are with the child the most, cannot be overstated. Because the MEISR is long and requires literacy skills for parents to complete independently, it can be a uniting activity to have a professional go through it with the family. The MEISR subtly shapes thinking: It gets professionals thinking about what really matters in children's development—the skills that help the child participate in everyday life in a meaningful way. It frees them from the shackles of nonfunctional skills on tests, curricula, and checklists. Families usually already know the importance of functional skills, because the absence of these skills causes low engagement on their child's part. However, professionals and Internet sources sometimes overemphasize discrete developmental milestones and test item completion, which can confuse families and cause them to worry about the child's ability to perform test items. The MEISR helps keep everyone on track with meaningful outcomes and meaningful interventions—determined by the people already teaching the child, in the contexts where the skills are needed.

# CHAPTER 5

# MEISR and the Child Outcomes Summary Process

In 2005, the Office of Special Education Programs (OSEP) started requiring state early intervention and preschool special education programs to measure outcomes of children served in the programs. Early intervention programs are required to report annually the percentage of infants and toddlers receiving early intervention services on an IFSP who have demonstrated improved functioning in three outcome areas: 1) positive social relationships, 2) acquisition and use of knowledge and skills, and 3) taking appropriate action to meet their needs. States use a variety of approaches to measure these three child outcomes, but the majority of states and territories use the COS process (Early Childhood Technical Assistance Center [ECTA], 2017).

The COS process is a team effort that involves gathering information about a child's functioning across a range of situations and settings. A team of professionals collects the information with the family, synthesizes it by the three outcomes, and converts the information to ratings, using the 7-point COS scale anchored by a continuum of foundational to age-expected functioning (Center for IDEA Early Childhood Data Systems [DaSy] & ECTA, 2017). A snapshot of the COS scale is shown in Figure 5.1, and it is available online through the ECTA web site at the following link: http://ectacenter.org/eco/assets/pdfs/Definitions_Outcome _Ratings.pdf.

The COS process yields a rating for each of the three outcomes, which defines where the child's skills are relative to the skills and behaviors expected for the child's chronological age. These ratings are determined as children enter early intervention programs, in some states at annual review meetings, and again as children exit the program. Each child's entry ratings are compared with his or her exit ratings to identify the extent of improvement in each of the three outcomes. These data are then aggregated and reported to the OSEP as part of state reporting requirements.

The data early intervention programs gather through the COS process are not only needed for federal reporting, but also can identify program improvement opportunities and show the success of early intervention. Data quality is a foundational component of the COS process, and it requires strong evidence to support every COS rating. Having good functional data from quality assessment tools can help ensure the quality of child outcomes data.

# Definitions for Child Outcomes Summary (COS) Ratings

| | | |
|---|---|---|
| **Overall Age-Appropriate** | 7 | • Child shows functioning expected for his or her age in all or almost all everyday situations that are part of the child's life.<br>• No one on the team has concerns about the child's functioning in this outcome area. |
| | 6 | • Child's functioning generally is considered appropriate for his or her age, but there are some significant concerns about the child's functioning in this outcome area.<br>• Although age-appropriate, the child's functioning may border on not keeping pace with age expectations. |
| **Overall Not Age-Appropriate** | 5 | • Child shows functioning expected for his or her age some of the time and/or in some settings and situations.<br>• Child's functioning is a mix of age-expected and not age-expected behaviors and skills.<br>• Child's functioning might be described as like that of a slightly younger child. |
| | 4 | • Child shows occasional age-appropriate functioning across settings and situations.<br>• More functioning is not age-expected than expected. |
| | 3 | • Child does not yet show functioning expected of a child of his or her age in any situation.<br>• Child uses immediate foundational skills most or all of the time across settings and situations.<br>• Functioning might be described as like that of a younger child. |
| | 2 | • Child occasionally uses immediate foundational skills across settings and situations.<br>• More functioning reflects skills that are not immediate foundational than are immediate foundational. |
| | 1 | • Child does not yet show functioning expected of a child of his or her age in any situation.<br>• Child's functioning does not yet include immediate foundational skills upon which to build age-appropriate functioning.<br>• Child's functioning might be described as like that of a much younger child. |

**Figure 5.1.** The 7-point Child Outcomes Summary (COS) scale. (Reprinted from Center for IDEA Early Childhood Data Systems & Early Childhood Technical Assistance Center. [2017]. *Definitions for Child Outcomes Summary [COS] ratings.* Retrieved from http://ectacenter.org/eco/assets/pdfs/Definitions_Outcome_Ratings.pdf)

## THE MEISR–COS CONNECTION

A research project examining COS meetings and the validity of COS ratings identified several best practices (Barton, Taylor, Spiker, & Hebbeler, 2016). The ENHANCE project extensively examined the COS processes by collecting data via an online survey, child assessment data, coding and analysis of actual COS meetings, and analysis of child outcome data from 18 states. Data from this study helped define COS process quality indicators (SRI International, 2013). The MEISR includes several characteristics that correspond with COS process best practices. Table 5.1 highlights the goodness of fit between several COS best practice characteristics and the MEISR. Accordingly, the MEISR is a natural tool to assist teams with determining high-quality child outcome ratings as part of the COS process.

**Table 5.1.** How characteristics of the MEISR correspond with best practice characteristics for the Child Outcomes Summary (COS) process

| Best Practice Characteristics | |
| --- | --- |
| COS . . . | MEISR . . . |
| Was established based on children's integrated and functional development rather than isolated skills | Is completely composed of functional skills |
| Requires team consideration of functional skills across settings and situations | Consists of functional skills across common routines assessed by or with the family |
| Calls for team consideration of the full breadth of skills associated with each outcome | Includes a span of functional skills for each of the three outcomes |
| Requires teams to think about the developmental progression of skills including those the child is not yet demonstrating | Contains a progression of functional skills across the birth-to-3-year-old age span for team consideration |
| Expects teams to age anchor skills correctly | Provides functional skill age anchors based upon valid and reliable resources |
| Stipulates that information about a child's functioning should come from the people who know the child best | Focuses on caregivers and authentic assessment as information sources |
| Acknowledges that assessment tools are typically organized around domains | Crosswalks skills with child outcomes |

## COS ESSENTIAL KNOWLEDGE AND THE MEISR

To complete the COS process effectively, teams need several essential knowledge components: 1) the child's functioning across settings and situations, 2) the content of the three child outcomes, 3) age-expected development and age anchoring, 4) age expectations for child functioning within the family's culture, and 5) use of the COS Decision Tree for the 7-point rating scale (DaSy & ECTA, 2017). (This decision tree is available in the online module titled "Session 5: More Information About Determining a Rating," available at the following address: http://dasyonline.org//olms2/5054208.) The MEISR supports each of these COS essential knowledge factors.

### Child Functioning Across Settings

Determining how a child functions across settings requires finding out how the child participates in day-to-day routines, how independently the child achieves his or her needs and desires, and how he or she interacts with other children, adults, and the environment. Notice that these dimensions of children's functioning encompass EISR and align with the three child outcomes. Assessing children's functioning also means focusing on the whole child versus isolated skills or separate domains, focusing on routines and activities in which the child participates, and focusing on the purpose and function of skills. For example, using a finger in a pointing motion is an isolated skill. To understand if the pointing has a function, we must consider the context in which the child is participating: Perhaps the child is having lunch with her mother, points at the bag of cookies on the table, and then looks back at her mother. The child's pointing has a function to request a cookie. If the child is walking outside with her older brother and pointing at the garbage truck, saying "Uck," the pointing action is now being used to draw her brother's attention to the truck that she sees. The child may also extend her finger in a pointing motion to activate a favorite toy while playing independently on the living room floor, pointing in response to a question asked about the book she is looking at, and so on. Skills can have different functions, but without gathering information about children's EISR across settings, we cannot fully understand how a child is using skills in a functional manner. If teams rely primarily on standardized, domain-based assessment instruments, they can miss out on understanding a child's true functioning. The MEISR, however, is organized by functional skills that are meaningful in the context of family routines.

## Content of Child Outcomes

A key challenge with measuring the three child outcomes is that assessment tools are nearly always organized around developmental domains (e.g., cognitive, communication, motor, adaptive, social-emotional). To mitigate this challenge, the ECTA (2019) developed crosswalks that cross-reference the skills listed on developmental assessments with the three child outcomes. (These are available through the ECTA web site at the following link: http://ectacenter .org/eco/pages/crosswalks.asp.) For example, skills related to how a child initiates interaction with peers are aligned with Outcome 1, positive social relationships; preliteracy skills are associated with Outcome 2, acquire and use knowledge and skills; and skills demonstrating the ability to move around independently are aligned with Outcome 3, take appropriate action to meet needs. Although these crosswalks are helpful, developmental assessments typically include decontextualized skills not easily translated to functional skills that are meaningful in children's and families' day-to-day activities. Accordingly, the crosswalks are helpful with the domain-to-outcome translation but do not necessarily include the vital functional aspect addressed earlier in this chapter and earlier in this manual. Unlike traditional tools, the MEISR includes an embedded crosswalk identifying the relationship of each routines-based functional item to a child outcome.

## Age Anchoring

Another essential knowledge point in the COS process is understanding age-expected development and age anchoring. Age anchoring is "the process of examining a child's functional abilities skills and behaviors and determining how close that functioning is to the functioning expected for the child's chronological age" (ECTA & DaSy, 2018a, p. 4). In light of the child's functional skills, the team considers the developmental progression of skills, determines what is expected for the child's age, and determines how close to or how far from the age expectations the child's functioning is using the categories of *age-expected* (AE), *immediate foundational* (IF), and *foundational* (F). The developmental continuum from F to AE can be thought of as a staircase, with earlier skills serving as the foundation for IF and AE skills, as shown in Figure 5.2 (ECTA & DaSy, 2018a, p. 10).

The MEISR includes starting ages for all of the routines-based skills included, thus making it a valuable resource for age anchoring. The following AE, IF, and F examples show how the MEISR can assist teams with age anchoring.

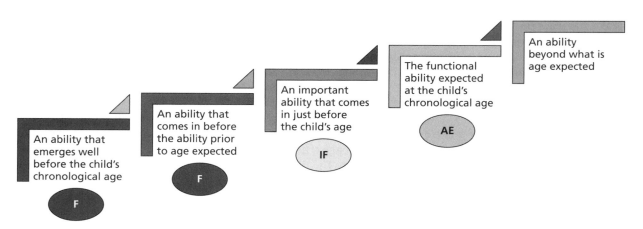

**Figure 5.2.** The developmental continuum from foundational (F) skills to immediate foundational (IF) and age-expected (AE) skills. (Reprinted from Early Childhood Technical Assistance Center & Center for IDEA Early Childhood Data Systems. [2018a]. *Age anchoring guidance for determining child outcomes summary [COS] ratings: Guidance for EI/ECSE practitioners and trainers* [p. 10]. Retrieved from http://ectacenter.org/~pdfs/eco/COS_Age _Anchoring_Guidance.pdf)

**AE** skills and behaviors are those expected for a child at a specific age. For example, Danielle, the mother of 5-month-old Ellie, says she puts Ellie in the high chair for breakfast, and Ellie sits up in it without slumping over. Using the MEISR, we see that the functional skill *Sitting in a high chair upright without slumping over* (3.06) is one that a child might have starting around 5 months of age. Therefore, in this example, we'd say this is an AE skill for Ellie.

**IF** skills and behaviors are those that occur just prior to AE skills and can be thought of as functional abilities like those of a slightly younger child. For example, Josie's child care teacher told Josie's dad that 30-month-old Josie shows interest in playing with the other children by going to where they are playing, but she is not yet initiating play with them or talking to them. Using the MEISR, we see that *Showing interest in playing with other children (e.g., going to where they are)* (6.25) emerges around 24 months of age, and *Initiating play with other children and talking to others with words* (6.32) is a 30-month-old ability. Considering Josie and this information, we would say this is an IF skill for Josie, because what she is doing develops just before what's expected of a child her age with regard to interacting with peers.

**F** skills and behaviors are those that start at a much earlier age and are the functional skills of a much younger child. For example, during the RBI, Heinz explains how his 19-month-old son, Dieter, plays with his favorite toys (i.e., wooden train, texture blocks, and a squeaky giraffe), mostly by picking them up, holding them, and then mouthing them. Using the MEISR, we see that *Exploring objects with hands and mouth* (9.03) is a skill that starts around 3 months of age. When asked more about play, Heinz said he had not seen Dieter dump toys and, although he had tried to encourage him to build with the blocks, he mostly just mouthed the blocks. Knowing this, we see that Dieter is not yet *Putting toys in and out of containers (e.g., dumping and filling)* (9.14), which is a skill that emerges at 12 months. We also know that he is not *Constructing things during play* (9.23), which is an AE skill for a 19-month-old child. With this knowledge, we can say that the way Dieter is exploring objects with his hands and mouth is considered a skill at the foundational level. This means that it is an important foundational ability to build upon, but he will need to develop several skills before he demonstrates the AE skill of constructing with toys.

Although knowledge of child development is important for early interventionists, it is unrealistic to expect these professionals to remember the age at which every functional skill or ability emerges. This is why using resources such as developmental guidelines, criterion-referenced instruments, and shared expertise from team members is essential for the COS process. As seen in the previous examples, the MEISR can be instrumental in helping teams age anchor the functional skills a child demonstrates across situations and settings. The precise nature of the skills reported and observed, however, might not be stated or seen exactly the same way as they are documented in the MEISR. Under these circumstances, teams must look for the underlying function of the skill and anchor it to the paired routines-based skill on the MEISR. For example, suppose that on a library outing with the family, you and Benny's mom observed how 16-month-old Benny walked independently across the large library open area without support, but he held his arms low and slightly out to his sides and took wide but controlled steps. The MEISR does not (nor will any single assessment tool) have exact matches for every nuance of all the functional skills teams observe children doing. But often there is an equivalent routines-based skill on the MEISR. For this example of Benny at the library, the MEISR skill would be item 12.12, *Walking with or without help when given the opportunity,* and this skill develops around 12 months of age. Knowing that Benny is 16 months old, we cannot say what he is doing is an AE skill, but it is an important ability that emerges just before his age, so we would identify it as an IF skill. If Benny were 30 months of age in this example, we would identify this skill as an F skill because it would have typically developed at a much younger age (12 months).

The COS process requires a synthesis of all the information known about the child's functioning, and no single assessment tool can provide all the information needed. Rather, the richness of information gathered through the early intervention process, including parent input and team observations, must be considered when teams decide upon COS ratings using the 7-point scale. Therefore, although the MEISR includes a rich array of functional skills and provides valuable information about a child's functional abilities, it should not be used as the sole source of information for the COS process. There will be instances when teams have to draw upon other resources to assist with age anchoring functional skills that are not included in the MEISR. Furthermore, the routines in the MEISR might not capture all those occurring in a child's life (Dunst et al., 2000). Information from the MEISR and details from other assessments, reports about the child's progress, and input from parents, caregivers, and other professionals provide the multiple data sources needed to understand a child's functional abilities across settings relative to the three child outcomes.

## Functioning Within the Family Culture

Cultural diversity is ever increasing, and assessment practices must be culturally competent to obtain valid information. The tendency for bias occurs when professionals unfamiliar with the family culture are the primary assessors, when the assessment relies upon instruments that do not include children of the same culture in the norming sample, and when the people who know the child and culture best are not key players in the assessment process. The MEISR reduces cultural bias because the family is providing the information. On occasion, an item on the MEISR may not be something the family encourages their child to do; in these situations, the family can simply skip that item, and doing so does not factor against the child or the family.

## Decision Tree

Using the COS Decision Tree for the 7-point scale (ECTA & DaSy, 2018b) is essential in the COS process. It is used to guide the COS rating discussion, to help teams accurately apply COS rating criteria, and to ensure careful distinctions among these seven points on the COS rating scale. Use of the Decision Tree is considered essential for implementing uniform application of the COS process (Younggren, Barton, Jackson, Swett, & Smyth, 2016). In fact, the *Child Outcomes Summary–Team Collaboration Quality Practices Checklist and Descriptions* (Younggren et al., 2016) specifically defines use of the Decision Tree as a quality practice in building team consensus for a high-quality COS rating. When using the Decision Tree, teams answer questions related to a child's functioning, such as *Does the child ever function in ways that would be considered age expected with regard to this outcome? Does the child function in ways that would be considered age expected across all or almost all settings and situations? To what extent does the child function in ways that are age expected across settings and situations? Does the child use any immediate foundational skills related to this outcome upon which to build age-expected functioning across settings and situations?* This is yet another point in the COS process where the MEISR can be particularly useful because it can provide a profile of the child's functioning organized by age and by child outcome area that teams can refer to when discussing the questions embedded in the Decision Tree to generate quality COS ratings.

For example, suppose an intervention team were to examine the MEISR profile for Bobby, a child who is 12 months old. They examine items related to the early childhood outcome of *acquiring and using knowledge and skills* (K). In so doing, they realize that Bobby

- Has several IF skills, as shown by his scores of 3 on several items with a typical starting age of 9 months within the routines of Toileting/Diapering, Going Out, Play With Others, Play by Him- or Herself, Nap Time, and Bath Time

- Has some AE skills, as shown by his scores of 3 on several items with a typical starting age of 12 months within the routines of Play by Him- or Herself and Hangout – TV – Books

- Is missing some AE skills, as shown by his scores of 1 or 2 on several items with a typical starting age of 12 months within the routines of Meal Times, Going Out, Play With Others, Play by Him- or Herself, Nap Time, and Hangout – TV – Books

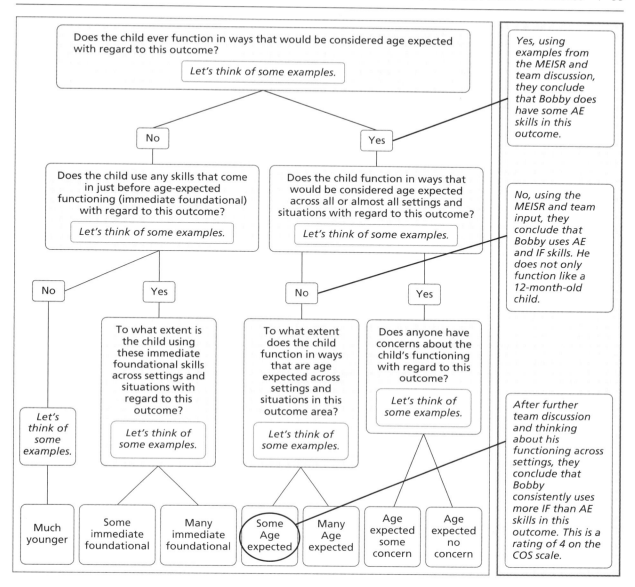

**Figure 5.3.** Sample of a Decision Tree a team could use to identify Bobby's Child Outcomes Summary (COS) rating for the outcome *acquiring and using knowledge and skills*, based on his MEISR scores and other information about his functioning. (*Key:* AE, age expected; IF, immediate foundational.) (Adapted from Early Childhood Technical Assistance Center & Center for IDEA Early Childhood Data Systems. [2018b]. *Decision tree for summary rating discussions.* Retrieved from http://ectacenter.org/eco/assets/pdfs/Decision_Tree.pdf)

Using information from the MEISR profile as well as other team information about Bobby's functioning in this outcome area, the team can collaboratively use the Decision Tree to identify the COS rating. Shown in Figure 5.3 is a version of the Decision Tree and excerpts from a team discussion, using, in part, the information from Bobby's MEISR.

For example, starting at the top of the Decision Tree, the team engages in a discussion to determine if the "child ever functions in ways that would be considered age expected." Their response is *yes* (see the top discussion box). They then follow the Decision Tree process down to the next question, "Does the child function in ways that would be considered age expected across all or almost all settings and situations?" Their response is *no* (see the middle discussion box). The next question on the Decision Tree is, "To what extent does the child function in ways that are age expected across settings and situations?" The team engages in further discussion before agreeing upon a rating (see the bottom discussion box).

The MEISR was not originally developed with the COS process in mind, but it clearly is a complement to the COS process.

## MEISR AS A LEARNING RESOURCE

Beyond its value for understanding a child's functional skills and age anchoring as part of the COS process, the MEISR is a helpful learning tool for reinforcing the difference between functional and nonfunctional skills. Functional skills represent integrated abilities that allow the child to interact with others meaningfully, effectively engage in various activities, and appropriately meet their needs in the context of day-to-day happenings. Reviewing functional skills in meaningful contexts, like those included in the MEISR, can serve as a learning activity for teams, individuals, and students interested in children's functional skill development. The MEISR is also a resource for building or rekindling understanding of typical development, another critical skill associated with the COS process.

## DATA QUALITY

As seen in this chapter, the MEISR includes functional information essential for determining high-quality COS ratings, making it a valuable part of the COS process. The COS data that programs are required to collect and report help them understand how programs are doing with children and families, define program improvement targets, and record successes for children, families, programs, and entire early intervention systems. For these reasons, having high-quality data is imperative. The MEISR is an ideal assessment for informing the COS process and consequently improving the quality of the data used in the COS process.

## SUMMARY

This chapter explained how the MEISR can support the COS process that early childhood programs use to measure the outcomes of the children they serve. The COS process is used to report information about children's functioning in three areas: 1) positive social relationships, 2) acquisition and use of knowledge and skills, and 3) taking appropriate action to meet their needs. The MEISR supports five knowledge components a team needs to complete the COS process: 1) the child's functioning across settings and situations, 2) the content of the three child outcomes, 3) age-expected development and age anchoring, 4) age expectations for child functioning within the family's culture, and 5) use of the COS Decision Tree for the 7-point rating scale. Because the MEISR includes starting ages for all of the skills included within each of 14 routines, it is useful for age anchoring and for identifying what F, IF, and AE skills a child has. This chapter explained how a team can collaboratively use a Decision Tree to complete a COS rating for a child in a given area, based on the child's MEISR scores and other information about his or her functioning.

# Implementation, Scoring, and Working With Data

CHAPTER 6

# Introducing the MEISR to Families and Collecting Data

When introducing the MEISR, the professional should discuss its specific purpose and benefits as they apply to each family. Although the process is straightforward, professionals might feel more confident presenting this comprehensive instrument to families if they have some guidance. This chapter offers such guidance; if the MEISR is being completed in conjunction with the RBI, review also the RBI guidelines in Chapter 3. In addition, Chapters 7 and 8 provide an in-depth discussion of how to score the MEISR and interpret results. Depending on how the professional and family choose to work together to complete the MEISR, the professional will likely want to share this information with caregivers.

Throughout this chapter, we use the example of Shawn to demonstrate the collaborative exchange that takes place between families and professionals when using the MEISR. Let's begin with an introduction to Shawn and his family.

### Meet Shawn and His Parents, Shanika and Jamal

Shawn is a 12-month-old boy who enjoys music and loud toys that he can activate by batting his arms. Shawn is not sitting up yet. He has increased muscle tone in his legs, which are often in full extension, tightly stretched out, and crossed over one another ("scissored"). His arms are also tight but bent at the elbow. His hands are mostly held in a fisted position, with his thumbs tucked inside his hands. Shawn flips himself over when he is lying on the floor. He cries quite a lot, but he also laughs when his parents play silly games with him. His mother, Shanika, stays home with him. Shawn's father, Jamal, delivers heating oil and is out of the house from 7 a.m. to 6 p.m. weekdays. When he's home, Jamal spends time with Shawn, mostly holding him while playing video games or watching TV.

An early intervention professional, Isabel García, visits the family regularly. During her first visit to the home, Isabel took note of details about Shawn. She planned to introduce the MEISR to the family during her third visit. In this case, the MEISR was not used in IFSP development but for monitoring child progress and for discussion of functioning with Shawn's family.

## INTRODUCING THE MEISR

The early intervention team can introduce the MEISR to the family at different points during the intervention process, including before, during, and after the development of the IFSP. As noted earlier, the caregiver and the professional complete the MEISR collaboratively; "caregiver" is defined, for our purposes, as someone who has observed the child often in the home, such as a parent or other adult family member who lives with the child. Key points for professionals to review prior to introducing the MEISR are as follows.

---

## Administration Guidelines for Intervention Professionals

1. Have the caregiver complete the MEISR, or ensure you complete it based on the caregiver's interview responses, your observation of the child in the home, or both. Under no circumstances should the MEISR be completed without a caregiver's input.

2. Before administering the MEISR, explain to the caregiver the specific purpose for using it. Explain that it will take about 45 minutes to complete.

3. Briefly review the MEISR's structure and content with the caregiver, along with the criteria for rating an item 1, 2, or 3.

4. Briefly explain the purpose of the following parts of the form (see Figure 6.1). Point out that they are for professional use and do not need to be completed by the caregiver.

   a. The three rightmost columns in each routine, which crosswalk the items with functional domains, developmental domains, and national child outcomes. (See Figure 6.1a.)

   b. Rows A, B, and C at the bottom of each routine, used for calculating mastery percentages. (See Figure 6.1b.)

   c. The MEISR Scoring Summary on page 2 of the MEISR. (See Figure 6.1b.)

5. Review the directions on page 1 of the MEISR form and complete this page. (See Figure 6.1c.)

6. Have caregivers rate all items within each routine, including those with a typical starting age beyond the child's age.

7. Follow scoring instructions at the bottom of each routine to determine the percentage of items mastered by age and by routine. Do not expect the caregiver to do this.

8. Once completed, transfer scores for all routines to the MEISR Scoring Summary page.

---

The dialogue below illustrates how a professional might answer the family's basic questions upon initially seeing the MEISR. The sections that follow provide detail about why the professional might introduce the MEISR at any of various points in the IFSP process.

### Introducing the MEISR and Responding to Shanika's Initial Questions

When Isabel introduced the MEISR to Shawn's family, she discussed how the assessment is organized by 14 everyday routines, pointed out some of the specific items within different routines, and explained that for each item, Shanika could circle 1, 2, or 3, depending on what Shawn usually did. Shanika listened to Isabel's description of the MEISR while she flipped through its pages. "What are all these numbers and letters for?" Shanika asked. The early interventionist explained, "The numbers and letters help us see patterns and connections in Shawn's development. What's most important for you are the columns with 1, 2, and 3."

Shanika examined the page in front of her. Isabel saw she was looking at the Bath Time page, so she pointed to skill 10.05 and asked, "Does Shawn splash in the water?"

"Sometimes."

"Then you'd circle 2. See: 'Sometimes.'"

"So this is what Shawn can and can't do?" asked Shanika.

"Yes, this will give us a picture of what Shawn can do in different activities throughout the day that are part of your regular family life."

| 1. Waking Up   Participates in waking up time by . . . | Typical starting age in months | Not yet | Sometimes | Often or Beyond this | Func | Dev | Out |
|---|---|---|---|---|---|---|---|
| 1.01  Making vocal sounds | 0 | 1 | 2 | 3 | S | CM | K |
| 1.02  Showing enjoyment when held, rocked, touched by caregiver | 0 | 1 | 2 | 3 | S | S | S |
| 1.03  Looking at caregiver and making eye contact | 0 | 1 | 2 | 3 | S | S | S |
| 1.04  Easily turning head to both sides | 1 | 1 | 2 | 3 | I | M | A |
| 1.05  Acting happy to see or hear caregiver | 1 | 1 | 2 | 3 | S | S | S |
| 1.06  Showing interest in crib toys (e.g., watching mobile) | 2 | 1 | 2 | 3 | E | CG | K |
| 1.07  Turning over from side to tummy or side to back | 2 | 1 | 2 | 3 | I | M | A |
| 1.08  Smiling, kicking, moving arms excitedly when sees caregiver | 2 | 1 | 2 | 3 | S | S, M | S |
| 1.09  Reaching out for or batting at toys, repeating action with enjoyment | 3 | 1 | 2 | 3 | E | CG, M | K |
| 1.10  Playing with hands and feet, touching and watching movements | 3 | 1 | 2 | 3 | E | CG | K |
| 1.11  Turning toward the sound of caregiver's voice | 3 | 1 | 2 | 3 | S | S | S |
| 1.12  Maintaining sitting at least briefly | 5 | 1 | 2 | 3 | I | M | A |
| 1.13  Raising arms to be picked up when caregiver reaches for child | 5 | 1 | 2 | 3 | S | CM, S | S |
| 1.14  Sitting when placed in sitting | 6 | 1 | 2 | 3 | I | M | A |
| 1.15  Moving up and down by bending knees when supported in standing | 6 | 1 | 2 | 3 | I | M | A |
| 1.16  Calling out for caregivers (e.g., shouting, vocalizing) | 7 | 1 | 2 | 3 | S | CM, S | A |
| 1.17  Waking up without crying immediately (calming self) | 8 | 1 | 2 | 3 | E | S | S |
| 1.18  Standing and cruising around crib | 10 | 1 | 2 | 3 | I | M | A |
| 1.19  Saying "mama" or "dada" when sees Mama or Dada | 12 | 1 | 2 | 3 | S | CM, S | S |
| 1.20  Standing for several seconds without support | 12 | 1 | 2 | 3 | I | M | A |
| 1.21  Playing with toys momentarily until caregiver comes (i.e., coping) | 18 | 1 | 2 | 3 | E | S | S |
| 1.22  Responding to caregiver's greeting with a sign or word | 18 | 1 | 2 | 3 | S | CM | S |
| 1.23  Leaving room to find caregiver | 24 | 1 | 2 | 3 | I | S | A |
| 1.24  Letting caregiver know how he/she is feeling (e.g., happy) by saying so or responding to a question | 30 | 1 | 2 | 3 | S | S | S |
| 1.25  Following directions involving descriptions (e.g., get the *big* pillow; be *quiet*, Sissy is still sleeping) | 33 | 1 | 2 | 3 | S | CG, CM | K |

A.  Total items scored 3 (Often or Beyond this): _____

B1.  Total items scored for child's age: _____

B2.  Percentage of items mastered by age (A / B1 * 100): _____ %

C1.  Total items scored for full routine: _____

C2.  Percentage of items mastered by routine (A / C1 * 100): _____ %
*Add scores to the MEISR Scoring Summary page*

3

**Figure 6.1a.**   Review with caregivers how to rate each item in a routine with a 1, 2, or 3. Point out that caregivers do not need to complete the Func[a], Dev[b], or Out[c] columns at right or the rows at the bottom used for calculating mastery percentages.

## MEISR Scoring Summary

| MEISR Routines (number of items in routine) | A. Total Number of 3s | B1. Total Number of Items Scored for Child's Age | B2. Percentage of Items Mastered by Child's Age (A/B1 * 100 = %) | C1. Total Number of Items Scored for Routine | C2. Percentage of Items Mastered by Routine (A/C1 * 100 = %) |
|---|---|---|---|---|---|
| 01. Waking Up (25) | | | % | | % |
| 02. Toileting/Diapering (20) | | | % | | % |
| 03. Meal Times (47) | | | % | | % |
| 04. Dressing Time (29) | | | % | | % |
| 05. Hangout – TV – Books (38) | | | % | | % |
| 06. Play With Others (38) | | | % | | % |
| 07. Nap Time (14) | | | % | | % |
| 08. Outside Time (26) | | | % | | % |
| 09. Play by Him- or Herself (35) | | | % | | % |
| 10. Bath Time (30) | | | % | | % |
| 11. Bedtime (16) | | | % | | % |
| 12. Going Out (35) | | | % | | % |
| 13. Grocery Shopping (18) | | | % | | % |
| 14. Transition Time (15) | | | % | | % |
| TOTALS | | | % | | % |

2

**Figure 6.1b.**   After the caregiver has rated all items in a routine and mastery percentages have been determined, transfer scores for all routines to the MEISR Scoring Summary on page 2.

**MEISR™ Measure of Engagement, Independence, and Social Relationships**

The MEISR™ is a list of skills that infants and toddlers (birth to 3 years of age) typically display in everyday routines within the home and community. To complete the MEISR, caregivers assess a child's level of functional participation in 14 different routines. For the purposes of the MEISR, a caregiver is defined as someone who has observed the child often in the home. Caregivers may work together with a professional to complete the MEISR.

The MEISR has many benefits within the context of early intervention. Prior to administration, professionals should discuss the specific purpose and benefits as they apply to each child and family.

**Directions to professionals:** Ask caregivers to rate **all items** within each routine, including items with a typical starting age beyond the child's age. Follow instructions at the bottom of each routine to determine scoring. Scores indicate a child's level of mastery by age (relative to typical starting age for skills) and by routine (relative to all skills for that routine up to 36 months of age). Once completed, transfer scores for all routines to the MEISR Scoring Summary page. See the manual for complete administration instructions (Chapters 4 and 6) and scoring instructions (Chapter 7).

**Directions to caregivers:** On a scale from 1 to 3 (Not yet, Sometimes, Often or Beyond this), rate your child's level of functioning in performing activities. Circle 1, 2, or 3 for each skill. Depending on the child's age, some activities may be beyond your child's capability. This is expected. The MEISR takes about 45 minutes to complete.

| | | |
|---|---|---|
| Child's name: | Child's DOB:<br><br>Child's age in months: | Today's date:<br><br>Date(s) of previous MEISR use (if applicable): |
| Caregiver(s) name and relationship to child:<br><br>Caregiver(s) contact information: | | |
| Professional(s) name and affiliation:<br><br>Professional(s) contact information: | | |

**KEY:**

**Func**[a] Functional Domains: **E** = engagement, **I** = independence, **S** = social relationships

**Dev**[b] Developmental Domains: **A** = adaptive, **CG** = cognitive, **CM** = communication, **M** = motor, **S** = social

**Out**[c] National Child Outcomes: **S** = positive social relationships, **K** = acquiring and using knowledge and skills, **A** = taking appropriate action to meet needs

 

**Figure 6.1c.** Review the directions on page 1 before completing this page with information about the intervention professional(s), caregiver(s), child, and date(s) of MEISR administration.

Shanika nodded to show she understood. Isabel explained that the MEISR helps Shanika and Jamal figure out what Shawn can do as well as track his progress over time. Shanika furrowed her brow and asked, "You want Shawn to do all these things?"

Isabel replied, "We want to figure out whether Shawn is learning the skills that your family finds useful for your life at home. Shawn doesn't have to do all the things listed here. That's up to your family. This tool helps us see how well Shawn is progressing."

The two women agreed that Shanika would complete the MEISR for Shawn before Isabel's next visit.

The MEISR can be used at several different points in the IFSP development process to assess a child's functioning and inform the intervention team's decisions. The sections that follow explain in detail the different options for when to introduce the MEISR in the IFSP development process and the underlying rationale for each option.

## Option 1. Before IFSP Development

The MEISR reinforces the functional nature of skills. Thus, introducing the family to the MEISR at referral or evaluation can help them review their child's functional development and share that important information with the rest of the intervention team to help guide intervention decisions. Inviting the family to complete the MEISR early in the IFSP process has several other benefits. First, it ensures that the family has ample time to complete the assessment. For example, some families may need assistance with completing the MEISR (i.e., because the family needs English-language support), and introducing it early allows more time for the family to obtain the resources needed. A second benefit is that the information gleaned from the

MEISR can be used for important next-step decisions. Even if the child is not eligible for intervention, the MEISR is an informative tool to help families understand their child's functional skill strengths, while reinforcing the varied learning opportunities in common, everyday family and community routines.

## Option 2. During IFSP Development

The MEISR can be used with or without the RBI. Because the RBI is the preferred method of obtaining outcomes and goals for the IFSP, the MEISR is best used either with the RBI or after it (see the later section titled "Option 3. Within 30 Days After **Initial IFSP**").

### Using the MEISR With the RBI
If the family completes the MEISR during the development of the initial IFSP, the service coordinator managing the IFSP process or the *most likely primary service provider* (MLPSP) would introduce it.

A note on the MLPSP: We have coined this term for the professional who will most likely be appointed to work with the family on an ongoing basis. That person cannot be appointed until goals have been decided, or it's considered predetermination of services. Hence, we use the phrase "most likely." This practice ensures continuity from needs assessment (e.g., RBI) through outcome and goal selection, and continuity between service decisions and actual service delivery. The same professional is involved. An MLPSP is needed only in situations where the service provider is not also the service coordinator. When the two roles are blended in one professional, there is continuity through the process. When "dedicated" service coordinators are used, an MLPSP is recommended. Other professionals who could introduce the MEISR to the family are those involved in the evaluation process.

Regardless of whether an MLPSP is working with the family, professionals conducting an RBI can use the MEISR to prepare for the interview or to score the child's functioning as reported by the family during the interview. Because the MEISR has many skills organized by routines, it can give an interviewer a list of questions to ask the family. Interviewers need to take care, however, to use the instrument as a guide to questions and not as a script for asking whether the child can do each skill. Using the MEISR as a script would change the RBI's intended purpose as a semistructured, conversational interview.

Another option for using the RBI during initial IFSP development is for a professional to score it based on the caregiver's report of what is happening in routines. At the end of the interview, the MEISR might not be completely scored because some items and even routines might not have been addressed during the RBI. Professionals can ask the family about those missing items later. The professional would probably not do so immediately after the interview, because the family would now have outcomes/goals (discussed during the last part of the RBI) and the meeting would already have taken 2 hours.

### Using the MEISR for Reviews and Annual IFSPs
For 6-month reviews and annual revisions of the IFSP, the service coordinator or ongoing service provider (if that's a different professional) may give the MEISR to the family about 30 days before the IFSP meeting. Doing so helps the intervention team, and especially the family, use the information to make decisions about changes to outcomes/goals or strategies.

### Using the MEISR Without the RBI
If the RBI is not used to assess needs and choose outcomes/goals, the MEISR can be substituted. The family can complete it, discuss the results with the intervention team, and then choose outcomes/goals based on that review. The review should include the child's strengths and weaknesses. Using the MEISR this way is not likely to produce outcomes/goals for routines not represented by the MEISR or for skills not included on the MEISR's extensive list. It is important to note that the MEISR will probably not elicit family outcomes/goals.

### Option 3. Within 30 Days After Initial IFSP

Instead of asking the family to complete the MEISR during the development of the initial IFSP, professionals can ask the family to complete it within the first 30 days of service delivery. Doing so may be less overwhelming for families during the busy and sometimes rushed period of IFSP development. This option is still early enough in service delivery to count as baseline, and it also ensures that the family's service provider can provide any necessary assistance. In the United States, IFSPs must be developed in 45 days, so professionals often seek ways to eliminate unnecessary paperwork. Unless the MEISR is essential to the program's process—for COS purposes, for example—completion of the MEISR could be delayed until after services have begun. In states employing dedicated service coordinators (i.e., states where the service coordinator is not the family's service provider), it might make sense to have the provider, rather than the service coordinator, help the family with the MEISR. Because service providers technically are not chosen until goals are decided, having the family complete the MEISR within the first 30 days of services means the provider would have been selected. One of the benefits of the first MEISR is that it captures baseline data, so that, later, the family and professionals involved with a child can see what impact early intervention has had on child functioning. No miracles would have occurred in the first 30 days, so the family's completing it in that time would provide an adequate baseline.

## EXPLAINING WHY WE USE THE MEISR

It is important for any professional implementing the MEISR with a family to understand the MEISR's purpose and uses thoroughly and to communicate this information clearly to the family. The professional should explain that the MEISR is different from a developmental test designed to find out whether a child is behind in development. Rather, the MEISR allows families and early intervention teams to document a child's present functioning and track child progress—that is, to see what functional skills the child has mastered since the last time the family completed the MEISR. By documenting what a child can and cannot do in daily life, the family can thoughtfully consider intervention priorities. The professional should explain to the family that the purposes of the MEISR are 1) to help families, as members of intervention teams, assess the child's competence in everyday situations, which might help them decide on intervention priorities; 2) to help professionals ask families relevant questions about child functioning in home routines (e.g., when conducting an RBI); and 3) to monitor a child's progress.

### To Help Families

The MEISR helps families assess child competence and guide decision making about intervention priorities and goals.

***Assess Child Competence***   When the family has completed the MEISR, the professional can go over the results with them, celebrating what the child can do and discussing skills the child doesn't yet have. The family might ask questions about whether their child should be doing certain skills, especially those that typically emerge at an age younger than the child's age. Professionals should explain that children master skills at different ages, but they should also be honest if a child is not yet demonstrating skills expected for his or her age.

***Guide Decision Making***   Professionals might tell the family that the MEISR helps identify outcomes/goals they might not have thought about with the RBI. Sometimes the RBI doesn't cover all routines, or the interviewer might not think about all the skills needed for meaningful participation in the routine. The MEISR can prompt the family to think about additional goals for their child to master.

## To Help Professionals and Programs

The MEISR helps professionals ask families relevant questions about child functioning in home routines. The MEISR can also benefit programs as a progress monitoring tool (see Chapter 8). In our experience, most early intervention programs collect little information to document how well children are doing as a function of intervention. The MEISR, aggregated across children, provides a functional index of the impact of early intervention.

## The Value of Routines

When introducing the MEISR to families, professionals should have strong arguments for the value of routines for needs assessment, for intervention, and for progress monitoring. The sections that follow sum up the points a professional might raise about these benefits.

***Needs Assessment***    Routines are valuable for assessing a child's needs. Meaningful participation in everyday life is a useful definition of *functioning*—and this meaningful participation occurs within routines. Explaining how it is important for children to be busy (engagement), be independent, and have social relationships will resonate with families—much better than will scores on a developmental test. In addition, that's the ticket into early intervention for many children and families. Everyday life can be chunked into the different times of the day—not literally the time on a clock, but the events and activities that tend to happen in daily life. We call these times of the day routines. Every family has them. To find out what the child needs to function well, we go through routines and ask the family what the child does and doesn't do. The MEISR contributes to this assessment of what the child needs in different routines.

***Intervention***    Routines are also valuable for intervention. Intervention consists of the teaching and support the child receives. The strategies the child's regular caregivers use to teach the child skills and to provide other supports that promote his or her functioning are intervention. We explain to families that they already provide learning opportunities for their child, and they do not need to set aside other, separate times to "work on goals," "give him his physical therapy," or "do his early intervention." Daily routines provide opportunities for teaching many different types of skills. The MEISR shows families how rich their existing routines are, in terms of the number of skills children at about their child's developmental age might be able to do.

***Progress Monitoring***    Finally, routines are valuable for monitoring a child's progress in particular skill areas. Does a given child follow directions? Well, perhaps he does pretty well during times when he's contained in a chair, such as at meals, but not well during times when he has the freedom to run away, such as play time at home and outside. Because behavior can vary by routine, monitoring performance of skills by routines is helpful. Therefore, it is important to discuss with families where and when children function.

*Using the MEISR for Monitoring Progress and Setting New Goals*

When Shawn and his family had been in early intervention for 5 months, Isabel asked Shanika to complete the MEISR again. The 6-month review was looming. Isabel said, "Can you please update this with a differently colored pen, Shanika? It will be fun for you to see what new things Shawn has learned to do. Also check to see if Shawn isn't doing any of the skills he could do before. If so, give that skill a 2 or a 1 with a differently colored pen."

After Shanika completed the MEISR again, Isabel reviewed her ratings, mostly to celebrate the skills Shawn had acquired. "Wow!" she said. "At 18 months, Shawn can walk with help when you guys go out! Six months ago, he couldn't do that. That's great progress! You said he doesn't point to draw your attention to things (12.16). Is this important to you?"

"Yes, I wish he would show me what he's interested in," said Shanika.

"Okay, we can consider adding that as an outcome/goal."

## Community Settings

The MEISR includes important home routines as well as grocery shopping and outings, which are some family routines that may take place in other community settings. Professionals introducing the MEISR should acknowledge that. These other settings might include a relative's house, restaurants, the grocery store, a place of worship, or a child care program. If it is a child care program and the team is implementing the RBM, the staff there—and anyone else caring for the child for 15 hours a week or more—will receive an RBI. Therefore, a professional will complete a needs assessment for those routines. In this model, the professional working with the family week in and week out will talk to the family about routines not on the MEISR to determine if the family has outcomes/goals pertaining to those routines.

(Note that the assessment of the child's functioning in child care is done using the RBI with the teacher or child care provider. Although a companion piece to the MEISR for classroom routines exists for children age 3 to 5 years, the Classroom Measure of Engagement, Independence, and Social Relationships [ClaMEISR; McWilliam, 2014], it is not applicable to children under age 3.)

As professionals introduce the MEISR to families, therefore, they discuss the importance of routines in the home and in other community settings.

### Reinforcing the Importance of Routines

On one visit, Shanika said, "I don't know which Shawn you're going to see today—the one who wants to play and smile or the one who cries and fusses."

"What's that like, when you can't tell which Shawn you're going to have?" Isabel replied. (A rule in the RBM is that we deal with feelings before facts.)

"It's frustrating. Shawn can be good as gold at breakfast and then a monster at play time."

"Is this pretty predictable?" asked Isabel.

"Yes. Most days."

Isabel said, "We might have to come up with some ideas for making sure your breakfast routine keeps going well and for improving play time routines."

Indeed, we have found that engagement varies by routine (Dunst et al., 1986; McWilliam et al., 1985), but also that engagement can be a trait carried across routines (Aguiar & McWilliam, 2013). In the previous vignette example, the professional working with Shanika is reinforcing the idea that routines set the stage for different amounts of meaningful participation. Shanika is learning that the kind of EISR she can expect from Shawn at breakfast might be different from his EISR at play time.

## COMPLETING THE MEISR: ASSESSING ROUTINES AND TROUBLESHOOTING

When completing the MEISR, professionals ask families to score all items; alternatively, the professional should score all items based on information gleaned from interviews or authentic observation. Professionals should explain to families that this will allow the score to reflect the percentage of skills the child has, out of all the skills for that routine, up to 36 months of age. For example, Tyrone, at age 17 months, would be expected to have about 50% of the skills, if he were typically developing. On reassessment at 23 months, the family would be asked to score all the items again. Suppose that at 17 months, Tyrone actually had only 30% of the skills listed for the Meal Times routine, as shown by the items within that routine that were scored 2 ("Sometimes") or 3 ("Often or Beyond this"). At 23 months, he might have additional items scored 2 or 3, totaling 45% of the items, for example. Scoring this way, the percentage almost always increases.

It can be tedious for a caregiver to score all the items a child can already do, especially if the child is 24 months old or older. When a professional gives the MEISR to the family and explains how to complete it, he or she can provide guidance on basal and ceiling scores. Use of these scores is described in Chapter 7.

Families vary in their comfort with scoring. Professionals can help families by reviewing the routines and items together. Professionals can also help families apply the basal and ceiling as described in the next chapter (note: basal and ceiling are to be used only with the guidance of and at the discretion of a professional). Professionals can do the same for families who are English language learners or for caregivers who may struggle with literacy.

Families might use people in their own network to help them complete the MEISR, which would be an excellent use of their own assets. It is empowering for families to figure out a solution rather than relying on the early intervention professional. However, if the professional and caregiver have already bonded, the caregiver might freely ask the professional for help. In conclusion, how the professional introduces the MEISR can make a difference in how the family perceives completing it and in how completely and thoughtfully the family completes it. Therefore, professionals should think about when to introduce it, describe it, explain the rationale for it, discuss routines, and provide scoring guidance.

## SUMMARY

Families and early intervention professionals work collaboratively to complete the MEISR. Therefore, it is important to introduce the MEISR thoughtfully and to provide families with clear information about the following topics:

- What the intended purpose of the MEISR is

- How the MEISR is structured and what skills it assesses (i.e., organization by 14 everyday routines; items within each routine)

- Why the "Typical starting age in months" column is included

- What is meant by the scores "Not yet" or 1, "Sometimes" or 2, and "Often or Beyond this" or 3

- How to assign their child a score of 1, 2, or 3 for each item

- How the three rightmost columns are used by professionals to identify patterns in the child's skill development (It is not necessary to explain these columns in detail.)

- How the professional determines the mastery percentages for each routine and completes the Scoring Summary sheet, and the purpose of these components

Throughout this chapter, the vignettes featuring Shawn, Shanika, and Jamal illustrate how a professional might address these topics with the family. For additional guidance on assigning scores and identifying patterns in the child's skill development, see Chapter 7.

Professionals should also know, and be prepared to explain to families, the reasons for completing the MEISR at various points during the IFSP process: before IFSP development, during IFSP development, or within 30 days afterward. The MEISR can support the IFSP process as follows:

1. Completing the MEISR before developing the IFSP helps the family review their child's functional development and guide intervention decisions.

2. Completing it during IFSP development (with or without the RBI) can help the family and the rest of the intervention team assess needs and determine goals/outcomes. As preparation for 6-month reviews and annual IFSP revisions, a professional may also have the family complete the MEISR about 30 days beforehand.

3. Completing the MEISR after the IFSP is created, within the first 30 days of service delivery, captures baseline data about the child's functional skills, which will later be useful for determining the intervention's impact.

When discussing the MEISR with families, emphasize the value of using routines for assessing the child's needs, providing day-to-day intervention, and monitoring progress.

Finally, when discussing scoring, explain to families that all items are to be scored, so the total score will reflect the percentage of skills the child has, out of all skills for that routine. In addition, professionals may choose to explain the use of basal and ceiling scores, as described in Chapter 7.

# Scoring the MEISR

MEISR scores can be summarized in a number of ways to show different profiles of child functioning. In this chapter, we will address the basic scoring of the MEISR as well as the calculation of mastery scores (by child's age and by the total items for a given routine). In addition, this chapter will discuss how to complete the MEISR Scoring Summary on page 2 of the MEISR protocol. As with any assessment, the purpose of the assessment should guide the tool chosen and selection of the scoring calculations needed. For example, if you want to know about a child's progress over time, you will want an assessment that can measure progress, and you will want to analyze those scores in light of child progress. Conversely, if you want to know the mix of functional behaviors the child demonstrated within a particular national outcome area, you will want to glean information from tools like the MEISR that can provide that information. As another example, if you want an analysis of children's progress across a program, you will want to look at tools that can be aggregated across children and provide program-level scoring calculations. However, knowing the purpose of assessment is a critical first consideration. Before discussing how to interpret a child's MEISR scores for different assessment purposes, let's first review the basic scoring instructions for the MEISR.

## BASIC SCORING

The basic scoring of the MEISR is relatively straightforward. This basic scoring can be completed by the caregiver independently, by the caregiver and the early intervention professional together, or by the early intervention professional using information gleaned from interviews and observation with the family. Essentially, the person or people completing the MEISR rate each functional skill using the 1–3 rating scale of *not yet* (1), *sometimes* (2), and *often or beyond this* (3) that is included in the MEISR. Each of these ratings is described next.

- **Rating of 1:** *Not yet* implies a belief that all children will acquire all of these skills, eventually. If the caregiver has never seen the child do the skill, the item receives a 1. If the child has done it once or twice, perhaps by accident, consider it a skill the child is "not yet" doing.

- **Rating of 2:** *Sometimes* means the child performs the skill inconsistently. This can mean the child can do what the item says but doesn't do it all the time, or it can mean the child approximates doing what the item says.

- **Rating of 3:** This rating applies to two distinct scenarios: 1) often and 2) beyond this. *Often* means the child has mastered the skill and therefore usually does what the item says.

*Beyond this* means the child has mastered the skill but no longer does what the item says, because he or she has replaced the skill with something more advanced. For example, if at meal times the child demonstrates *drinking appropriate amount from open cup at one time (with each sip)* (3.25), he would receive a score of 3 ("Beyond this") for the preceding item *drinking appropriate amount from bottle or when nursing* (3.03). When scoring the MEISR, remember that items rated 3 (Often or Beyond this) are equally regarded as mastered items.

## Using a Four-Item Basal

It can be tedious for a caregiver to score all the items a child can already do, especially if the child is 24 months old or older. Families can use a four-item basal, which means that, working up the MEISR from a point younger than the child's age, once four items in a row are marked with a 3, all the items listed for younger ages are assumed to be 3s. The caregiver doesn't have to complete them. The professional computing the scores will give credit for those younger items.

In the example shown in Figure 7.1, a family is completing the Hangout–TV–Books routine for Renee. At hanging-out time, Renee could attend to objects (5.10), but couldn't play with books (5.09) or pull up to stand on furniture consistently (5.08). But she could do the four skills immediately preceding 5.08 (i.e., for younger ages): 5.04 to 5.07. Because, in this routine, four items in a row are marked with a 3, the family does not have to score the items for younger ages, which, in this case, are only three items. The person computing the percentages will give Renee credit for items 5.01 to 5.03.

## Using a Four-Item Ceiling

A ceiling works the other way. Families can use a four-item ceiling: Once four items in a row are marked with a 1, all the remaining items are assumed to be 1s. The caregiver does not have to complete them. The professional computing the scores will give credit for those items listed for older ages. Using the example of Renee in Figure 7.1, she could only inconsistently

| 5. Hangout – TV – Books   Participates in hanging-out time by . . . | Typical starting age in months | Not yet | Sometimes | Often or Beyond this | EnR* | Dev* | Diff* |
|---|---|---|---|---|---|---|---|
| 5.01 Responding positively to being held and cuddled | 0 | 1 | 2 | 3 | S | S | S |
| 5.02 Responding differently to the voice of a stranger from that of caregiver | 3 | 1 | 2 | 3 | S | S | S |
| 5.03 Looking at an object and watching it move in different directions (up, down, left, right) | 3 | 1 | 2 | 3 | E | CG | K |
| 5.04 Pushing up on hands when lying on tummy | 5 | 1 | 2 | ③ | I | M | A |
| 5.05 Reaching forward to get toys when supported in sitting | 5 | 1 | 2 | ③ | I | M | A |
| 5.06 Having fun pointing to and pulling on facial features of caregivers | 5 | 1 | 2 | ③ | S | S | S |
| 5.07 Rolling back to tummy and tummy to back both directions | 7 | 1 | 2 | ③ | I | M | A |
| 5.08 Pulling up to stand on furniture | 8 | 1 | ② | 3 | I | M | A |
| 5.09 Playing with books (e.g., looking at, touching, mouthing) | 8 | ① | 2 | 3 | E | CG | K |
| 5.10 Attending to objects mentioned during conversation (e.g., looking at dog when mentioned, looking at ball) | 10 | 1 | 2 | ③ | E | CG | K |
| 5.11 Moving about to explore, looking back to caregiver | 12 | 1 | ② | 3 | S | S | S |
| 5.12 Showing interest looking at pictures in a book | 12 | ① | 2 | 3 | E | CG | K |
| 5.13 Staying with caregiver looking at a book at least a few minutes | 12 | ① | 2 | 3 | E | S | S |
| 5.14 Vocalizing to get caregiver attention to start or change activity | 12 | ① | 2 | 3 | S | CM | A |
| 5.15 Exploring drawers and cabinets | 13 | ① | 2 | 3 | E | CG, M | K |
| 5.16 Turning pages in books (might be several at a time) | 14 | 1 | 2 | 3 | I | M | K |
| 5.17 Figuring out how to activate/get a toy (e.g., turning toy on, climbing to get toy) | 18 | 1 | 2 | 3 | I | CG | K |
| 5.18 Showing clear preference for picture/book/show | 18 | 1 | 2 | 3 | E | CG | K |
| 5.19 Recognizing him- or herself in a picture by pointing or looking | 19 | 1 | 2 | 3 | E | CG | K |

9

**Figure 7.1.** Hangout – TV– Books routine for Renee that incorporates four-item basal.

SCORING THE MEISR | 111

move about to explore (5.11) and she couldn't yet do the next four items (i.e., for older ages): items 5:12 to 5.15. Because, in this routine, four items in a row are marked with a 1, the family does not have to score the items listed for older ages.

## Skipping Items

On rare occasions, it could happen that an item on the MEISR is not something that a family encourages their child to do or try. When this happens, it is possible not to score that item on the MEISR. When determining whether to skip an item, however, it is important to consider if the functional ability is used or needed in other settings in which the child participates, such as daycare or with another caregiver. If that's the case, then the item should be scored; otherwise, it could be skipped. When you skip an item, be sure to omit that item from the total number of items scored when calculating the child's mastery of skills in routines or in routines up to and including the child's age. Be sure also to make note on the MEISR that the item was purposefully skipped rather than just leaving it blank.

## CALCULATING MASTERY SCORES

Upon completion of the MEISR, you can generate different child- and program-level scoring profiles. Mastery of skills in routines provides a profile of the percentage of functional skills a child has mastered (scored 3) for each of the 14 routines included in the MEISR. Mastery scores represent simple calculations of the percentage of items scored 3. These are considered simple calculations because they do not require a spreadsheet or statistical software program to compute; these percentages can be calculated directly on the MEISR protocol using a simple calculator. Mastery of skills in routines can be calculated by determining

- Mastery of skills within routines for the child's age

- Mastery of total skills within routines

The phrase "For the child's age" refers to skills for which the typical starting age is the same as, or younger than, the age of the child being assessed. "Total skills within routines" refers to all skills within the routine, for which the typical starting ages range from 0 to 36 months.

These two profiles measure different things. The difference is that one includes only the items up to and including the child's age, and the other includes all items in each routine. Completing all items does make the MEISR a bit more time consuming to complete, especially for very young children. However, it can identify possible splinter skills a child may demonstrate. Splinter skills are atypically advanced skills within a child's profile, either because they typically emerge well past the child's chronological age or they are far more advanced than other skills the child demonstrates.

## Mastery of Skills Within Routines for Age

Mastery of skills within routines for the child's age is the actual percentage of items a child has mastered within each of the 14 different routines up to and including the child's age. When calculating this percentage for a child's age, a line is drawn after the last skill for the child's age in each routine, and the MEISR is completed up to the drawn lines in each routine. In the following example of 24-month-old Lucas, shown in Figure 7.2, notice how the line is drawn between MEISR items 4.20 and 4.21; this is done to indicate that all of the items before the line are skills for Lucas's age. In this particular example, there are 20 items in the Dressing Time routine for 24-month-old Lucas. If Lucas were 15 months of age, the line would be drawn between items 4.12 and 4.13.

| 4. Dressing Time  Participates in dressing time by . . . | Typical starting age in months | Not yet | Sometimes | Often or Beyond this | Freq | Dev | Out |
|---|---|---|---|---|---|---|---|
| 4.01  Attending to sound of caregiver's voice | 0 | 1 | 2 | ③ | S | S | S |
| 4.02  Allowing caregiver to dress him or her without getting overly upset or showing strong discomfort for clothing or touch | 0 | 1 | 2 | ③ | E | S | S |
| 4.03  Responding positively to physical contact and holding | 0 | 1 | 2 | ③ | E | S | S |
| 4.04  Inspecting his or her hands | 2 | 1 | 2 | ③ | E | CG | K |
| 4.05  Communicating with vocal sounds | 2 | 1 | 2 | ③ | S | CM | K |
| 4.06  Responding to own name when called (e.g., pausing, alerting, vocalizing) | 6 | 1 | 2 | ③ | S | CM | S |
| 4.07  Babbling with adult-like inflection (e.g., baba, mama, or different syllables together, mado, bada) | 8 | 1 | 2 | ③ | S | CM | K |
| 4.08  Assisting by extending an arm or leg for a sleeve or pants leg | 11 | 1 | 2 | ③ | I | A | A |
| 4.09  Pointing correctly to one body part on self when asked | 15 | 1 | 2 | ③ | S | CM, CG | K |
| 4.10  Removing an article of clothing by him- or herself (e.g., socks, hat) | 15 | 1 | 2 | ③ | I | A | A |
| 4.11  Indicating he or she understands the name of an article of clothing (e.g., looking at or otherwise acknowledging when caregiver says shoes, shirt) | 15 | 1 | ② | 3 | S | CM | K |
| 4.12  Recognizing self in mirror (e.g., pointing at self) | 15 | 1 | 2 | ③ | E | CG, S | K |
| 4.13  Indicating what he or she wants to wear (gesturing/verbalizing when given choice) | 18 | 1 | ② | 3 | S | CM | A |
| 4.14  Undoing fasteners (e.g., unzipping large zipper, snaps) | 18 | 1 | 2 | ③ | I | A | A |
| 4.15  Helping undress self (e.g., removing shoes) | 18 | 1 | 2 | ③ | I | A | A |
| 4.16  Using gestures or words to identify two or more body parts | 18 | 1 | ② | 3 | S | CM | K |
| 4.17  Using some signs or words to comment or respond | 18 | 1 | ② | 3 | S | CM | K |
| 4.18  Following directions to fetch something (e.g., go get your shoes) | 18 | ① | 2 | 3 | S | CM | K |
| 4.19  Persisting with trying to put on/take off some clothes (might still need help to complete task) | 24 | 1 | ② | 3 | I | A | A |
| 4.20  Identifying five or more body parts (e.g., pointing at oneself, others, or doll) | 24 | ① | 2 | 3 | E | CG | K |
| 4.21  Following two-step directions (e.g., first shoes on, then outside) | 25 | 1 | 2 | 3 | E | CM | K |
| 4.22  Dressing him- or herself with assistance (i.e., helping) | 28 | 1 | 2 | 3 | I | A | A |

**Figure 7.2.**   Dressing Time routine for 24-month-old Lucas; the line between items 4.20 and 4.21 indicates that all of the items before the line are skills for Lucas's age.

To calculate the percentage of functional skills mastered for the child's age, we work through the following calculations.

1. Add up the number of items scored a 3, up to the drawn line.

2. Then divide that number (number of mastered items) by the number of items in the routine that were included and scored for the child's age. *Note: If an item is skipped because it is not part of the family culture, be sure to reduce the number of scored items accordingly.*

3. Last, multiply that number by 100 to produce the percentage of items mastered in the routine for the child's age.

Using the example from Lucas in the Dressing Time routine, we would calculate the percentage as follows. (See Figure 7.3.)

1. Add up the items scored 3. This includes 13 items scored Often or Beyond this, which totals 13 mastered items.

2. Divide the 13 mastered items by the 20 total items for Lucas's age. This gives us 0.65. *Note: No items were skipped, so the total number of items is 20.*

3. Multiply 0.65 by 100 to get 65%.

From this, we can conclude that in the getting dressed routine, Lucas has mastered 13 (65%) of the 20 functional skills for his age (24 months).

Remember too that when calculating percentages, it is wise to cross-check your work by adding up all the marked items in each column to make certain they add up to the total items included. In this example, there are 2 items scored Not yet, 5 scored Sometimes, and 13 scored Often or Beyond this. Adding these together (2 + 5 + 13 = 20) should equal the number of items

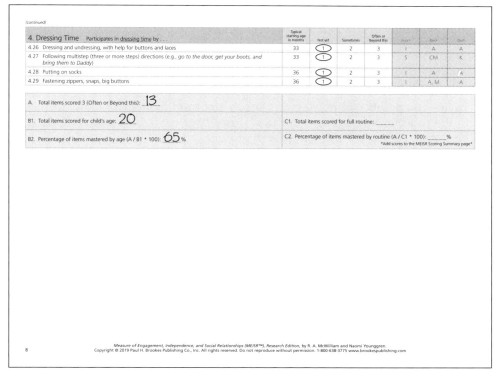

| 4. Dressing Time — Participates in dressing time by . . . | Typical starting age in months | Not yet | Sometimes | Often or Beyond this | Func | Dev | Out |
|---|---|---|---|---|---|---|---|
| 4.01 Attending to sound of caregiver's voice | 0 | 1 | 2 | (3) | S | S | S |
| 4.02 Allowing caregiver to dress him or her without getting overly upset or showing strong discomfort for clothing or touch | 0 | 1 | 2 | (3) | E | S | S |
| 4.03 Responding positively to physical contact and holding | 0 | 1 | 2 | (3) | E | S | S |
| 4.04 Inspecting his or her hands | 2 | 1 | 2 | (3) | E | CG | K |
| 4.05 Communicating with vocal sounds | 2 | 1 | 2 | (3) | S | CM | K |
| 4.06 Responding to own name when called (e.g., pausing, alerting, vocalizing) | 6 | 1 | 2 | (3) | S | CM | S |
| 4.07 Babbling with adult-like inflection (e.g., baba, mama, or different syllables together, mado, bada) | 8 | 1 | 2 | (3) | S | CM | K |
| 4.08 Assisting by extending an arm or leg for a sleeve or pants leg | 11 | 1 | 2 | (3) | I | A | A |
| 4.09 Pointing correctly to one body part on self when asked | 15 | 1 | 2 | (3) | S | CM, CG | K |
| 4.10 Removing an article of clothing by him- or herself (e.g., socks, hat) | 15 | 1 | 2 | (3) | I | A | A |
| 4.11 Indicating he or she understands the name of an article of clothing (e.g., looking at or otherwise acknowledging when caregiver says shoes, shirt) | 15 | 1 | (2) | 3 | S | CM | K |
| 4.12 Recognizing self in mirror (e.g., pointing at self) | 15 | 1 | 2 | (3) | E | CG, S | K |
| 4.13 Indicating what he or she wants to wear (gesturing/verbalizing when given choice) | 18 | 1 | (2) | 3 | S | CM | A |
| 4.14 Undoing fasteners (e.g., unzipping large zipper, snaps) | 18 | 1 | 2 | (3) | I | A | A |
| 4.15 Helping undress self (e.g., removing shoes) | 18 | 1 | 2 | (3) | I | A | A |
| 4.16 Using gestures or words to identify two or more body parts | 18 | 1 | (2) | 3 | S | CM | K |
| 4.17 Using some signs or words to comment or respond | 18 | 1 | (2) | 3 | S | CM | K |
| 4.18 Following directions to fetch something (e.g., go get your shoes) | 18 | (1) | 2 | 3 | S | CM | K |
| 4.19 Persisting with trying to put on/take off some clothes (might still need help to complete task) | 24 | 1 | (2) | 3 | I | A | A |
| 4.20 Identifying five or more body parts (e.g., pointing at oneself, others, or doll) | 24 | (1) | 2 | 3 | E | CG | K |
| 4.21 Following two-step directions (e.g., first shoes on, then outside) | 25 | (1) | 2 | 3 | E | CM | K |
| 4.22 Dressing him- or herself with assistance (i.e., helping) | 28 | (1) | 2 | 3 | I | A | A |
| 4.23 Putting shoes on (maybe on wrong feet and not tied) | 30 | (1) | 2 | 3 | I | A | A |
| 4.24 Putting on coat with assistance | 30 | (1) | 2 | 3 | I | A | A |
| 4.25 Describing clothing preference (e.g., want dinosaur jammies, princess skirt) | 30 | (1) | 2 | 3 | S | CM | A |

*(continued)*

7

**Figure 7.3.** Scoring for Lucas's Dressing Time routine showing percentage of functional skills mastered for his age.

*(continued)*

| 4. Dressing Time — Participates in dressing time by . . . | Typical starting age in months | Not yet | Sometimes | Often or Beyond this | Func | Dev | Out |
|---|---|---|---|---|---|---|---|
| 4.26 Dressing and undressing, with help for buttons and laces | 33 | (1) | 2 | 3 | I | A | A |
| 4.27 Following multistep (three or more steps) directions (e.g., go to the door, get your boots, and bring them to Daddy) | 33 | (1) | 2 | 3 | S | CM | K |
| 4.28 Putting on socks | 36 | (1) | 2 | 3 | I | A | (A) |
| 4.29 Fastening zippers, snaps, big buttons | 36 | (1) | 2 | 3 | I | A, M | A |

A. Total items scored 3 (Often or Beyond this): **13**

B1. Total items scored for child's age: **20**

C1. Total items scored for full routine: _____

B2. Percentage of items mastered by age (A / B1 * 100): **65** %

C2. Percentage of items mastered by routine (A / C1 * 100): _____ %
*Add scores to the MEISR Scoring Summary page*

**Figure 7.3.** Scoring for Lucas's Dressing Time routine showing percentage of functional skills mastered for his age.

MEISR Scoring Summary

| MEISR Routines *(number of items in routine)* | A. Total Number of 3s | B1. Total Number of Items Scored for Child's Age | B2. Percentage of Items Mastered by Child's Age (A/B1 * 100 = %) | C1. Total Number of Items Scored for Routine | C2. Percentage of Items Mastered by Routine (A/C1 * 100 = %) |
|---|---|---|---|---|---|
| 01. Waking Up (25) | | | % | | % |
| 02. Toileting/Diapering (20) | | | % | | % |
| 03. Meal Times (47) | | | % | | % |
| 04. Dressing Time (29) | 13 | 20 | 65 % | | % |

2

*Measure of Engagement, Independence, and Social Relationships (MEISR™), Research Edition,* by R. A. McWilliam and Naomi Younggren.


**Figure 7.4.** Scoring Summary page showing scoring for Dressing Time routine, with the percentage of items mastered for child's age.

scored, which in this example is 20. This type of cross-checking helps ensure that the percentages are calculated accurately.

Using the MEISR Scoring Summary on page 2 of the MEISR, enter the data from each routine in columns A, B1, and B2 to see the results easily, as shown in Figure 7.4. The MEISR Scoring Summary can also be helpful for reviewing a child's progress across time. Ultimately, a child's mastery percentages would increase over time.

## Mastery of Total Skills Within Routine

Mastery of total skills within routine is the percentage of all items the child has mastered within each of the 14 different routines. This calculation includes all the skills within each routine, which means that all items on the MEISR are completed.

To calculate the percentage of functional skills mastered, we work through the following steps.

1. Add up the number of items scored a 3.
2. Divide the number of mastered items by the total number of items included and scored in the routine. ***Note:*** *If an item is skipped because it is not part of the family culture, be sure to reduce the number of scored items accordingly.*
3. Multiply that number by 100 to produce the percentage of items mastered in the routine for the child's age.

Using the example from Lucas in the Dressing Time routine, we calculate his scores as follows. (See Figure 7.5.)

1. Add up the items scored 3. This includes 13 items scored Often or Beyond this, meaning there are 13 mastered items.
2. Divide the 13 mastered items by the total 29 items in the routine. This gives us 0.448, which we can round up to 0.45. ***Note:*** *No items were skipped so the total is 29.*
3. Multiply 0.45 by 100 to get 45%.

From this, we can conclude that in the Dressing Time routine, Lucas has mastered 13 (45%) of the 29 functional skills.

Using the MEISR Scoring Summary on page 2 of the MEISR, enter the data from each routine in columns C1 and C2, as shown in Figure 7.6.

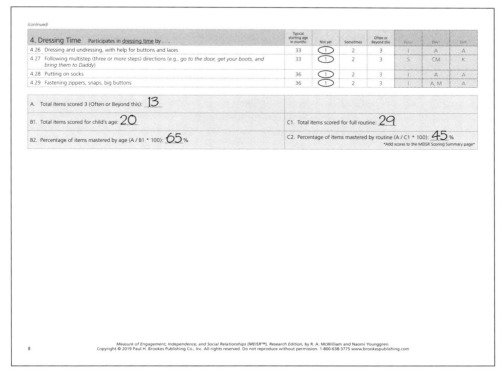

| 4. Dressing Time  Participates in dressing time by . . . | Typical starting age in months | Not yet | Sometimes | Often or Beyond this | Env | Dev | Out |
|---|---|---|---|---|---|---|---|
| 4.01  Attending to sound of caregiver's voice | 0 | 1 | 2 | (3) | S | S | S |
| 4.02  Allowing caregiver to dress him or her without getting overly upset or showing strong discomfort for clothing or touch | 0 | 1 | 2 | (3) | E | S | S |
| 4.03  Responding positively to physical contact and holding | 0 | 1 | 2 | (3) | E | S | S |
| 4.04  Inspecting his or her hands | 2 | 1 | 2 | (3) | E | CG | K |
| 4.05  Communicating with vocal sounds | 2 | 1 | 2 | (3) | S | CM | K |
| 4.06  Responding to own name when called (e.g., pausing, alerting, vocalizing) | 6 | 1 | 2 | (3) | S | CM | S |
| 4.07  Babbling with adult-like inflection (e.g., baba, mama, or different syllables together, mado, bada) | 8 | 1 | 2 | (3) | S | CM | K |
| 4.08  Assisting by extending an arm or leg for a sleeve or pants leg | 11 | 1 | 2 | (3) | I | A | A |
| 4.09  Pointing correctly to one body part on self when asked | 15 | 1 | 2 | (3) | S | CM, CG | K |
| 4.10  Removing an article of clothing by him- or herself (e.g., socks, hat) | 15 | 1 | 2 | (3) | I | A | A |
| 4.11  Indicating he or she understands the name of an article of clothing (e.g., looking at or otherwise acknowledging when caregiver says shoes, shirt) | 15 | 1 | (2) | 3 | S | CM | K |
| 4.12  Recognizing self in mirror (e.g., pointing at self) | 15 | 1 | 2 | (3) | E | CG, S | K |
| 4.13  Indicating what he or she wants to wear (gesturing/verbalizing when given choice) | 18 | 1 | (2) | 3 | S | CM | A |
| 4.14  Undoing fasteners (e.g., unzipping large zipper, snaps) | 18 | 1 | 2 | (3) | I | A | A |
| 4.15  Helping undress self (e.g., removing shoes) | 18 | 1 | 2 | (3) | I | A | A |
| 4.16  Using gestures or words to identify two or more body parts | 18 | 1 | (2) | 3 | S | CM | K |
| 4.17  Using some signs or words to comment or respond | 18 | 1 | (2) | 3 | S | CM | K |
| 4.18  Following directions to fetch something (e.g., go get your shoes) | 18 | (1) | 2 | 3 | S | CM | K |
| 4.19  Persisting with trying to put on/take off some clothes (might still need help to complete task) | 24 | 1 | (2) | 3 | I | A | A |
| 4.20  Identifying five or more body parts (e.g., pointing at oneself, others, or doll) | 24 | (1) | 2 | 3 | E | CG | K |
| 4.21  Following two-step directions (e.g., first shoes on, then outside) | 25 | (1) | 2 | 3 | E | CM | K |
| 4.22  Dressing him- or herself with assistance (i.e., helping) | 28 | (1) | 2 | 3 | I | A | A |
| 4.23  Putting shoes on (maybe on wrong feet and not tied) | 30 | (1) | 2 | 3 | I | A | A |
| 4.24  Putting on coat with assistance | 30 | (1) | 2 | 3 | I | A | A |
| 4.25  Describing clothing preference (e.g., want dinosaur jammies, princess skirt) | 30 | (1) | 2 | 3 | S | CM | A |

(continued)

7

**Figure 7.5.** Scoring for Lucas's Dressing Time routine showing percentage of functional skills mastered within the routine.

(continued)

| 4. Dressing Time  Participates in dressing time by . . . | Typical starting age in months | Not yet | Sometimes | Often or Beyond this | Env | Dev | Out |
|---|---|---|---|---|---|---|---|
| 4.26  Dressing and undressing, with help for buttons and laces | 33 | (1) | 2 | 3 | I | A | A |
| 4.27  Following multistep (three or more steps) directions (e.g., go to the door, get your boots, and bring them to Daddy) | 33 | (1) | 2 | 3 | S | CM | K |
| 4.28  Putting on socks | 36 | (1) | 2 | 3 | I | A | A |
| 4.29  Fastening zippers, snaps, big buttons | 36 | (1) | 2 | 3 | I | A, M | A |

A.  Total items scored 3 (Often or Beyond this): 13

B1.  Total items scored for child's age: 20

B2.  Percentage of items mastered by age (A / B1 * 100): 65 %

C1.  Total items scored for full routine: 29

C2.  Percentage of items mastered by routine (A / C1 * 100): 45 %
*Add scores to the MEISR Scoring Summary page*

8

**Figure 7.5.** Scoring for Lucas's Dressing Time routine showing percentage of functional skills mastered within the routine.

| MEISR Scoring Summary | | | | | |
|---|---|---|---|---|---|
| MEISR Routines (number of items in routine) | A. Total Number of 3s | B1 Total Number of Items Scored for Child's Age | B2. Percentage of Items Mastered by Child's Age (A/B1 * 100 = %) | C1. Total Number of Items Scored for Routine | C2. Percentage of Items Mastered by Routine (A/C1 * 100 = %) |
| 01. Waking Up (25) | | | % | | % |
| 02. Toileting/Diapering (20) | | | % | | % |
| 03. Meal Times (47) | | | % | | % |
| 04. Dressing Time (29) | 13 | 20 | 65 % | 29 | 45 % |

**Figure 7.6.** Scoring Summary page showing scoring for Dressing Time routine, with the percentage of items mastered for age and for the routine.

## SUMMARY

Scoring of the MEISR, as described in this chapter, is straightforward. The child's home caregiver has three options for rating each skill. From this, professionals and families can develop the child's competence profile for different routines and overall. Looking at the percentage of skills mastered for each routine helps you see where the child is more or less competent. The scoring can also be calculated in terms of the percentage of skills mastered, up to the child's age. On the MEISR form itself, items are crosswalked with the functional outcomes of EISR; the five developmental domains required on IFSPs in the United States; and the three federal child outcomes. Users can subdivide the scores by these subscales. For example, you can determine what percentage of all the engagement items the child has mastered in each routine or what percentage of engagement items up to the child's age the child has mastered in each routine.

# CHAPTER 8

# Interpreting and Reviewing the MEISR With Families

Assessment is a process. It is not simply a completed tool or product. It is a practice that must start with a purpose. Questions to ask include *Why are we conducting the assessment? What questions are we trying to answer? What are the decisions we need to make?* Knowing why assessment is being done is essential to ensure the right type of information is gathered for the purpose identified. If the answer to the *why* question is unknown, the assessment process can go astray, produce confusion, result in insufficient or inaccurate information, involve the wrong tools, and generate extra work on the part of any or all team members. Quality assessment practices include four important processes: determining the assessment purpose, collecting the information needed, reviewing and analyzing the information collected, and acting upon the information in light of the purpose.

Assessment must be purpose driven. Different tools have distinct purposes and answer different types of questions. The MEISR is an assessment tool that generates ecologically valid assessment results to help teams answer assessment questions about a child's functional skills and abilities. To address how the results of the MEISR can be used in early intervention, in this chapter, we will 1) explore the varied assessment purposes and questions the MEISR can help answer and 2) discuss how the information can be applied and acted upon in light of different assessment purposes and within early intervention.

## REVIEWING THE ASSESSMENT PURPOSE

The assessment purpose can be thought of as the questions the team hopes to answer. As teams use assessment processes, those processes can become familiar and even, unfortunately, automatic for professionals. Yet it is crucial to remember that although the professionals may be very familiar and skilled with the critical components of the assessment process, the family might not be. Rather, assessment is often a new process for families, especially families of very young children entering an early intervention system. Professionals must explain each assessment so all team members are on the same page and moving together as a team. Taking time to review the assessment purpose is an essential practice for effectively engaging and empowering families, building partnerships, and sharing the assessment responsibility.

Following is a collection of questions the MEISR can help teams answer:

1. *How is the child functioning across routines?* Being uniquely organized by a wide variety of routines-based skills, the MEISR yields a comprehensive picture of the child's functioning. This is an essential question for teams to answer as part of the early intervention process in order to understand a child's functional strengths and needs, which traditional evaluations do not capture.

2. *How is the child demonstrating EISR abilities?* EISR abilities are the core of children's learning and successful participation in day-to-day routines. Included in the MEISR is a cross-reference of each item to EISR. When reviewing the MEISR, teams can visually analyze the child's scores, item by item, using the cross-references to determine whether a child has particular strengths in one or more of these functional domains. This can further assist the team's understanding of a child's learning style as well as strengths and needs.

3. *How is the child demonstrating functional abilities across the different domains of development (e.g., the five developmental domains)?* Similar to the way the MEISR items are cross-referenced with EISR, so too are the items crosswalked with the five domains of development. Teams can visually analyze the child's MEISR scores, item by item, using the crosswalk to explore a child's functioning relative to a particular domain or domains.

4. *How is the child demonstrating functional abilities within the context of the three national outcomes?* Aligning functional skills with the three national outcomes continues to present some challenges. Because the functional items on the MEISR are cross-referenced with the three national outcomes, teams can accurately associate different skills with the outcomes, which is essential for high-quality COS ratings. Teams can examine the child's MEISR scores for each item, together with the cross-referencing provided, to visually analyze the mix of routines-based skills a child demonstrates relative to each of the three national outcomes.

5. *How is the child functioning relative to starting age expectations?* Each item on the MEISR includes a starting age. These starting ages are useful for all team members to understand a child's functioning relative to age expectations. These age anchors are not intended for eligibility purposes or high-stakes decisions, but they do provide teams an understanding of developmental progressions in routines-based functioning.

6. *What is a baseline for intervention?* The MEISR can be scored at the start of intervention and periodically thereafter to get a snapshot of the child's functional progress regarding his or her participation in day-to-day routines.

7. *How has the child's functioning changed over time?* As noted earlier, the MEISR scores can be used to broadly review a child's progress. Additionally, when the MEISR is completed periodically, the detail in the MEISR will provide teams a closer look at just how a child's functioning has changed over time.

When identifying assessment purposes, it is possible to have more than one purpose. Therefore, it is possible to have combinations of the following questions. In any case, the early interventionist working with the family will need to make sure they clearly understand the purpose(s) for using the MEISR and which question(s) the team hopes to answer. These questions are further discussed in the sections that follow.

## 1. How Is the Child Functioning Across Routines?

The MEISR helps teams address this question, as it is primarily organized around common family and community routines. As mentioned earlier, the MEISR is not a replacement for the RBI, but it most certainly helps teams understand a child's functioning within the context of common routines. Within the early intervention process, this question might be asked as part of the referral, eligibility determination, IFSP development, service delivery, or transition.

In fact, the team needs a rich and detailed understanding of the child's routines-based skills at many points in early intervention.

At referral, the professional can show the MEISR to the family to help them understand the great mix of functional skills their child does and what skills the child will be ready for next. As noted earlier, the MEISR is not intended for use as an eligibility determination tool, but it can help team members recognize the child's functional skills. The team might also use information about the child's routines-based functioning as part of providing an informed opinion, depending on their program guidance.

As part of IFSP development, the MEISR is particularly useful to help the team know how the child is functioning across routines, because that information might help the family identify their priorities for intervention.

As part of ongoing service delivery, teams often ask how the child is progressing and benefit from periodic review of the child's functioning to celebrate and monitor progress and revise intervention. As early interventionists work with families on children's engagement in routines, they can consult the MEISR for skills typically found in that routine. For example, if you're working with the family of a 24-month-old child on singing snippets of songs during play time with others (item 6.23), it might be helpful to see whether the child is also indicating ownership over toys or items with peers (e.g., might grab toy—item 6.22) or whether the child maintains motor control over his or her body in relationship to others (e.g., walks well, moves around others—item 6.24). These are other skills emerging at about the same time as the target one in the same routine, Play With Others. Therefore, the MEISR helps the early interventionist and the family consider functioning in the routine, not just an isolated skill. When it comes time for transition, teams ponder this question again as they work together to facilitate a smooth change of services. When teams engage in assessment to understand a child's functioning across routines, the MEISR can be a go-to tool.

## 2. How Is the Child Demonstrating EISR Abilities?

EISR abilities embody core components of learning, as discussed in Chapter 2. Therefore, when considering a child's functioning, it can be particularly useful to consider these functional areas of development. By asking this question, teams can begin to understand how sophisticated a child's participation is in the context of common family and community routines. By visually analyzing the scoring data for the different items within routines, together with the crosswalking of each item to EISR abilities, teams can understand how the child is demonstrating these critical aspects of participation. For example, the team might learn that, within particular routines, a child has relative strengths in independence, but fewer important social relationship and engagement abilities. Teams can use that information as they continue to promote the child's independence and identify increased opportunities to facilitate social engagement in the context of routines. Considering these functional domains is likely new for teams not actively using the RBI, as they are core questions in the RBI. Yet, these domains are valuable for understanding a child's functional abilities and successful participation in day-to-day activities.

## 3. How Is the Child Demonstrating Functional Abilities Across the Different Domains of Development (the Five Developmental Domains)?

Skills organized exclusively by developmental domain are not inherently functional, because they are not contextually based, lack apparent purpose or meaning, and are isolated or inflexible measures of discrete skills. Yet, if a team is trying to understand a child's functioning around a particular domain, it can be useful to consider the functional skills that align with domains. For example, a team might need to explore a child's functioning in a particular domain or domains as part of giving an informed opinion or to consider a child's *functional* abilities in a domain. Because the items included in the MEISR are naturally functional, they often align with more than one discrete developmental domain. For example, participating in waking up time by raising arms to be picked up when the caregiver reaches for the child (1.13) aligns with the communication and social domains of development. When the team's assessment purpose includes understanding a child's functioning by developmental domain, the MEISR adds an important functional view of a child's skills.

### 4. How Is the Child Demonstrating Functional Abilities Within the Context of Each of the Three National Outcomes?

This question is asked as part of the federal requirement for measuring child outcomes. As mentioned in Chapter 5, programs using the COS process will be particularly interested in using the MEISR to assist teams with determining high-quality COS ratings.

### 5. How Is the Child Functioning Relative to Starting Age Expectations?

The starting ages embedded in the MEISR can be useful when teams have questions about a child's functioning relative to age expectations. As noted earlier, this line of inquiry might be examined when looking at a child's functioning relative to routines, functional domains, developmental domains, or the three national outcomes. The age ranges are general starting ages and are not designed to convert to age equivalences needed in some programs to assist with eligibility determination. Yet, they are useful for helping teams understand age expectations and recognize the mix of functional skills that emerge around the same time and within the context of routines.

### 6. What Is a Baseline for Intervention?

Determining baselines is important for teams to understand and reflect on progress made, and the MEISR uniquely provides a baseline of functioning. Teams can calculate MEISR scores of all items or all items up to the child's age within or across routines to understand the child's functioning when starting intervention and subsequently examine assessment results to understand how the child progresses over time. When exploring baseline measures, it is important to consider how the measure will be used and to be certain the same measure is used at a subsequent interval. For example, if the early intervention team working with a family of a child named Arno took his baseline MEISR measure to include the percentage of all MEISR skills he demonstrates across routines, they will need to do the same when measuring progress at a later point, rather than, for instance, measuring the percentage of items only up to and including his age. Baseline measures are useful for snapshot reviews of progress, relative to entry measures. Yet, they do not equate to other measures, such as percentages of delay or age equivalences.

### 7. How Has the Child's Functioning Changed Over Time?

Teams often ask this question as part of ongoing intervention, for progress monitoring, and at transition times. The MEISR provides a unique lens for looking at functioning over time because the items are routines based, capturing a child's genuine functioning. For example, the MEISR can tell us the percentage of skills, within a routine, that a child can do. It can also tell us the percentage of skills, up to and including the child's age, that the child can do. For example, at going-out time, 20-month-old Rachel was doing 80% of the skills up to and including those listed for her age. When the team compared that to her earlier measure, which was completed when she was only 14 months old, they saw that at that time she was doing 40% of the items up to and including those listed for her age. These types of MEISR-generated measures can help teams explore a child's meaningful routines-based functioning over time.

## ANALYSIS QUESTIONS AND CONSIDERATIONS

To assist teams with analyzing assessment information, the MEISR tool can be reviewed as it is completed. Depending upon the assessment purpose and questions, the team will visually analyze the completed MEISR as described earlier, paying particular attention to different items and routines and the different cross-referencing included (e.g., EISR, five domains, three national outcomes, starting ages). Using the seven assessment questions reviewed earlier, we will highlight how the MEISR information can be reviewed to provide further information for deeper analysis.

In addition, we provide a few deeper analysis questions that teams might consider as they examine the MEISR to help answer assessment questions. The deeper analysis questions help teams determine if there are particular patterns that might provide insight about the child's learning, the child's strengths and needs, the child's participation, and more. We also include some "so what" examples of how the deeper analysis might inform intervention or next steps for the team.

## 1. How Is the Child Functioning Across Routines?

***MEISR Profile***     The completed MEISR tool might be sufficient for teams to examine this question. It is possible to explore the functional skills the child is demonstrating by simply reviewing the routines-based skills a child does often, sometimes, and not yet. The team can understand much about how the child is functioning by reviewing the MEISR. For example, Figure 8.1 shows how Ishmael's team reviewed his participation in dressing by looking at the completed MEISR. In doing so, they noticed several things:

- He is not yet doing all of the skills we might expect for his age, 24 months, as shown by his receiving a Not yet (MEISR score 1) for several skills with a starting age of 24 months or younger.

- When the team looked at the functional domains of EISR (marked with E, I, or S on the form), they noticed that the skills he is doing are mostly related to engagement and social relationships, as shown by the letters E and S, respectively, in the column headed Func[a].

| 4. Dressing Time   Participates in dressing time by . . . | Typical starting age in months | Not yet | Sometimes | Often or Beyond this | Func | Dev? | Out? |
|---|---|---|---|---|---|---|---|
| 4.01 Attending to sound of caregiver's voice | 0 | 1 | 2 | (3) | S | S | S |
| 4.02 Allowing caregiver to dress him or her without getting overly upset or showing strong discomfort for clothing or touch | 0 | 1 | 2 | (3) | E | S | S |
| 4.03 Responding positively to physical contact and holding | 0 | 1 | 2 | (3) | E | S | S |
| 4.04 Inspecting his or her hands | 2 | 1 | 2 | (3) | E | CG | K |
| 4.05 Communicating with vocal sounds | 2 | 1 | 2 | (3) | S | CM | K |
| 4.06 Responding to own name when called (e.g., pausing, alerting, vocalizing) | 6 | 1 | 2 | (3) | S | CM | S |
| 4.07 Babbling with adult-like inflection (e.g., baba, mama, or different syllables together, mado, bada) | 8 | 1 | 2 | (3) | S | CM | K |
| 4.08 Assisting by extending an arm or leg for a sleeve or pants leg | 11 | (1) | 2 | 3 | I | A | A |
| 4.09 Pointing correctly to one body part on self when asked | 15 | 1 | 2 | 3 | S | CM, CG | K |
| 4.10 Removing an article of clothing by him- or herself (e.g., socks, hat) | 15 | (1) | 2 | 3 | I | A | A |
| 4.11 Indicating he or she understands the name of an article of clothing (e.g., looking at or otherwise acknowledging when caregiver says shoes, shirt) | 15 | 1 | 2 | (3) | S | CM | K |
| 4.12 Recognizing self in mirror (e.g., pointing at self) | 15 | 1 | 2 | (3) | E | CG, S | K |
| 4.13 Indicating what he or she wants to wear (gesturing/verbalizing when given choice) | 18 | 1 | 2 | (3) | S | CM | A |
| 4.14 Undoing fasteners (e.g., unzipping large zipper, snaps) | 18 | (1) | 2 | 3 | I | A | A |
| 4.15 Helping undress self (e.g., removing shoes) | 18 | (1) | 2 | 3 | I | A | A |
| 4.16 Using gestures or words to identify two or more body parts | 18 | 1 | 2 | (3) | S | CM | K |
| 4.17 Using some signs or words to comment or respond | 18 | 1 | 2 | (3) | S | CM | K |
| 4.18 Following directions to fetch something (e.g., go get your shoes) | 18 | 1 | (2) | 3 | S | CM | K |
| 4.19 Persisting with trying to put on/take off some clothes (might still need help to complete task) | 24 | (1) | 2 | 3 | I | A | A |
| 4.20 Identifying five or more body parts (e.g., pointing at oneself, others, or doll) | 24 | 1 | (2) | 3 | E | CG | K |
| 4.21 Following two-step directions (e.g., first shoes on, then outside) | 25 | 1 | 2 | 3 | E | CM | K |
| 4.22 Dressing him- or herself with assistance (i.e., helping) | 28 | 1 | 2 | 3 | I | A | A |
| 4.23 Putting shoes on (maybe on wrong feet and not tied) | 30 | 1 | 2 | 3 | I | A | A |
| 4.24 Putting on coat with assistance | 30 | 1 | 2 | 3 | I | A | A |
| 4.25 Describing clothing preference (e.g., want dinosaur jammies, princess skirt) | 30 | 1 | 2 | 3 | S | CM | A |

(continued)

7

**Figure 8.1.**   Ishmael's scores for the Dressing Time routine.

- When the team looked at developmental domains, they noticed that the skills he is not yet doing are mostly aligned with the adaptive domain, as shown by their being marked A in the column headed Dev[b].

- When the team looked even more closely at the routines-based skills, they easily recognized how Ishmael's motor impairment is impacting his ability to participate in dressing by being more independent. However, although he is not yet doing tasks related to assisting with dressing and undoing fasteners, he does participate in dressing by responding to questions related to body parts, following directions, and using words to communicate.

Knowing this helped the team understand, in greater detail, Ishmael's functional participation in dressing time. This will be useful as the family identifies their IFSP outcomes and as the team works with the family to identify and enhance Ishmael's natural learning opportunities. For example, the team might find ways to capitalize on Ishmael's understanding of directions and identify what directions and adaptations they might make to promote his independence with dressing.

***Analysis*** Beyond the question about the child's functioning across routines, teams can also explore deeper analysis questions to understand further details and identify possible patterns in the child's functioning. Following are further analysis questions that might help teams explore a child's functioning across routines:

- Across routines, how similar is the child's participation?

- Across routines, how similar is the age range for the skills the child does always, sometimes, and not yet?

- Are there particular routines in which the child is more or less successful?

- What do we know about the child's natural learning opportunities?

- Are there particular functional area skills (EISR) that are more or less consistently demonstrated (strengths/needs)?

- Considering the child's participation in each routine, are there any not-yet-mastered skills that will be important to promote the child's successful participation in the routine? (These may or may not be skills included on the MEISR.)

***So What?*** By reviewing a child's skills in the different routines in the MEISR, teams can gain a more detailed picture of how the child is participating in routines. They can identify any patterns that might provide insight into the child's interests and learning style, so that intervention can capitalize upon these patterns.

## 2. How Is the Child Demonstrating EISR Abilities?

***MEISR Profile*** It is possible to explore this question further by viewing the MEISR tool as it is completed and paying particular attention to how the items are cross-referenced with EISR abilities. (These abilities are indicated by E, I, or S on the MEISR form.)

***Analysis*** As teams consider the question about the child's EISR abilities, they might explore several additional considerations to fully understand how a child is demonstrating these abilities across routines. Included here are some deeper analysis questions teams can examine.

- Is the child demonstrating more or fewer EISR skills?

- Across routines, how similar is the child's mix of mastered, sometimes, and not yet EISR skills across routines?

- Across routines, how similar is the age range for mastered, sometimes, and not yet skills by EISR?

- Are there particular strengths with regard to one or more functional EISR areas?

- What percentage of EISR skills is the child demonstrating for his or her age and/or for all MEISR items?

*So What?*     Knowing more about the pattern of a child's EISR skills can help inform intervention. For example, if the team recognizes that a child demonstrates particular strengths with skills in the functional area of engagement in all routines except bath time, the team could review those routines-based skills more closely to understand what might be happening.

## 3. How Is the Child Demonstrating Functional Abilities Across the Different Domains of Development (i.e., the Five Developmental Domains)?

*MEISR Profile*     As with the other questions, it is possible to view the completed MEISR and explore skills by a domain by paying attention to how the items are cross-referenced with the different developmental domains.

*Analysis*     When reviewing functional skills by domain, teams can benefit from considering the following further analysis questions.

- Is the child demonstrating more or fewer skills in different developmental domains?

- How similar is the child's mix of mastered, sometimes, and not yet skills across developmental domains?

- How similar is the age range for mastered, sometimes, and not yet skills across developmental domains?

- Are the child's skills more or less age expected by different domains?

- Are there particular strengths with regard to one or more developmental domains?

- What degree of skills is the child demonstrating across domains, for the child's age, and/ or for all MEISR items?

*So What?*     Knowing more about the child's routines-based abilities within the context of developmental domains can provide the detail about functioning that traditional, norm-referenced tools often lack. It can also help teams understand how a child's domain-based areas of strength or need affect the child's functional participation in routines.

## 4. How Is the Child Demonstrating Functional Abilities Within the Context of Each of the Three National Outcomes?

*MEISR Profile*     When reviewing this question, examining the MEISR by the three national outcomes and by age is remarkably useful. Doing so provides the team practical information for determining skills that are age expected (AE), immediate foundational (IF), and foundational (F). These determinations are necessary when completing the COS process and working through the decision tree to determine COS ratings for each of the three national outcomes. By closely reviewing the MEISR items and how these items are crosswalked with the three outcomes, teams can identify examples of different functional skills that fall within each of the three national child outcomes.

*Analysis*     When exploring functional skills by the three national outcomes and for the COS rating process, teams can find it useful to ask the following analysis questions.

- Is the mix of mastered, sometimes, and not yet skills more or less consistently demonstrated across the three outcomes?

- Does the child demonstrate age-expected skills for any of the three outcomes?

- Looking at the skills and age expectations, does the child have any IF skills in each outcome area? (Recall that IF skills are those that come in just before AE skills.)

- Looking at skills and age expectations, does the child have any F skills in each outcome area? (Recall that F skills are those that come in much earlier than AE skills.)

- What, if any, are important AE skills that the child has not yet mastered? How is this affecting his or her ability to participate successfully in the routine?

*So What?*     Inclusion of this type of analysis can further help programs facilitate an analogous review of age-anchored, routines-based skills by each of the three national child outcomes, which is in part critical to quality COS ratings.

## 5.  How Is the Child Functioning Relative to Starting Age Expectations?

*MEISR Profile*     Teams can review the completed MEISR to begin answering this question as well. By attending to the starting ages associated with each MEISR item, teams can illustrate examples of the child's functioning relative to age expectations.

*Analysis*     When exploring functional skills by age, teams can benefit from considering the following analysis questions:

- Is the mix of mastered, sometimes, and not yet skills more or less consistently demonstrated across broad age ranges?

- What type of age-expected skills is the child demonstrating?

- What age-expected functioning is the child not yet demonstrating? Is that impacting his or her successful participation in the routine? If so, how?

- What functional skills appear to be relative age-related strengths or needs?

- How close or far is the child's functioning from age expectations across routines?

*So What?*     Knowing the general starting ages of a child's current functional skills can help teams target intervention attention and monitor progress.

## 6.  What Is a Baseline for Intervention?

*MEISR Profile*     Measuring baseline skills as children get started in programs provides a good benchmark to measure against later. The MEISR lends nicely to baseline measures of a child's functional skills across common family and community routines. Percentages of mastered items across routines and for the child's age provide a summative account of functional skills that teams can reexamine at later points in the program. The cumulative scoring tables in the MEISR Scoring Summary on page 2 of the form provide teams a quick glance at the percentage of mastered items by routine and overall, by all MEISR items, or by MEISR items up to and including the child's age. It is important to note that the percentage scores do not equate to measures beyond the percentage of mastered MEISR items. They *do not* translate to other scores, such as percentage of delay. They are, however, sensitive to a child's

| MEISR Scoring Summary | | | | | |
|---|---|---|---|---|---|
| MEISR Routines *(number of items in routine)* | A. Total Number of 3s | B1. Total Number of Items Scored for Child's Age | B2. Percentage of Items Mastered by Child's Age (A/B1 * 100 = %) | C1. Total Number of Items Scored for Routine | C2. Percentage of Items Mastered by Routine (A/C1 * 100 = %) |
| 01. Waking Up (25) | 17 | 25 | 68 % | 25 | 68 % |
| 02. Toileting/Diapering (20) | 5 | 20 | 25 % | 20 | 25 % |
| 03. Meal Times (47) | 22 | 47 | 47 % | 47 | 47 % |
| 04. Dressing Time (29) | 9 | 29 | 31 % | 29 | 31 % |
| 05. Hangout – TV – Books (38) | 16 | 38 | 42 % | 38 | 42 % |
| 06. Play With Others (38) | 13 | 38 | 34 % | 38 | 34 % |
| 07. Nap Time (14) | 10 | 14 | 71 % | 14 | 71 % |
| 08. Outside Time (26) | 18 | 26 | 69 % | 26 | 69 % |
| 09. Play by Him- or Herself (35) | 25 | 35 | 71 % | 35 | 71 % |
| 10. Bath Time (30) | 12 | 30 | 40 % | 30 | 40 % |
| 11. Bedtime (16) | 8 | 16 | 50 % | 16 | 50 % |
| 12. Going Out (35) | 13 | 35 | 37 % | 35 | 37 % |
| 13. Grocery Shopping (18) | 6 | 18 | 33 % | 18 | 33 % |
| 14. Transition Time (15) | 4 | 15 | 27 % | 15 | 27 % |
| TOTALS | 178 | 386 | 46 % | 386 | 46 % |

**Figure 8.2.** Sample completed Scoring Summary page.

developmental change over time. Figure 8.2 shows a sample completed Scoring Summary with the percentage of mastered items for all MEISR items up to and including the child's age, as well as the percentage of all items mastered within each routine.

***Analysis*** As teams consider MEISR baseline measures, they are encouraged to consider the following analysis questions.

- What percentage of all MEISR items has the child mastered for each routine?

- What percentage of MEISR items has the child mastered up to and including his or her age for each routine?

- What is the overall total percentage of all MEISR items the child has mastered?

- What is the total percentage of MEISR items the child has mastered for his or her age?

***So What?*** It is this type of baseline data that can help teams review an individual child's progress from a broad aggregate perspective.

## 7. How Has the Child's Functioning Changed Over Time?

***MEISR Profile*** The MEISR is sensitive to developmental change, and completing it at subsequent intervals provides teams an easy visual illustration of newly mastered functional skills. In addition, teams can examine aggregate results from the MEISR, such as the percentage of items mastered, percentage of items mastered for age, or percentage of items mastered by routine.

*Analysis*    When exploring a child's functional skills over time, teams can benefit from considering the following analysis questions.

- How has the child's participation in routines changed?

- What, if any, changes are particularly noteworthy? What might have influenced these changes?

- Is the mix of mastered, sometimes, and not yet skills more or less consistently demonstrated across broad age ranges?

- Have the child's skills moved closer to age expectations?

- What type of age-expected skills is the child demonstrating now that he or she wasn't demonstrating before?

- What functional skills appear to be relative age-related strengths or needs?

- How close or far is the child's functioning from age expectations across routines?

*So What?*    Examining children's progress over time is valuable for all stakeholders involved. This too could lead teams into further examination or analysis using some of the earlier questions addressed in this chapter. For example, are there particular areas in which the child progressed?

## TAKING ACTION

After identification of assessment purpose, completion of the MEISR, and analysis of results, it is time for action: What action will the team take? When thinking about action steps, it is essential to regard and respect families as key decision makers. They know what will and will not work, while professionals on the team can share information to support family-informed decision making.

As teams consider action options, it is important to consider the full mix of understandings the team has about the child and about the child in the context of his or her family. If action steps are exclusively based on one single assessment, even the MEISR, it is highly likely that the team is missing essential information about the child and/or family. The child's temperament, health, behaviors, strength, and interests, for example, are important factors to consider in order to understand the child's functioning. Family priorities, values, beliefs, circumstances, experiences, and understanding must also be considered, as they too have an influence on the child's functional development, actions, interactions, and learning opportunities.

Based upon the assessment questions (purpose), careful analysis of results, and steps in the early intervention/IFSP process, team action steps can be varied. These steps may include decisions about IFSP outcomes, choices about intervention strategies, and clarifications about next steps in the process. Decisions about IFSP outcomes can involve identifying new outcomes, refining existing IFSP outcomes, or discontinuing outcomes, because they have been met or because perhaps they are no longer a priority. Choices about intervention strategies can also include deciding upon new strategies or refining, building upon, or discontinuing strategies for intervention. Clarifications about next steps include team decisions about how to proceed. The matrix in Table 8.1 shows how the assessment questions discussed earlier fit within the early intervention process; the right column includes some activity strategies for sharing and using the MEISR.

## REVIEWING WITH FAMILIES

Birbili and Tzioga (2014) observed, "When parents are provided with opportunities to observe, record, and reflect on their children's learning they are able both to see the 'acts and products' of learning and to appreciate their child's progress, efforts, successes, and achievements over

**Table 8.1.** Using the MEISR to address assessment questions throughout the early intervention process

| Early Intervention Process | Assessment Purpose/Questions | Ways to Use and Share the MEISR |
|---|---|---|
| Referral | Q-1 | • Give the MEISR to the family and introduce the importance of routines-based skills and learning. <br> • Invite the family to begin completing the MEISR, noting that you will review it together at a subsequent visit. |
| Evaluation for Eligibility | Q-1 <br> Q-3 <br> Q-5 | • Use the results of the MEISR, along with information from other resources, to describe the child's functional strengths and needs as part of the team eligibility determination process. |
| Individualized Family Service Plan (IFSP) Development | Q-1 <br> Q-2 <br> Q-4 <br> Q-5 | • Use the MEISR to help the family identify IFSP outcomes. <br> • Use the MEISR items' crosswalking to the three outcomes and the items' starting ages to assist with the Child Outcomes Summary (COS) rating process. <br> • Use the MEISR to ensure inclusion of functional routines-based skills in the IFSP present levels of development (PLOD). |
| Service Delivery | Q-1 <br> Q-6 | • Use the MEISR as baseline information at the start of ongoing services. <br> • Use the MEISR on an ongoing basis to monitor and track progress and guide intervention decisions. <br> • Use the MEISR to understand natural learning opportunities. <br> • Use the MEISR to understand the dynamic skills that are part of children's participation in day-to-day routines, and identify strategies to promote the child's routines-based participation and learning. |
| Progress Monitoring | Q-7 | • Use the MEISR to assess how the child's functioning has changed over time. |
| Transition | Q-1 <br> Q-2 <br> Q-7 | • Use the MEISR to assess progress. <br> • Use the MEISR to assist the team with identifying goals in the child's next setting. |

• Q-1: *How is the child functioning across routines?*
• Q-2: *How is the child demonstrating engagement, independence, and social relationship (EISR) abilities?*
• Q-3: *How is the child demonstrating functional abilities across the different domains of development (i.e., the five developmental domains)?*
• Q-4: *How is the child demonstrating functional abilities within the context of each of the 3 national outcomes?*
• Q-5: *How is the child functioning relative to starting age expectations?*
• Q-6: *What is a baseline for intervention?*
• Q-7: *How has the child's functioning changed over time?*

time" (p. 161). Because the MEISR is completed entirely by or with families, they are inherently familiar with the results. When going over assessment data, such as MEISR results, with families, it is important to review the purpose and analysis discoveries in order for the team to work together to determine what action to take.

Best practices for engaging families in assessment review include sharing results in an understandable and respectful manner (Division for Early Childhood, 2014) while keeping a focus on the family-centered foundations of early intervention. Professionals must share assessment discoveries in a manner that is understandable to families and respectful. This includes the following:

• Respecting families as partners in the process

• Talking about the results in descriptive terms

• Avoiding professional jargon, or defining any jargon used

• Looking at the MEISR together

• Reflecting together about observations and discoveries to determine the next steps collaboratively based upon family priorities.

We know adults have varied learning styles. When reviewing MEISR profiles with families, be sure to take the time needed and encourage questions and observations. In cases when it would be helpful to share write-ups ahead of time, do this so the family can also prepare for team meetings.

Family-centered practices comprise two distinct subcategories, relational and participatory (Dunst, Trivette, & Hamby, 2007). When reviewing assessments with families, both dimensions should be apparent. From a relational perspective, professionals must convey their respect and understanding of the family's values, cultural strengths, and child-rearing beliefs by showing compassion, by being empathetic, and by listening actively and reflectively. The family is the constant in the child's life, and professionals must communicate their understanding for each family and their unique situations and circumstances by being sensitive and not judgmental. From a participatory lens, professionals must actively involve the family by acknowledging and promoting family confidence and competence and engaging the family as partners. This means empowering families by being flexible and responsive and encouraging their input, participation, and active decision making.

The unique design of the MEISR easily aligns it with these best practices, because families are the active participants completing the MEISR in a partnership relationship facilitated by the early intervention providers, all as part of the four quality assessment processes discussed in the beginning of this chapter (determining the assessment purpose, collecting the information needed, reviewing and analyzing the information collected, and acting upon the information in light of the purpose).

## MEISR Applied Practice: Meeting the Brook Family

Chapter 6 provided examples of how a professional might introduce the MEISR to a family—Shawn and his parents, Shanika and Jamal—and guide them to complete it. The following case study presents a more in-depth example of how the MEISR can inform an intervention team's decisions. The case study describes how one team used the MEISR at different steps in the IFSP process to help answer varied questions and help the team determine intervention priorities and monitor progress.

*Referral*     Amber Brook was 25 months old when the pediatrician referred her to Little Steps early intervention. Upon receipt of the referral, the Little Steps manager assigned Viola, the early childhood special educator, as the initial service coordinator. The Little Steps program uses a primary services provider model, whereby providers also function as service coordinators.

*First Contact*     Viola contacted the Brook family via telephone to determine their interest in early intervention. Lomita Brook, Amber's mother, answered the phone and spent about 15 minutes talking with Viola about the referral and her concerns about Amber's development. Viola was interested in learning about Amber's functioning within the context of the things that the family does. Lomita talked about how Amber did not seem to talk like other children her age; she mostly said vowel sounds and "sing-song" sounds and only a few words. When Viola asked about how Amber responded to questions or responded when given directions to do something, Lomita explained that Amber sometimes responded but needed lots of reminders. Lomita noted that sometimes, "It's like she is looking through me."

Viola also asked about Amber's favored activities, as she was interested in knowing what motivates her and sparks her engagement. Viola asked these questions to get a better understanding of Amber's participation in day-to-day routines, referring to the MEISR as Lomita talked about what Amber does. Viola thought too about how the completed MEISR would provide even more detail. Lomita described how Amber loved her little ponies and how Amber carried them around and rubbed the hair of their manes against her cheeks. Lomita stated that Amber seemed to like the feel of the hair against her cheeks. Lomita also talked about how

Amber loved bath time and was generally easy to take on outings but did not wave bye-bye or show interest in others.

As they talked more, Viola discussed the program and outlined the steps involved. During the conversation, Viola also learned that Lomita was a stay-at-home mom and that her husband, Evan, was an Army sergeant working field artillery and was often gone on exercises for 2 to 3 weeks at a time. Lomita reviewed Evan's schedule and her upcoming doctor appointments, as she was 6 months pregnant with their second child. Together, Lomita and Viola decided upon an appointment for the evaluation, which would include Viola and Ben, the speech-language pathologist.

During this step in the early intervention process, the team referred to the MEISR to begin to help answer the following questions:

Q-1: *How is the child functioning across routines?*

Q-3: *How is the child demonstrating functional abilities across the different domains of development (i.e., the five developmental domains)?*

**Evaluation**     When it came time for the evaluation visit, Viola explained the evaluation process and got the family's permission to proceed. Evan was able to be home during the evaluation, so Viola invited Evan to discuss his observations and questions about Amber. Viola also shared the MEISR with the family and discussed how they might be able to complete part of it as they discussed Amber's participation in day-to-day routines. During the discussion, Evan talked about going to the playground with Amber. At this point, Viola referred to the MEISR, and together they were able to complete the items for the Outside Time routine about walking, running, jumping, playing outside without fussing, and playing purposefully (8.04, 8.05, 8.07, 8.11, and 8.10, respectively). Viola also asked a few more detailed questions about how Amber was moving ride-on toys with her feet (8.06), using the slide (8.08), using the sandbox (8.09), having favored playground toys (8.12), and catching balls (8.13). Viola also inquired a bit further about Amber's use of stairs and jumping and her understanding of descriptions such as hot and cold (MEISR items 8.15–8.19) so that the team could see where her skills in this routine plateaued. By listening to Evan and asking a few questions, the team was able to complete the Outside Time routine section of the MEISR. They also used this information as they completed the evaluation. The Outside Time section of Amber's completed MEISR is shown in Figure 8.3. Her full completed MEISR appears as Appendix 8.1.

Viola shared this page of the MEISR with Lomita and Evan and explained that they would refer to this more later. Meanwhile, Ben sat back and observed what Amber was doing with her own toys. Ben took notes, in the form of a running record, of what he observed Amber doing. Before transitioning to completion of the evaluation instrument, Ben reviewed his observations with Lomita and Evan to determine if what he had observed were abilities they too had seen Amber demonstrate, which they had. Ben asked a few more questions to complete the Play by Him- or Herself section of the MEISR. This completed section of Amber's MEISR is shown in Figure 8.4. Ben asked Lomita and Evan how Amber interacts with books (9.19), and they shared that she really showed little interest in books other than sometimes turning pages and looking at or patting at pictures, like the ones in her Little Pony book. So together they scored this item as *sometimes*. Ben also asked if Amber understood where things belong, such as knowing where to find things or put things away. Lomita said, "Well, she knows where we put her ponies at bed time, and she goes to get them the next day. She also knows we put the iPad on top of the fridge now—where she can't get it when we take it away from her. Funny, I never thought about this before. She really does know where things belong, even does things like putting her cup in the sink and getting snacks from the snack drawer." So together they scored that item (9.24) as *often*. Ben asked a couple more questions, and together they completed this section of the MEISR.

| 8. Outside Time  Participates in outside time by . . . | Typical starting age in months | Not yet | Sometimes | Often or Beyond this | Func | Dev | Out |
|---|---|---|---|---|---|---|---|
| 8.01 Looking at object 8–10 inches away | 0 | 1 | 2 | 3 | E | CG | K |
| 8.02 Holding object placed in his or her hand | 2 | 1 | 2 | 3 | I | M | A |
| 8.03 Holding one and reaching for a second toy or object | 6 | 1 | 2 | 3 | I | M | A |
| 8.04 Walking independently at least a few steps | 13 | 1 | 2 | (3) | I | M | A |
| 8.05 Running (might look like fast walk) | 16 | 1 | 2 | (3) | I | M | A |
| 8.06 Moving ride-on wheeled toys (no pedals) with feet | 20 | 1 | 2 | (3) | I | M | A |
| 8.07 Jumping up so that both feet are off the ground | 24 | 1 | 2 | (3) | I | M | A |
| 8.08 Going up the ladder and down small slide | 24 | 1 | 2 | (3) | I | M | A |
| 8.09 Using sandbox toys appropriately (e.g., not throwing or eating sand) | 24 | 1 | 2 | (3) | E | CG | K |
| 8.10 Playing purposefully with playground toys (figuring out their best use) | 24 | 1 | (2) | 3 | E | CG | K |
| 8.11 Playing outside without fussing (with supervision for ~30 minutes) | 24 | 1 | 2 | (3) | E | S | S |
| 8.12 Showing interest in the playground (might have favorite toy/activity) | 24 | 1 | 2 | (3) | E | CG | K |
| 8.13 Catching a large ball (e.g., beach ball) | 24 | (1) | 2 | 3 | I | M | A |
| 8.14 Walking upstairs alone (both feet on each step), using rail if needed | 24 | 1 | 2 | (3) | I | M | A |
| 8.15 Walking downstairs alone (both feet on each step), using rail if needed | 26 | 1 | 2 | (3) | I | M | A |
| 8.16 Jumping off small step or bottom of slide with both feet together | 27 | (1) | 2 | 3 | I | M | A |
| 8.17 Walking forward and backward with balance while playing | 28 | (1) | 2 | 3 | I | M | A |
| 8.18 Walking upstairs alone (alternating feet—one foot on each step) | 30 | (1) | 2 | 3 | I | M | A |
| 8.19 Understanding descriptions such as hot, cold, dirty, wet (e.g., *the ball is dirty, the sand is wet*) | 30 | (1) | 2 | 3 | S | CM, CG | K |
| 8.20 Riding on toy with pedals at least a short distance | 33 | 1 | 2 | 3 | I | M | A |
| 8.21 Climbing on jungle gyms with hands and feet | 33 | 1 | 2 | 3 | I | M | A |
| 8.22 Engaging with others in a game with turn taking (e.g., jumping over rope, chalk line; might need caregiver guidance) | 34 | 1 | 2 | 3 | S | S | S |
| 8.23 Understanding simple rules (but might still test limits) | 34 | 1 | 2 | 3 | E | S | S |
| 8.24 Following caregiver's directions given from a distance | 36 | 1 | 2 | 3 | S | CM | K |
| 8.25 Using big slides (about 6 feet/2 meters high) | 36 | 1 | 2 | 3 | I | M | A |
| 8.26 Swinging on regular swing (might still not pump feet effectively) | 36 | 1 | 2 | 3 | I | M | A |

A. Total items scored 3 (Often or Beyond this): 13

B1. Total items scored for child's age: 14

B2. Percentage of items mastered by age (A / B1 * 100): 93 %

C1. Total items scored for full routine: 26

C2. Percentage of items mastered by routine (A / C1 * 100): 50 %
*Add scores to the MEISR Scoring Summary page*

**Figure 8.3.** Amber's scores for the Outside Time routine.

| 9. Play by Him- or Herself  Participates in play time by him- or herself by . . . | Typical starting age in months | Not yet | Sometimes | Often or Beyond this | Func | Dev | Out |
|---|---|---|---|---|---|---|---|
| 9.01 Lying on back turning head (might prefer one side but can do both) | 0 | 1 | 2 | 3 | I | M | A |
| 9.02 Repeating actions with toys (e.g., banging at toys, kicking legs to move toy) | 3 | 1 | 2 | 3 | E | CG | K |
| 9.03 Exploring objects with hands and mouth | 3 | 1 | 2 | 3 | E | CG | K |
| 9.04 Grasping own foot and taking it to mouth to explore | 5 | 1 | 2 | 3 | E | CG, M | K |
| 9.05 Lying on tummy and reaching for toys with one hand | 6 | 1 | 2 | 3 | I | M | A |
| 9.06 Seeking partly hidden items, such as pacifier or bottle or favored toy | 6 | 1 | 2 | 3 | E | CG | K |
| 9.07 Working to get out-of-reach toy by pivoting, rolling, stretching | 7 | 1 | 2 | 3 | E | M | A |
| 9.08 Sitting independently (not propped with hands) | 8 | 1 | 2 | 3 | I | M | A |
| 9.09 Making toys work by self (e.g., pushing to reactivate action) | 9 | 1 | 2 | 3 | E | CG | K |
| 9.10 Dropping or throwing objects while exploring objects | 9 | 1 | 2 | 3 | E | M, CG | K |
| 9.11 Moving from sitting to hands and knees to crawl on hands and knees | 9 | 1 | 2 | 3 | I | M | A |
| 9.12 Crawling on hands and knees to get toys or objects of interest | 9 | 1 | 2 | 3 | I | M | A |
| 9.13 Picking up small objects effectively, with tip of index finger and thumb | 10 | 1 | 2 | (3) | I | M | A |
| 9.14 Putting toys in and out of containers (e.g., dumping and filling) | 12 | 1 | 2 | (3) | E | CG | K |
| 9.15 Watching where toy moves out of sight and going to get it (e.g., ball, car) | 12 | 1 | 2 | (3) | E | M, CG | K |
| 9.16 Using both hands equally well in play to explore | 12 | 1 | 2 | (3) | E | M | A |
| 9.17 Playing with toys, showing awareness of toy functions (e.g., banging on drum, drinking from cup) | 12 | 1 | 2 | (3) | E | CG | K |
| 9.18 Using nonwords to express emotion (e.g., uh-oh, oops, ah) whee on swings | 12 | 1 | (2) | 3 | S | CM | S |
| 9.19 Patting at pictures in books, turning one or more pages at a time | 15 | 1 | (2) | 3 | E | M, CG | K |
| 9.20 Picking up toys/objects from floor while standing | 15 | 1 | 2 | (3) | I | M | A |
| 9.21 Selecting favorite toy or object and going to get it by him- or herself | 15 | 1 | 2 | (3) | I | CG | A |
| 9.22 Sustaining play by self for a few minutes without caregiver in clear sight | 18 | 1 | 2 | (3) | E | S | S |
| 9.23 Constructing things during play (e.g., build or stacks blocks) | 19 | (1) | 2 | 3 | E | CG, M | K |
| 9.24 Indicating understanding of where toys or other things belong (e.g., goes to shelf to find specific toy, puts toy away) | 21 | 1 | 2 | (3) | E | CG | K |
| 9.25 Holding crayon with three fingers to color | 23 | (1) | 2 | 3 | I | M | A |
| 9.26 Jabbering and saying true words too during play | 24 | (1) | 2 | 3 | E | CM | K |
| 9.27 Pretending by linking two or more actions (e.g., feeding, burping, and putting doll down for nap) | 24 | (1) | 2 | 3 | E | CG | K |
| 9.28 Pretending objects are something else (e.g., block to represent food) | 24 | (1) | 2 | 3 | E | CG | K |
| 9.29 Matching two or more identical shapes or colors (e.g., putting round blocks together, picking out same-colored cars) | 24 | (1) | 2 | 3 | E | CG | K |

(continued)

**Figure 8.4.** Amber's scores for the Play by Him- or Herself routine.

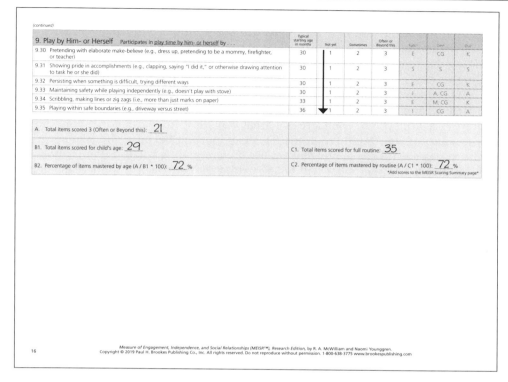

**Figure 8.4.**   Amber's scores for the Play by Him- or Herself routine.

The team evaluation instrument was then completed, and before the end of the visit, the team was able to determine that Amber had a significant delay in development and was eligible for early intervention. The team members discussed their observations and the results of the evaluation tool. Following the discussion about eligibility, Viola talked about next steps and how important it was to have a rich understanding of Amber's functional skills. Viola took this opportunity to review the MEISR more closely with the family. Viola said, "The MEISR, which we briefly showed you earlier, is a kind of assessment that you as Amber's parents can complete, because you know her better than anyone. This tool helps all of us understand how Amber participates in your day-to-day routines, which is the natural context for young children's learning. Let's look at it a bit closer now so that we can answer any questions you might have." Viola referred again to the page they had completed for the Outside Time routine. Viola pointed out how the items are organized around common family routines; she then pointed out the starting age column and highlighted the fact that some of the skills they had previously talked about and scored were on target for Amber's age.

Viola also explained the scoring process, saying, "The scoring of this tool is simply circling the number 1 if she is *not yet* doing the item, 2 if she does it *sometimes*, or 3 if she does it *often*. This 'Often or Beyond this' column also includes skills that she did but now no longer needs to do—for instance, she used to crawl, but doesn't do that anymore because she can walk now. That is what *beyond this* means." Viola then asked Lomita and Evan, "What additional questions do you have right now about the MEISR?" Lomita stated, "It's pretty straightforward. I don't have any questions right now," and Evan concurred.

Next, Ben took the opportunity to review the conversation they had had earlier about the notes he had taken as he watched Amber play. Ben said, "As we briefly discussed earlier, I was watching Amber play, and you also stated that some of the things I was seeing her do are things you have also noticed. Let's look at these on the MEISR and score them together." Together, Lomita, Evan, Ben, and Viola discussed Amber's independent play and completed MEISR items for the Play by Him- or Herself routine (9.13–9.29) as shown in Figure 8.4. (Arrows marking the items before 9.13 and after 9.29 illustrate the team's use of the four-item basal and ceiling, as described in Chapter 7.)

At this point, Viola asked Lomita and Evan if they felt comfortable completing the rest of the MEISR, and they agreed to do so prior to their next appointment. Viola recapped, "This tool we're asking you to complete is a great way for us to learn more about the things Amber does as part of your family routines. This is important because children learn in the context of the things you do day in and day out. By understanding what Amber is and is not yet doing, we can decide together what will be important for her to learn to increase her participation and learning in her day-to-day experiences."

Viola discussed the next steps in the process, and they scheduled the next appointment, which would include reviewing the MEISR, discussing family routines, and identifying the family's priorities for intervention.

During this step in the process, the team used the MEISR to gather information toward answering the following questions:

Q-1: *How is the child functioning across routines?*

Q-3: *How is the child demonstrating functional abilities across the different domains of development (i.e., the five developmental domains)?*

Q-4: *How is the child demonstrating functional abilities within the context of each of the three national outcomes?*

Q-5: *How is the child functioning relative to starting age expectations?*

**IFSP Development**     At the IFSP development meeting, the team reviewed the MEISR together and talked about the family's day-to-day routines and Amber's participation. They also talked about Amber's EISR abilities and highlighted that she demonstrates more age-expected independent skills. During the course of their conversation, Lomita and Evan identified the following concerns that would become outcomes on their IFSP. These priorities mostly emerged through their discussion and review of the MEISR:

1. Saying "mama" and "dada" when she sees us in the morning (1.19)

2. Pointing clearly to indicate her food preference at meal times (3.23)

3. Saying "more" or "finished" at meal times (3.28 and 3.29)

4. Pointing to and naming pictures in books (5.21)

5. Singing some words in familiar songs (6.23)

6. Jabbering and saying true words too during play (9.26)

7. Waving bye on outings and at home when friends are leaving (12.11)

8. Understanding directions and names of body parts at bath time, like wash your feet (10.15)

In addition, Viola asked the family about child care and their ability to do the things they enjoy. During this conversation, the family identified the following priorities that would be included in their IFSP.

1. Find a playgroup that is not too big for Amber to participate in.

2. Figure out how to explain Amber's development and delays to Lomita's parents.

3. Figure out ways to engage Amber in the Saturday morning Facetime calls with Lomita's sister.

After identifying the priorities the family wanted to address, Viola explained how she and Ben would enter these concerns as outcomes on the family's IFSP. Viola also discussed how they would write up this information. She explained how, at their next appointment, they could review the entire IFSP and also decide upon initial ratings about Amber's functioning as part of the COS process. Viola explained more about the COS process and answered the family's questions. The team scheduled their next appointment, and Viola mentioned that she would share a draft of the IFSP prior to their next meeting.

Back at the office, Viola and Ben reviewed the MEISR, paying particular attention to the skills Amber demonstrated within the context of the three national child outcomes, because that is how they write up the PLOD section of the IFSP. They used the MEISR and other tools to categorize some of Amber's skills as AE, IF, and F. They drafted the IFSP and shared a copy with the family. Appendix 8.1 shows Amber's completed MEISR, whereas Appendix 8.2 shows her PLOD.

During this step in the process, the team used the MEISR to help answer the following questions:

Q-1: *How is the child functioning across routines?*

Q-2: *How is the child demonstrating EISR abilities?*

Q-4: *How is the child demonstrating functional abilities within the context of each of the three national outcomes?*

Q-5: *How is the child functioning relative to starting age expectations?*

### IFSP Completion Meeting

At this meeting, the team reviewed the PLOD and determined the COS ratings. Viola explained more about the COS process, including why and how the three child outcomes are measured. Viola explained that the PLOD includes a review of the information they shared about Amber's functioning on the MEISR and during their earlier interactions and observations and how that information combined was organized into the three child outcome areas as shown on the PLOD. Together the team reviewed each of the PLOD paragraphs, engaged in some further discussion about Amber's functioning, and completed the COS rating process. Next they reviewed each of the IFSP outcomes and discussed services. The team agreed that Viola would be the family's primary provider and Ben would join her on visits once a month for the first 3 months. Upon completion of the meeting, the family signed the IFSP and made an appointment to start IFSP implementation.

During this step in the process, the team used the MEISR to help answer the following questions:

Q-4: *How is the child demonstrating functional abilities within the context of each of the three national outcomes?*

Q-6: *What is a baseline for intervention?*

### IFSP Implementation

On their next visit, Viola met the family at their home. She explained how the ongoing intervention visits would generally flow, emphasizing that they would work together to address the IFSP outcomes. Viola invited Lomita to ask questions and comment on her expectations for their ongoing visits. Then the team started working on the family's first priority, for Amber to participate in meal times by pointing or vocalizing to indicate what she wanted to eat. Viola learned more about what Lomita and Evan had tried and how, when they could not make out what she wanted, they would bring Amber to the fridge or cupboard for her to choose. Together they tried this as it was nearing snack time. As Viola watched how Lomita brought Amber to the cupboard, she wondered out loud how easy this was for Amber. Lomita commented, referring to the snack shelf, "She likes lots of the things on this shelf." Viola asked, "How do you think we could make it easier for Amber to choose?"

After some further discussion—with Viola discussing how choosing from two options is easier and also allows caregivers to limit the child's options—they tried offering Amber two choices rather than going to the cupboard. It didn't work at first, but after a few more trials, they were able to get Amber's attention so she could make a choice. Viola also discussed how it can be easier for children to choose from two options rather than several. Lomita shared that she liked how Amber responded when she was given a choice of two items, making sure one item was one she wanted and the other was not. Viola offered more feedback, and Lomita stated that she was comfortable with this strategy and would try it during meal times. They also discussed how choice making might be used in other times during the day. Lomita thought for a bit and talked about maybe giving Amber choices of bath toys. Viola agreed that was a great idea, and together they went into the bathroom to look at the toys and determine how that might go. Lomita also said she could use choices at dressing time. Viola applauded her ideas and reinforced how having more opportunities to make choices will build Amber's ability to do so and how making it part of day-to-day activities provides natural practice opportunities for both her and Amber. Just then it was time for a diaper change. Viola observed how Lomita gave Amber a toy to distract her while on the changing table and asked Lomita if this might be another time to offer Amber a choice. Viola smiled and they tried offering Amber a choice between two toys. Lomita excitedly commented that she could probably think of many other opportunities to offer Amber choices. Lomita shared her excitement and expressed how she looked forward to hearing about how it went on their next visit. As they wrapped up the visit, Lomita shared what she wanted to do between now and their next visit. Then, together they identified the IFSP outcome they would focus on during their next visit and how they would follow up on the choice-making strategy during snacks, bath, dressing, diapering, and other times of day that Lomita indicates.

The ongoing visits continued in this manner. Periodically, Viola would review the MEISR before, during, or after her visits with the family. She also purposefully reviewed the MEISR with Lomita and Evan, sometimes as they were discussing a particular routine or reviewing Amber's progress.

During this step in the process, the team used the MEISR to help answer the following questions:

Q-1: *How is the child functioning across routines?*

Q-2: *How is the child demonstrating EISR abilities?*

Q-5: *How is the child functioning relative to starting age expectations?*

Q-7: *How has the child's functioning changed over time?*

**Six-Month Review**    Just prior to the 6-month IFSP review, Viola invited Lomita and Evan to review and update the MEISR, asking them to complete it this time with a different-colored pen. At the 6-month review meeting, the team reviewed the progress toward the family's IFSP outcomes and then reviewed the MEISR. Lomita and Evan were excited to share how Amber had made progress on many of the MEISR items that they had initially marked as "Sometimes." The team also looked at the MEISR to guide their discussion as they chose to develop a few new outcomes.

During this step in the process, the team used the MEISR to help answer the following questions:

Q-1: *How is the child functioning across routines?*

Q-7: *How has the child's functioning changed over time?*

**Transition**    In preparation for the transition process, Lomita and Evan updated the MEISR using a different-colored pen. To help discuss progress, Viola took the completed MEISR and analyzed Amber's progress by looking at the percentage of items within each routine that

Amber was now doing. Viola and Lomita reviewed this together, along with other updated testing at the transition meeting. With the family's permission, Viola shared a copy of the MEISR with the preschool team and also shared some of the things the family would like to see Amber be able to do as she transitioned out of early intervention.

During this step in the process, the team used the MEISR to help answer the following questions:

Q-1: *How is the child functioning across routines?*

Q-3: *How is the child demonstrating functional abilities across the different domains of development (i.e., the five developmental domains)?*

Q-4: *How is the child demonstrating functional abilities within the context of each of the three national outcomes?*

Q-5: *How is the child functioning relative to starting age expectations?*

Q-7: *How has the child's functioning changed over time?*

Engaging families in assessment processes, as Amber's team did with the Brook family, is an essential practice in early intervention. After all, families know their children best and have the greatest long-lasting impact on their children's development. The inclusion of a functional assessment tool, such as the MEISR, promotes family engagement in the ongoing assessment process in a way that easily guides their sharing of the rich information they know about their child's functioning in their day-to-day routines. Having and updating this functional assessment information throughout the early intervention process helps all team members share in the process. It also helps families know their child's functional abilities, identify and enhance natural learning opportunities, and advocate for their child and family needs. The MEISR is not an assessment that the professional administers to the child in a clinical way; rather, it is a tool used with families and by families.

## SUMMARY

This chapter addressed the different purposes of assessment in early intervention, the questions the MEISR can help answer, and ways caregivers and professionals can apply and act upon information from the MEISR. Questions the MEISR can help teams answer include the following: 1) How is the child functioning across routines? 2) How is the child demonstrating EISR abilities? 3) How is the child demonstrating functional abilities across the different domains of development (e.g., the five developmental domains)? 4) How is the child demonstrating functional abilities within the context of the three national outcomes? 5) How is the child functioning relative to starting age expectations? 6) What is a baseline for intervention? and 7) How has the child's functioning changed over time? This chapter described how MEISR scoring data can help intervention teams answer these questions and listed deeper analysis questions for the team to consider. It also provided guidance for professionals about how to review the MEISR with families and determine what action to take next. Throughout the chapter, we emphasized the 1) importance of working with the family to make sure they clearly understand the purpose(s) for using the MEISR and the question(s) the team hopes to answer and 2) the importance of respecting the family as key decision makers.

# Amber's Completed MEISR

# MEISR™  Measure of Engagement, Independence, and Social Relationships

The MEISR™ is a list of skills that infants and toddlers (birth to 3 years of age) typically display in everyday routines within the home and community. To complete the MEISR, caregivers assess a child's level of functional participation in 14 different routines. For the purposes of the MEISR, a caregiver is defined as someone who has observed the child often in the home. Caregivers may work together with a professional to complete the MEISR.

The MEISR has many benefits within the context of early intervention. Prior to administration, professionals should discuss the specific purpose and benefits as they apply to each child and family.

**Directions to professionals:** Ask caregivers to rate **all items** within each routine, including items with a typical starting age beyond the child's age. Follow instructions at the bottom of each routine to determine scoring. Scores indicate a child's level of mastery by age (relative to typical starting age for skills) and by routine (relative to all skills for that routine up to 36 months of age). Once completed, transfer scores for all routines to the MEISR Scoring Summary page. See the manual for complete administration instructions (Chapters 4 and 6) and scoring instructions (Chapter 7).

**Directions to caregivers:** On a scale from 1 to 3 (Not yet, Sometimes, Often or Beyond this), rate your child's level of functioning in performing activities. Circle 1, 2, or 3 for each skill. Depending on the child's age, some activities may be beyond your child's capability. This is expected. The MEISR takes about 45 minutes to complete.

| Child's name: Amber Brook | Child's DOB: June 1, 2015 | Today's date: July 1, 2017 |
| | Child's age in months: 25 months | Date(s) of previous MEISR use (if applicable): n/a |

| Caregiver(s) name and relationship to child: Lomita and Evan Brook – Amber's parents |
| Caregiver(s) contact information: |
| Professional(s) name and affiliation: Viola Jackson and Ben Larsen, Little Steps |
| Professional(s) contact information: |

**KEY:**

**Func[a]** Functional Domains: **E** = engagement, **I** = independence, **S** = social relationships

**Dev[b]** Developmental Domains: **A** = adaptive, **CG** = cognitive, **CM** = communication, **M** = motor, **S** = social

**Out[c]** National Child Outcomes: **S** = positive social relationships, **K** = acquiring and using knowledge and skills, **A** = taking appropriate action to meet needs

1

## MEISR Scoring Summary

| MEISR Routines (number of items in routine) | A. Total Number of 3s | B1. Total Number of Items Scored for Child's Age | B2. Percentage of Items Mastered by Child's Age (A/B1 * 100 = %) | C1. Total Number of Items Scored for Routine | C2. Percentage of Items Mastered by Routine (A/C1 * 100 = %) |
|---|---|---|---|---|---|
| 01. Waking Up (25) | 21 | 23 | 91 % | 25 | 84 % |
| 02. Toileting/Diapering (20) | 6 | 12 | 50 % | 20 | 30 % |
| 03. Meal Times (47) | 24 | 37 | 65 % | 47 | 51 % |
| 04. Dressing Time (29) | 11 | 21 | 52 % | 29 | 38 % |
| 05. Hangout – TV – Books (38) | 16 | 24 | 67 % | 38 | 42 % |
| 06. Play With Others (38) | 18 | 27 | 67 % | 38 | 47 % |
| 07. Nap Time (14) | 9 | 11 | 82 % | 14 | 64 % |
| 08. Outside Time (26) | 13 | 14 | 93 % | 26 | 50 % |
| 09. Play by Him- or Herself (35) | 21 | 29 | 72 % | 35 | 60 % |
| 10. Bath Time (30) | 20 | 25 | 76 % | 30 | 63 % |
| 11. Bedtime (16) | 10 | 12 | 83 % | 16 | 63 % |
| 12. Going Out (35) | 15 | 26 | 58 % | 35 | 43 % |
| 13. Grocery Shopping (18) | 6 | 13 | 46 % | 18 | 33 % |
| 14. Transition Time (15) | 5 | 9 | 56 % | 15 | 33 % |
| TOTALS | 195 | 283 | 69 % | 386 | 51 % |

*Measure of Engagement, Independence, and Social Relationships (MEISR™), Research Edition*, by R. A. McWilliam and Naomi Younggren.
Copyright © 2019 Paul H. Brookes Publishing Co., Inc. All rights reserved. Do not reproduce without permission. 1-800-638-3775 www.brookespublishing.com

2

# 1. Waking Up — Participates in waking up time by . . .

| Item | Typical starting age in months | Not yet | Sometimes | Often or Beyond this | Func | Dev | Out |
|---|---|---|---|---|---|---|---|
| 1.01 Making vocal sounds | 0 | 1 | 2 | 3 | S | CM | K |
| 1.02 Showing enjoyment when held, rocked, touched by caregiver | 0 | 1 | 2 | 3 | S | S | S |
| 1.03 Looking at caregiver and making eye contact | 0 | 1 | 2 | 3 | S | S | S |
| 1.04 Easily turning head to both sides | 1 | 1 | 2 | 3 | I | M | A |
| 1.05 Acting happy to see or hear caregiver | 1 | 1 | 2 | 3 | S | S | S |
| 1.06 Showing interest in crib toys (e.g., watching mobile) | 2 | 1 | 2 | 3 | E | CG | K |
| 1.07 Turning over from side to tummy or side to back | 2 | 1 | 2 | 3 | I | M | A |
| 1.08 Smiling, kicking, moving arms excitedly when sees caregiver | 2 | 1 | 2 | 3 | S | S, M | S |
| 1.09 Reaching out for or batting at toys, repeating action with enjoyment | 3 | 1 | 2 | 3 | E | CG, M | K |
| 1.10 Playing with hands and feet, touching and watching movements | 3 | 1 | 2 | 3 | E | CG | K |
| 1.11 Turning toward the sound of caregiver's voice | 3 | 1 | 2 | 3 | S | S | S |
| 1.12 Maintaining sitting at least briefly | 5 | 1 | 2 | 3 | I | M | A |
| 1.13 Raising arms to be picked up when caregiver reaches for child | 5 | 1 | 2 | 3 | S | CM, S | S |
| 1.14 Sitting when placed in sitting | 6 | 1 | 2 | 3 | I | M | A |
| 1.15 Moving up and down by bending knees when supported in standing | 6 | 1 | 2 | (3) ← | I | M | A |
| 1.16 Calling out for caregivers (e.g., shouting, vocalizing) whines | 7 | 1 | 2 | (3) | S | CM, S | A |
| 1.17 Waking up without crying immediately (calming self) | 8 | 1 | 2 | (3) | E | S | S |
| 1.18 Standing and cruising around crib | 10 | 1 | 2 | (3) | I | M | A |
| 1.19 Saying "mama" or "dada" when sees Mama or Dada | 12 | (1) | 2 | 3 | S | CM, S | S |
| 1.20 Standing for several seconds without support | 12 | 1 | 2 | (3) | I | M | A |
| 1.21 Playing with toys momentarily until caregiver comes (i.e., coping) | 18 | (1) | 2 | 3 | E | S | S |
| 1.22 Responding to caregiver's greeting with a sign or word | 18 | 1 | 2 | 3 | S | CM | S |
| 1.23 Leaving room to find caregiver | 24 | 1 | 2 | (3) | I | S | A |
| 1.24 Letting caregiver know how he/she is feeling (e.g., happy) by saying so or responding to a question | 30 | (1) | 2 | 3 | S | S | S |
| 1.25 Following directions involving descriptions (e.g., get the *big pillow*; be *quiet*, Sissy is still sleeping) | 33 | (1) | 2 | 3 | S | CG, CM | K |

A. Total items scored 3 (Often or Beyond this): __21__

B1. Total items scored for child's age: __23__

B2. Percentage of items mastered by age (A / B1 * 100): __91__ %

C1. Total items scored for full routine: __25__

C2. Percentage of items mastered by routine (A / C1 * 100): __84__ %
*Add scores to the MEISR Scoring Summary page*

3

140

## 2. Toileting/Diapering  Participates in toileting/diapering time by . . .

| | Typical starting age in months | Not yet | Sometimes | Often or Beyond this | Func | Dev | Out |
|---|---|---|---|---|---|---|---|
| 2.01 Quieting when picked up by caregiver | 0 | 1 | 2 | (3) | E | S | S |
| 2.02 Cooperating with diaper change without being inconsolably fussy | 1 | 1 | 2 | (3) | S | S | S |
| 2.03 Paying attention to surroundings, including caregiver's face | 1 | 1 | 2 | (3) | E | CG | K |
| 2.04 Vocalizing frequently with apparent intent (short, loud, different pitches) | 9 | 1 | 2 | (3) | S | CM | K |
| 2.05 Indicating when he or she needs to be changed by vocalizing | 12 | 1 | (2) | 3 | S | CM | A |
| 2.06 Following routine directions with a prompt with items in sight (e.g., put diaper in bin) | 15 | 1 | (2) | 3 | S | CM | K |
| 2.07 Using a sign or word about toilet/diapering (e.g., to comment or respond) | 18 | (1) | 2 | 3 | S | CM | K |
| 2.08 Washing hands, completing the steps with prompting (might need help reaching things and rinsing off soap)  We do it for her | 24 | 1 | (2) | 3 | I | A | A |
| 2.09 Using the toilet (or potty chair) with assistance  before bath | 24 | 1 | (2) | 3 | I | A | A |
| 2.10 Lowering pants (may need help with fasteners or getting over diaper) | 24 | 1 | 2 | (3) | I | A | A |
| 2.11 Using two-word phrases to express self (e.g., me potty, go potty, me poop) | 24 | (1) | 2 | 3 | S | CM | K |
| 2.12 Staying dry for 3 hours | 25 | 1 | 2 | (3) | I | A | A |
| 2.13 Indicating a need to go to the bathroom and actually going, most of the time | 30 | (1) | 2 | 3 | I | A | A |
| 2.14 Indicating need to go in enough time to get to the bathroom, usually | 30 | (1) | 2 | 3 | I | A | A |
| 2.15 Responding to questions about bowel movement/urination (poop and pee—knows the difference) | 30 | (1) | 2 | 3 | S | CG | K |
| 2.16 Lasting the whole night without wetting | 33 | 1 | 2 | 3 | A | A | A |
| 2.17 Attempting to wipe self | 33 | 1 | 2 | 3 | I | A | A |
| 2.18 Talking about the toilet | 33 | 1 | 2 | 3 | S | CM | K |
| 2.19 Managing toileting mostly by self, may need reminders and help with wiping | 33 | 1 | 2 | 3 | I | A | A |
| 2.20 Doing several steps in toilet routine without being prompted (e.g., goes to potty, pulls pants down, sits on potty) | 33 | 1 | 2 | 3 | E | CG | K |

A. Total items scored 3 (Often or Beyond this): ___6___

B1. Total items scored for child's age: ___12___

B2. Percentage of items mastered by age (A / B1 * 100): ___50___ %

C1. Total items scored for full routine: ___20___

C2. Percentage of items mastered by routine (A / C1 * 100): ___30___ %
*Add scores to the MEISR Scoring Summary page*

*Measure of Engagement, Independence, and Social Relationships (MEISR™), Research Edition*, by R. A. McWilliam and Naomi Younggren.
Copyright © 2019 Paul H. Brookes Publishing Co., Inc. All rights reserved. Do not reproduce without permission. 1-800-638-3775 www.brookespublishing.com

4

## 3. Meal Times — Participates in meal times by . . .

Circled value indicates the selected rating.

| Item | Description | Typical starting age in months | Not yet (1) | Sometimes (2) | Often or Beyond this (3) | Func | Dev | Out |
|---|---|---|---|---|---|---|---|---|
| 3.01 | Opening mouth when caregiver gives bottle or breast for nursing | 0 | 1 | 2 | 3 ← | I | A | A |
| 3.02 | Sucking strongly enough when nursing or bottle feeding | 0 | 1 | 2 | 3 | I | A | A |
| 3.03 | Drinking appropriate amount from bottle or when nursing | 0 | 1 | 2 | 3 | I | A | A |
| 3.04 | Swallowing following a few sucks | 0 | 1 | 2 | 3 | I | A | A |
| 3.05 | Feeding on a fairly consistent schedule (e.g., every 3–4 hours) | 3 | 1 | 2 | 3 | I | A | A |
| 3.06 | Sitting in a high chair upright without slumping over | 5 | 1 | 2 | 3 | I | M | A |
| 3.07 | Remaining calm (at least briefly) while waiting for feeding when hungry | 6 | 1 | 2 | 3 | E | S | S |
| 3.08 | Holding own bottle (if bottle fed) | 6 | 1 | 2 | 3 | I | A | A |
| 3.09 | Beginning to eat solid food (e.g., teething cracker) | 6 | 1 | 2 | 3 | I | A | A |
| 3.10 | Raking foods with fingers to pick up and eat | 7 | 1 | 2 | 3 | I | A, M | A |
| 3.11 | Eating with little or no drooling (except for teething) | 7 | 1 | 2 | **③** | I | A | A |
| 3.12 | Feeding self with fingers (half or more of meal) | 9 | 1 | 2 | **③** | I | A | A |
| 3.13 | Chewing food (e.g., cracker, cookie) | 9 | 1 | 2 | **③** | I | A | A |
| 3.14 | Using thumb and forefinger to pick up small pieces of food (like pinching) | 10 | 1 | 2 | **③** | I | A, M | A |
| 3.15 | Following simple requests (e.g., eat more, drink your water) | 12 | 1 | **②** | 3 | S | CM | K |
| 3.16 | Following pointing by looking to person and object | 12 | 1 | 2 | 3 | S | CM | K |
| 3.17 | Drinking from a cup with a lid by him- or herself (e.g., trainer cup) | 12 | **①** | 2 | 3 | S | CM | K |
| 3.18 | Bringing spoon to mouth, eating some of the food from it | 12 | 1 | 2 | **③** | I | A | A |
| 3.19 | Using pointing to communicate (e.g., as if to say "look" or "I want") | 12 | **①** | 2 | 3 | S | CM | K |
| 3.20 | Saying "no" with meaning | 13 | 1 | **②** | 3 | S | CM | K |
| 3.21 | Using a spoon to eat sticky foods (e.g., mashed potatoes) (might include some spilling) | 15 | 1 | 2 | 3 | I | A | A |
| 3.22 | Indicating when hungry or thirsty with a sign or word | 15 | **①** | 2 | 3 | S | CM | A |
| 3.23 | Pointing or vocalizing clearly to indicate food preference | 16 | **①** | 2 | 3 | S | CM | A |
| 3.24 | Using a spoon independently for most of the meal | 18 | 1 | 2 | **③** | I | A | A |
| 3.25 | Drinking appropriate amount from open cup at one time (with each sip) | 18 | 1 | 2 | **③** | I | A | A |
| 3.26 | Staying seated for meal while he or she is eating with others | 18 | 1 | **②** | 3 | E | S | S |
| 3.27 | Using signs or words to ask for at least one specific food or drink | 18 | **①** | 2 | 3 | S | CM | A |
| 3.28 | Communicating "more" with signs or words | 18 | **①** | 2 | 3 | S | CM | A |
| 3.29 | Communicating "finished" with signs or words | 18 | **①** | 2 | 3 | S | CM | A |
| 3.30 | Putting an appropriate amount of food in mouth at a time | 18 | 1 | 2 | **③** | I | A | A |
| 3.31 | Climbing forward onto adult-sized chair or backing into a child-sized chair | 18 | 1 | 2 | **③** | I | M | A |
| 3.32 | Eating a variety of foods | 23 | 1 | **②** | 3 | I | A | A |

(continued)

(continued)

| 3. Meal Times — Participates in meal times by . . . | Typical starting age in months | Not yet | Sometimes | Often or Beyond this | Func | Dev | Out |
|---|---|---|---|---|---|---|---|
| 3.33 Removing easy wrappers or peels before eating (e.g., sliced orange peel)  opens candy | 23 | 1 | 2 | (3) | I | A | A |
| 3.34 Waiting for food for a few minutes, without fussing | 24 | 1 | 2 | (3) | E | S | S |
| 3.35 Handling fragile items carefully (e.g., drinking glass) | 24 | 1 | (2) | 3 | E | S, A | A |
| 3.36 Using words to ask for help (e.g., when opening drink box) | 24 | (1) | 2 | 3 | S | CM | A |
| 3.37 Following a two-part command (e.g., give me the plate and put cup in sink) | 25 | (1) | 2 | 3 | S | CM | K |
| 3.38 Using words (pronouns) "I," "me" to refer to self (e.g., I did it) | 27 | (1) | 2 | 3 | S | CM | K |
| 3.39 Biting off pieces of hard foods (e.g., apple slices, carrot stick) | 30 | 1 | 2 | (3) | I | A | A |
| 3.40 Using a napkin to clean mouth and hands | 30 | (1) | 2 | 3 | I | A | A |
| 3.41 Spreading with a knife with supervision and help | 30 | (1) | 2 | 3 | I | A | A |
| 3.42 Using a fork to stab food and eat it | 30 | (1) | 2 | 3 | I | A | A |
| 3.43 Serving him- or herself (e.g., sandwich from plate, scooping from bowl) | 33 | (1) | 2 | 3 | I | A, M | A |
| 3.44 Making choices about food (e.g., saying what's wanted, choosing desired food from menu pictures) | 33 | 1 | 2 | 3 | S | CG, CM | A |
| 3.45 Cooperating with caregivers' requests, most of the time | 33 | 1 | 2 | 3 | S | S | S |
| 3.46 Engaging in conversation using short sentences | 34 | 1 | 2 | 3 | S | CM | S |
| 3.47 Having the fork control to stab, dip in sauce, and get to mouth | 36 | 1 | 2 | 3 | I | A | A |

A. Total items scored 3 (Often or Beyond this): 24

B1. Total items scored for child's age: 37

B2. Percentage of items mastered by age (A / B1 * 100): 65 %

C1. Total items scored for full routine: 47

C2. Percentage of items mastered by routine (A / C1 * 100): 51 %

*Add scores to the MEISR Scoring Summary page*

6

## 4. Dressing Time — Participates in dressing time by . . .

| | Typical starting age in months | Not yet | Sometimes | Often or Beyond this | Func[a] | Dev[b] | Out |
|---|---|---|---|---|---|---|---|
| 4.01 Attending to sound of caregiver's voice | 0 | 1 | 2 | ③ | S | S | S |
| 4.02 Allowing caregiver to dress him or her without getting overly upset or showing strong discomfort for clothing or touch | 0 | 1 | 2 | ③ | E | S | S |
| 4.03 Responding positively to physical contact and holding | 0 | 1 | 2 | ③ | E | S | S |
| 4.04 Inspecting his or her hands | 2 | 1 | 2 | ③ | E | CG | K |
| 4.05 Communicating with vocal sounds | 2 | 1 | 2 | ③ | S | CM | K |
| 4.06 Responding to own name when called (e.g., pausing, alerting, vocalizing) babbles | 6 | 1 | ② | 3 | S | CM | S |
| 4.07 Babbling with adult-like inflection (e.g., baba, mama, or different syllables together, mado, bada) | 8 | 1 | 2 | ③ | S | CM | K |
| 4.08 Assisting by extending an arm or leg for a sleeve or pants leg | 11 | 1 | 2 | ③ | I | A | A |
| 4.09 Pointing correctly to one body part on self when asked | 15 | ① | 2 | 3 | S | CM, CG | K |
| 4.10 Removing an article of clothing by him- or herself (e.g., socks, hat) | 15 | 1 | 2 | ③ | I | A | A |
| 4.11 Indicating he or she understands the name of an article of clothing (e.g., looking at or otherwise acknowledging when caregiver says shoes, shirt) shoes | 15 | 1 | 2 | ③ | S | CM | K |
| 4.12 Recognizing self in mirror (e.g., pointing at self) | 15 | ① | 2 | 3 | E | CG, S | K |
| 4.13 Indicating what he or she wants to wear (gesturing/verbalizing when given choice) | 18 | 1 | ② | 3 | S | CM | A |
| 4.14 Undoing fasteners (e.g., unzipping large zipper, snaps) and seatbelts | 18 | 1 | 2 | ③ | I | A | A |
| 4.15 Helping undress self (e.g., removing shoes) | 18 | 1 | 2 | ③ | I | A | A |
| 4.16 Using gestures or words to identify two or more body parts | 18 | ① | 2 | 3 | S | CM | K |
| 4.17 Using some signs or words to comment or respond | 18 | ① | 2 | 3 | S | CM | K |
| 4.18 Following directions to fetch something (e.g., go get your shoes) | 18 | ① | 2 | 3 | S | CM | K |
| 4.19 Persisting with trying to put on/take off some clothes (might still need help to complete task) | 24 | 1 | ② | 3 | I | A | A |
| 4.20 Identifying five or more body parts (e.g., pointing at oneself, others, or doll) | 24 | ① | 2 | 3 | E | CG | K |
| 4.21 Following two-step directions (e.g., first shoes on, then outside) | 25 | ① | 2 | 3 | E | CM | K |
| 4.22 Dressing him- or herself with assistance (i.e., helping) | 28 | 1 | ② | 3 | I | A | A |
| 4.23 Putting shoes on (maybe on wrong feet and not tied) | 30 | ① | 2 | 3 | I | A | A |
| 4.24 Putting on coat with assistance | 30 | ① | 2 | 3 | I | A | A |
| 4.25 Describing clothing preference (e.g., want dinosaur jammies, princess skirt) | 30 | 1 | 2 | 3 | S | CM | A |

(continued)

(continued)

## 4. Dressing Time   Participates in dressing time by . . .

| | Typical starting age in months | Not yet | Sometimes | Often or Beyond this | Func¹ | Dev² | Out³ |
|---|---|---|---|---|---|---|---|
| 4.26 Dressing and undressing, with help for buttons and laces | 33 | (1) | 2 | 3 | I | A | A |
| 4.27 Following multistep (three or more steps) directions (e.g., go to the door, get your boots, and bring them to Daddy) | 33 | 1 | 2 | 3 | S | CM | K |
| 4.28 Putting on socks | 36 | 1 | 2 | 3 | I | A | A |
| 4.29 Fastening zippers, snaps, big buttons | 36 | 1 | 2 | 3 | I | A, M | A |

A.   Total items scored 3 (Often or Beyond this): _____

B1.   Total items scored for child's age: ___11___

B2.   Percentage of items mastered by age (A / B1 * 100): ___21___ %

C1.   Total items scored for full routine: ___29___

C2.   Percentage of items mastered by routine (A / C1 * 100): ___38___ %

*Add scores to the MEISR Scoring Summary page*

8

## 5. Hangout – TV – Books — Participates in <u>hanging-out time</u> by . . .

| | Typical starting age in months | Not yet | Sometimes | Often or Beyond this | Func^a | Dev^a | Out. |
|---|---|---|---|---|---|---|---|
| 5.01 Responding positively to being held and cuddled | 0 | 1 | 2 | 3 | S | S | S |
| 5.02 Responding differently to the voice of a stranger from that of caregiver | 3 | 1 | 2 | 3 ← | S | S | S |
| 5.03 Looking at an object and watching it move in different directions (up, down, left, right) | 3 | 1 | 2 | 3 | E | CG | K |
| 5.04 Pushing up on hands when lying on tummy | 5 | 1 | 2 | 3 | I | M | A |
| 5.05 Reaching forward to get toys when supported in sitting | 5 | 1 | 2 | 3 | I | M | A |
| 5.06 Having fun pointing to and pulling on facial features of caregivers | 5 | 1 | 2 | (3) | S | S | S |
| 5.07 Rolling back to tummy and tummy to back both directions | 7 | 1 | 2 | (3) | I | M | A |
| 5.08 Pulling up to stand on furniture | 8 | 1 | 2 | (3) | I | M | A |
| 5.09 Playing with books (e.g., looking at, touching, mouthing) | 8 | 1 | 2 | (3) | E | CG | K |
| 5.10 Attending to objects mentioned during conversation (e.g., looking at dog when mentioned, looking at ball)  iPad | 10 | 1 | 2 | (3) | E | CG | K |
| 5.11 Moving about to explore, looking back to caregiver | 12 | 1 | 2 | (3) | S | S | S |
| 5.12 Showing interest looking at pictures in a book | 12 | 1 | 2 | (3) | E | CG | K |
| 5.13 Staying with caregiver looking at a book at least a few minutes | 12 | 1 | 2 | (3) | E | S | S |
| 5.14 Vocalizing to get caregiver attention to start or change activity | 12 | 1 | (2) | 3 | S | CM | A |
| 5.15 Exploring drawers and cabinets | 13 | 1 | 2 | (3) | E | CG, M | K |
| 5.16 Turning pages in books (might be several at a time) | 14 | 1 | 2 | (3) | I | M | K |
| 5.17 Figuring out how to activate/get a toy (e.g., turning toy on, climbing to get toy)  ponies | 18 | 1 | 2 | (3) | I | CG | K |
| 5.18 Showing clear preference for picture/book/show | 18 | 1 | (2) | 3 | E | CG | K |
| 5.19 Recognizing him- or herself in a picture by pointing or looking | 19 | (1) | 2 | 3 | E | CG | K |
| 5.20 Naming a character when seen in a book/show | 24 | (1) | 2 | 3 | E | CG, CM | K |
| 5.21 Pointing to and naming pictures in a book/show (three or more pictures) | 24 | (1) | 2 | 3 | S | CM, CG | K |
| 5.22 Talking about books/shows when they are being read/watched | 24 | (1) | 2 | 3 | S | CM | K |
| 5.23 Responding to emotions of others, sometimes with prompting (e.g., laughing at another's laugh, approaching crying child) | 24 | 1 | 2 | 3 | S | S | S |
| 5.24 Using a word like "big" or "little" to describe things | 25 | (1) | 2 | 3 | E | CG, CM | K |
| 5.25 Understanding and naming actions of things in books/shows (e.g., running, eating, crying) | 30 | (1) | 2 | 3 | S | CM | K |
| 5.26 Attending while watching or listening to a show or book with caregiver | 30 | (1) | 2 | 3 | E | S | S |
| 5.27 Pretending to read | 30 | 1 | 2 | 3 | E | CG | K |
| 5.28 Talking about book/show characters when not visible | 30 | 1 → | 2 | 3 | S | CM | K |
| 5.29 Naming what book/show he or she would like to read/watch | 33 | 1 → | 2 | 3 | S | CM | A |

(continued)

9

(continued)

## 5. Hangout – TV – Books   Participates in hanging-out time by . . .

| | Typical starting age in months | Not yet | Sometimes | Often or Beyond this | Func* | Dev^ | Out^ |
|---|---|---|---|---|---|---|---|
| 5.30 Understanding "two" (e.g., you can pick two books/shows) | 33 | 1 | 2 | 3 | E | CG | K |
| 5.31 Responding to others' feelings with caring behavior, without adult prompting (e.g., patting crying baby, kissing hurt finger) | 33 | 1 | 2 | 3 | S | S | S |
| 5.32 Helping tell story by commenting/gesturing about what's happening | 33 | 1 | 2 | 3 | E | CM, CG | K |
| 5.33 Behaving appropriately when watching a show alone (~20 minutes) | 33 | 1 | 2 | 3 | E | S | S |
| 5.34 Responding to characters on a show (e.g., when character asks audience a question or directs audience to imitate) | 36 | 1 | 2 | 3 | E | CM | K |
| 5.35 Asking "wh" questions (what, when, why) | 36 | 1 | 2 | 3 | S | CM | K |
| 5.36 Cooperating when his/her show/game/program is changed | 36 | 1 | 2 | 3 | S | S | S |
| 5.37 Recognizing own name or a letter from own name when written | 36 | 1 | 2 | 3 | E | CG | K |
| 5.38 Saying what will happen next in the story | 36 | 1 | 2 | 3 | E | CG | K |

A.   Total items scored 3 (Often or Beyond this):   16

B1.   Total items scored for child's age:   24

B2.   Percentage of items mastered by age (A / B1 * 100):   67 %

C1.   Total items scored for full routine:   38

C2.   Percentage of items mastered by routine (A / C1 * 100):   42 %
*Add scores to the MEISR Scoring Summary page*

10

## 6. Play With Others — Participates in play time with others by . . .

| Item | Typical starting age in months | Not yet | Sometimes | Often or Beyond this | Func[a] | Dev[b] | Out |
|---|---|---|---|---|---|---|---|
| 6.01 Reacting to sounds (e.g., startling) | 0 | 1 | 2 | 3 | E | CG | K |
| 6.02 Following caregiver with his or her eyes | 3 | 1 | 2 | 3 | E | S | S |
| 6.03 Getting excited as caregiver approaches/starts playful game (e.g., squealing) | 3 | 1 | 2 | 3 | S | S | S |
| 6.04 Wiggling or vocalizing to continue social play (e.g., bouncing) with caregiver | 4 | 1 | 2 | 3 | S | S, CG | S |
| 6.05 Playing with others, without fussing or getting upset | 6 | 1 | 2 | 3 | S | S | S |
| 6.06 Rolling back to tummy | 6 | 1 | 2 | 3 | I | M | A |
| 6.07 Playing simple games with caregiver or older child (e.g., peek-a-boo) | 6 | 1 | 2 | 3 | S | CG, S | S |
| 6.08 Imitating others (e.g., patting, banging) | 6 | 1 | 2 | 3 | S | CG | K |
| 6.09 Showing interest in children (e.g., looking at, vocalizing, gesturing) | 9 | 1 | 2 | ③ | S | S | S |
| 6.10 Indicating he or she understands what "no" means | 9 | 1 | 2 | ③ | S | CM, S | K |
| 6.11 Talking or babbling back and forth in a sort of conversation with caregiver | 11 | 1 | 2 | ③ | S | CM, S | S |
| 6.12 Attempting to climb on things (e.g., onto furniture, in boxes) | 11 | 1 | 2 | ③ | I | M | A |
| 6.13 Repeating things (e.g., sounds, actions) when laughed at by others | 11 | 1 | ② | 3 | S | CM, S | S |
| 6.14 Indicating understanding of simple request with clear gestures (e.g., *come here, give me*) | 12 | 1 | ② | 3 | S | CM | K |
| 6.15 Playing a back-and-forth game (e.g., pushing ball, moving to get toy back) | 12 | 1 | 2 | ③ | S | S, CG | S |
| 6.16 Imitating actions using toys/objects (e.g., banging a drum, stirring with a spoon) | 12 | 1 | 2 | ③ | S | CG | K |
| 6.17 Playing apart from familiar caregiver (5 minutes or longer) | 15 | 1 | 2 | ③ | S | S | S |
| 6.18 Playing with a variety of toys in their intended manner (e.g., scribbling on paper, stacking rings on ring stacker toy) | 15 | 1 | 2 | ③ | E | CG | K |
| 6.19 Playing back-and-forth (early turn taking) game with another child (with caregiver assistance) | 18 | ① | 2 | 3 | S | S | S |
| 6.20 Playing side by side with other children, interacting with gestures | 18 | ① | 2 | 3 | S | S, CM | S |
| 6.21 Cleaning up toys, as part of routine, when asked (e.g., putting toy in box) *ponies to bed* | 22 | 1 | ② | 3 | S | CM, S | S |
| 6.22 Indicating ownership over toys or items with peers (e.g., might grab toy) | 23 | 1 | 2 | 3 | S | S | S |
| 6.23 Singing some words in familiar songs (e.g., "Happy Birthday," "Twinkle Twinkle") | 24 | ① | 2 | 3 | E | CM | K |
| 6.24 Maintaining motor control over his or her body in relationship to others (e.g., walks well, moves around others) | 24 | 1 | 2 | ③ | I | M | A |
| 6.25 Showing interest in playing with other children (e.g., going to where they are) | 24 | 1 | ② | 3 | S | S | S |
| 6.26 Playing simple make-believe with another (e.g., shopping, putting things in toy grocery cart, going to peer/adult to get more) | 24 | ① | 2 | 3 | E | CG, S | S |
| 6.27 Protecting own territory/toys/objects by saying "mine" | 24 | ① | 2 | 3 | I | CM | S |
| 6.28 Sustaining (~15 minutes) play with children, might need caregiver to help with disputes | 30 | ① | 2 | 3 | E | S | S |

*(continued)*

(continued)

## 6. Play With Others — Participates in play time with others by . . .

| | Typical starting age in months | Not yet | Sometimes | Often or Beyond this | Func[c] | Dev[b] | Out[a] |
|---|---|---|---|---|---|---|---|
| 6.29 Being bossy with other children (e.g., has ideas, might try to be in charge) | 30 | (1) | 2 | 3 | S | S | S |
| 6.30 Separating from parent without acting anxious, in familiar settings | 30 | (1) | 2 | 3 | S | S | S |
| 6.31 Playing with others but might have preferred play partners | 30 | (1) | 2 | 3 | S | S | S |
| 6.32 Initiating play with other children and talking to others with words | 30 | (1) | 2 | 3 | S | S, CM | S |
| 6.33 Playing group games with adult help (e.g., Ring Around the Rosie) | 30 | 1 | 2 | 3 | S | S | S |
| 6.34 Seeking caregiver help with conflicts (e.g., going to caregiver when peer grabs his or her toy) | 30 | 1 | 2 | 3 | S | S | S |
| 6.35 Playing without messing up others' creations (e.g., blocks, painting) | 36 | 1 | 2 | 3 | E | S | S |
| 6.36 Asking another child for a turn with a toy | 36 | 1 | 2 | 3 | S | S | S |
| 6.37 Using loud (including rough and tumble) and quiet play at appropriate times/in appropriate contexts | 36 | 1 | 2 | 3 | E | S | S |
| 6.38 Staying quiet when playing hide-and-seek with others | 36 | 1 | 2 | 3 | E | CG | S |

A. Total items scored 3 (Often or Beyond this): 18

B1. Total items scored for child's age: 27

B2. Percentage of items mastered by age (A / B1 * 100): 67 %

C1. Total items scored for full routine: 38

C2. Percentage of items mastered by routine (A / C1 * 100): 47 %

*Add scores to the MEISR Scoring Summary page*

12

## 13

## 7. Nap Time  Participates in nap time by . . .

| | Typical starting age in months | Not yet | Sometimes | Often or Beyond this | Func[c] | Dev[b] | Out[a] |
|---|---|---|---|---|---|---|---|
| 7.01 Falling asleep in response to caregiver's actions (e.g., nursing, rocking) | 0 | 1 | 2 | 3 | E | S | S |
| 7.02 Taking frequent naps (30 minutes to 4 hours at a time) | 0 | 1 | 2 | 3 | I | A | A |
| 7.03 Staying awake for periods during the day (e.g., 2–3 hours) | 3 | 1 | 2 | 3 | I | A | A |
| 7.04 Waking up, perhaps by rolling over (back to side), without crying immediately | 4 | 1 | 2 | 3 | E | S, M | S |
| 7.05 Napping at predictable times (establishing nap schedule) | 6 | 1 | 2 | **3** | I | A | A |
| 7.06 Playing with toys, beyond mouthing or banging | 9 | 1 | 2 | **3** | E | CG | K |
| 7.07 Using objects (e.g., blanket, stuffed toy) to self-soothe/regulate emotions | 12 | 1 | 2 | **3** | E | S | S |
| 7.08 Giving up one nap | 12 | **1** | 2 | **3** | I | A | A |
| 7.09 Giving hugs or kisses as part of sleep/nap routine  *puts ponies down* | 14 | 1 | 2 | 3 | S | S | S |
| 7.10 Taking one nap a day, which is typically enough | 18 | 1 | 2 | **3** | I | A | A |
| 7.11 Understanding directions, such as "Finish this (be specific), then it's nap time" | 24 | **1** | 2 | 3 | S | CM, CG | K |
| 7.12 Resting/playing quietly by self for a while (20+ minutes) | 30 | **1** | 2 | 3 | E | A | S |
| 7.13 Getting through the day without a nap | 33 | **1** | 2 | 3 | I | A | A |
| 7.14 Sleeping through the night and not taking a daytime nap | 36 | **1** | 2 | 3 | I | A | A |

(← arrow drawn in "Often or Beyond this" column at item 7.04)

A. Total items scored 3 (Often or Beyond this): _9_

B1. Total items scored for child's age: _11_

B2. Percentage of items mastered by age (A / B1 * 100): _82_ %

C1. Total items scored for full routine: _14_

C2. Percentage of items mastered by routine (A / C1 * 100): _64_ %

*Add scores to the MEISR Scoring Summary page*

| 8. Outside Time   Participates in outside time by . . . | Typical starting age in months | Not yet | Sometimes | Often or Beyond this | Func | Dev | Out |
|---|---|---|---|---|---|---|---|
| 8.01 Looking at object 8–10 inches away | 0 | 1 | 2 | 3 | E | CG | K |
| 8.02 Holding object placed in his or her hand | 2 | 1 | 2 | 3 | I | M | A |
| 8.03 Holding one and reaching for a second toy or object | 6 | 1 | 2 | 3 | I | M | A |
| 8.04 Walking independently at least a few steps | 13 | 1 | 2 | (3) | I | M | A |
| 8.05 Running (might look like fast walk) | 16 | 1 | 2 | (3) | I | M | A |
| 8.06 Moving ride-on wheeled toys (no pedals) with feet | 20 | 1 | 2 | (3) | I | M | A |
| 8.07 Jumping up so that both feet are off the ground | 24 | 1 | 2 | (3) | I | M | A |
| 8.08 Going up the ladder and down small slide | 24 | 1 | 2 | (3) | I | M | A |
| 8.09 Using sandbox toys appropriately (e.g., not throwing or eating sand) | 24 | 1 | 2 | (3) | E | CG | K |
| 8.10 Playing purposefully with playground toys (figuring out their best use) | 24 | 1 | (2) | 3 | E | CG | K |
| 8.10 Playing outside without fussing (with supervision for ~30 minutes) | 24 | 1 | 2 | (3) | E | S | S |
| 8.12 Showing interest in the playground (might have favorite toy/activity) | 24 | 1 | 2 | (3) | E | CG | K |
| 8.13 Catching a large ball (e.g., beach ball) | 24 | (1) | 2 | 3 | I | M | A |
| 8.14 Walking upstairs alone (both feet on each step), using rail if needed | 24 | 1 | 2 | (3) | I | M | A |
| 8.15 Walking downstairs alone (both feet on each step), using rail if needed | 26 | 1 | 2 | (3) | I | M | A |
| 8.16 Jumping off small step or bottom of slide with both feet together | 27 | (1) | 2 | 3 | I | M | A |
| 8.17 Walking forward and backward with balance while playing | 28 | (1) | 2 | 3 | I | M | A |
| 8.18 Walking upstairs alone (alternating feet—one foot on each step) | 30 | (1) | 2 | 3 | I | M | A |
| 8.19 Understanding descriptions such as hot, cold, dirty, wet (e.g., *the ball is dirty, the sand is wet*) | 30 | (1) | 2 | 3 | S | CM, CG | K |
| 8.20 Riding on toy with pedals at least a short distance | 33 | 1 | 2 | 3 | I | M | A |
| 8.21 Climbing on jungle gyms with hands and feet | 33 | 1 | 2 | 3 | I | M | A |
| 8.22 Engaging with others in a game with turn taking (e.g., jumping over rope, chalk line; might need caregiver guidance) | 34 | 1 | 2 | 3 | S | S | S |
| 8.23 Understanding simple rules (but might still test limits) | 34 | 1 | 2 | 3 | E | S | S |
| 8.24 Following caregiver's directions given from a distance | 36 | 1 | 2 | 3 | S | CM | K |
| 8.25 Using big slides (about 6 feet/2 meters high) | 36 | 1 | 2 | 3 | I | M | A |
| 8.26 Swinging on regular swing (might still not pump feet effectively) | 36 | 1 | 2 | 3 | I | M | A |

A.  Total items scored 3 (Often or Beyond this): ___13___

B1.  Total items scored for child's age: ___14___

B2.  Percentage of items mastered by age (A / B1 * 100): ___93___ %

C1.  Total items scored for full routine: ___26___

C2.  Percentage of items mastered by routine (A / C1 * 100): ___50___ %

*Add scores to the MEISR Scoring Summary page*

14

*Measure of Engagement, Independence, and Social Relationships (MEISR™), Research Edition*, by R. A. McWilliam and Naomi Younggren.

## 9. Play by Him- or Herself    Participates in play time by him- or herself by . . .

| | Typical starting age in months | Not yet | Sometimes | Often or Beyond this | Func | Dev | Out |
|---|---|---|---|---|---|---|---|
| 9.01 Lying on back turning head (might prefer one side but can do both) | 0 | 1 | 2 | 3 | I | M | A |
| 9.02 Repeating actions with toys (e.g., banging at toys, kicking legs to move toy) | 3 | 1 | 2 | 3 | E | CG | K |
| 9.03 Exploring objects with hands and mouth | 3 | 1 | 2 | 3 | E | CG | K |
| 9.04 Grasping own foot and taking it to mouth to explore | 5 | 1 | 2 | 3 | E | CG, M | K |
| 9.05 Lying on tummy and reaching for toys with one hand | 6 | 1 | 2 | 3 | I | M | A |
| 9.06 Seeking partly hidden items, such as pacifier or bottle or favored toy | 6 | 1 | 2 | 3 | E | CG | K |
| 9.07 Working to get out-of-reach toy by pivoting, rolling, stretching | 7 | 1 | 2 | 3 | E | M | A |
| 9.08 Sitting independently (not propped with hands) | 8 | 1 | 2 | 3 | I | M | A |
| 9.09 Making toys work by self (e.g., pushing to reactivate action) | 9 | 1 | 2 | 3 | E | CG | K |
| 9.10 Dropping or throwing objects while exploring objects | 9 | 1 | 2 | 3 | E | M, CG | K |
| 9.11 Moving from sitting to hands and knees to crawl on hands and knees | 9 | 1 | 2 | 3 | I | M | A |
| 9.12 Crawling on hands and knees to get toys or objects of interest | 9 | 1 | 2 | 3 | I | M | A |
| 9.13 Picking up small objects effectively, with tip of index finger and thumb | 10 | 1 | 2 | ③ | I | M | A |
| 9.14 Putting toys in and out of containers (e.g., dumping and filling) | 12 | 1 | 2 | ③ | E | CG | K |
| 9.15 Watching where toy moves out of sight and going to get it (e.g., ball, car) | 12 | 1 | 2 | ③ | E | M, CG | K |
| 9.16 Using both hands equally well in play to explore | 12 | 1 | 2 | ③ | I | M | A |
| 9.17 Playing with toys, showing awareness of toy functions (e.g., banging on drum, drinking from cup) | 12 | 1 | 2 | ③ | E | CG | K |
| 9.18 Using nonwords to express emotion (e.g., *uh-oh, oops, ah*) *whee* on swings | 12 | 1 | ② | 3 | S | CM | S |
| 9.19 Patting at pictures in books, turning one or more pages at a time | 15 | 1 | ② | 3 | E | M, CG | K |
| 9.20 Picking up toys/objects from floor while standing | 15 | 1 | 2 | ③ | I | M | A |
| 9.21 Selecting favorite toy or object and going to get it by him- or herself | 15 | 1 | 2 | ③ | I | CG | A |
| 9.22 Sustaining play by self for a few minutes without caregiver in clear sight | 18 | ① | 2 | 3 | E | S | S |
| 9.23 Constructing things during play (e.g., build or stacks blocks) | 19 | ① | 2 | 3 | E | CG, M | K |
| 9.24 Indicating understanding of where toys or other things belong (e.g., goes to shelf to find specific toy, puts toy away) | 21 | 1 | 2 | ③ | E | CG | K |
| 9.25 Holding crayon with three fingers to color | 23 | 1 | 2 | 3 | I | M | A |
| 9.26 Jabbering and saying true words too during play | 24 | ① | 2 | 3 | E | CM | K |
| 9.27 Pretending by linking two or more actions (e.g., feeding, burping, and putting doll down for nap) | 24 | ① | 2 | 3 | E | CG | K |
| 9.28 Pretending objects are something else (e.g., block to represent food) | 24 | ① | 2 | 3 | E | CG | K |
| 9.29 Matching two or more identical shapes or colors (e.g., putting round blocks together, picking out same-colored cars) | 24 | ① | 2 | 3 | E | CG | K |

*(continued)*

15

(continued)

## 9. Play by Him- or Herself  Participates in play time by him- or herself by . . .

| | Typical starting age in months | Not yet | Sometimes | Often or Beyond this | Func* | Dev* | Out* |
|---|---|---|---|---|---|---|---|
| 9.30 Pretending with elaborate make-believe (e.g., dress up, pretending to be a mommy, firefighter, or teacher) | 30 | 1 | 2 | 3 | E | CG | K |
| 9.31 Showing pride in accomplishments (e.g., clapping, saying "I did it," or otherwise drawing attention to task he or she did) | 30 | 1 | 2 | 3 | S | S | S |
| 9.32 Persisting when something is difficult, trying different ways | 30 | 1 | 2 | 3 | E | CG | K |
| 9.33 Maintaining safety while playing independently (e.g., doesn't play with stove) | 30 | 1 | 2 | 3 | I | A, CG | A |
| 9.34 Scribbling, making lines or zig zags (i.e., more than just marks on paper) | 33 | 1 | 2 | 3 | E | M, CG | K |
| 9.35 Playing within safe boundaries (e.g., driveway versus street) | 36 | 1 | 2 | 3 | I | CG | A |

A.  Total items scored 3 (Often or Beyond this):  21

B1.  Total items scored for child's age:  29

B2.  Percentage of items mastered by age (A / B1 * 100):  72  %

C1.  Total items scored for full routine:  35

C2.  Percentage of items mastered by routine (A / C1 * 100):  72  %

*Add scores to the MEISR Scoring Summary page*

## 10. Bath Time — Participates in <u>bath time</u> by . . .

| | | Typical starting age in months | Not yet | Sometimes | Often or Beyond this | Func | Dev | Out |
|---|---|---|---|---|---|---|---|---|
| 10.01 | Engaging with caregiver without fussing or getting upset | 0 | 1 | 2 | 3 | E | S | S |
| 10.02 | Sitting up propped with arms at least briefly and with head upright | 5 | 1 | 2 | 3 | I | M | A |
| 10.03 | Smiling at and playing with own image in mirror | 5 | 1 | 2 | 3 | E | S | S |
| 10.04 | Making eye contact, babbling (baba, dada), or otherwise interacting with caregiver | 6 | 1 | 2 | 3 | S | S, CM | S |
| 10.05 | Splashing in the water | 6 | 1 | 2 | 3 | E | CG | K |
| 10.06 | Reaching for and grasping toy, if sitting securely with support | 6 | 1 | 2 | 3 | I | M | A |
| 10.07 | Holding washcloth and imitating caregiver's washing actions | 9 | 1 | 2 | 3 | I | CG | K |
| 10.08 | Showing toy to caregiver but not necessarily releasing it | 9 | 1 | 2 | 3 | S | S | S |
| 10.09 | Retrieving toys that have fallen into the water | 9 | 1 | 2 | 3 | E | CG | K |
| 10.10 | Responding with gestures when asked "want up," "all done" | 9 | 1 | 2 | (3) | S | CM | K |
| 10.11 | Holding out arm to be washed | 11 | 1 | 2 | (3) | E | A | A |
| 10.12 | Walking with one or both hands held | 12 | 1 | 2 | (3) | I | M | A |
| 10.13 | Indicating understanding of a familiar word about bath (e.g., *up, splash*) | 12 | 1 | 2 | (3) | S | CM | K |
| 10.14 | Playing with objects in the tub using caregiver to help repeat enjoyable action (e.g., giving caregiver toy to pour, blow bubbles) | 12 | 1 | 2 | (3) | E | CG | K |
| 10.15 | Understanding directions and names of things (e.g., *wash feet, get cup*) | 18 | 1 | (2) | 3 | S | CG, CM | K |
| 10.16 | Letting caregiver brush his or her teeth (may hold or chew on brush) | 18 | 1 | 2 | (3) | E | A | A |
| 10.17 | Standing on one foot, with help (e.g., for drying, putting on pajama bottoms) | 18 | 1 | 2 | (3) | I | M | A |
| 10.18 | Cooperating (no fussing) with hair washing | 19 | 1 | 2 | (3) | S | S | S |
| 10.19 | Identifying him- or herself in mirrors (e.g., saying name or nickname) | 20 | (1) | 2 | 3 | E | CG | K |
| 10.20 | Indicating if the water temperature is uncomfortable (words or gestures) | 20 | (1) | 2 | 3 | S | CM | A |
| 10.21 | Putting away bath toys, as part of bath routine, on request with prompting | 22 | 1 | 2 | (3) | E | CM, S | S |
| 10.22 | Washing body parts independently (e.g., feet, hands, legs) | 24 | 1 | (2) | 3 | I | A | A |
| 10.23 | Cooperating with caregiver for hair brushing | 24 | 1 | 2 | 3 | S | S | S |
| 10.24 | Talking during bath time with caregiver understanding half or more of the words he or she says | 24 | (1) | 2 | 3 | S | CM | K |
| 10.25 | Brushing teeth with some help | 25 | 1 | 2 | (3) | S | A | A |
| 10.26 | Using towel to dry, making drying actions, but still needing help to get dry | 30 | (1) | 2 | 3 | I | A | A |

*(continued)*

*Measure of Engagement, Independence, and Social Relationships (MEISR™), Research Edition*, by R. A. McWilliam and Naomi Younggren.
Copyright © 2019 Paul H. Brookes Publishing Co., Inc. All rights reserved. Do not reproduce without permission. 1-800-638-3775 www.brookespublishing.com

(continued)

## 10. Bath Time — Participates in bath time by . . .

| | Typical starting age in months | Not yet | Sometimes | Often or Beyond this | Func* | Dev* | Out* |
|---|---|---|---|---|---|---|---|
| 10.27 Showing pride in accomplishments for things done independently | 30 | (1) | 2 | 3 | S | S | S |
| 10.28 Saying if he or she is a boy or a girl when asked | 33 | (1) | 2 | 3 | S | S | K |
| 10.29 Drying off independently (might need caregiver's final touch) | 36 | (1) | 2 | 3 | I | A | A |
| 10.30 Making some choices about toothpaste flavor, hair accessories, and so on | 36 | (1) | 2 | 3 | E | CG, CM | A |

A. Total items scored 3 (Often or Beyond this): __20__

B1. Total items scored for child's age: __25__

B2. Percentage of items mastered by age (A / B1 * 100): __76__ %

C1. Total items scored for full routine: __30__

C2. Percentage of items mastered by routine (A / C1 * 100): __63__ %

*Add scores to the MEISR Scoring Summary page*

## 11. Bedtime  Participates in bedtime by . . .

| | Typical starting age in months | Not yet | Sometimes | Often or Beyond this | Func* | Dev* | Out* |
|---|---|---|---|---|---|---|---|
| 11.01 Falling asleep in response to caregiver (e.g., nursing, rocking) | 0 | 1 | 2 | 3 ← | S | S | S |
| 11.02 Sleeping for a 4-hour interval at night | 2 | 1 | 2 | 3 | I | A | A |
| 11.03 Sleeping in his or her own crib or bed (i.e., able to do so) | 3 | 1 | 2 | ③ | I | A | A |
| 11.04 Sleeping for 6+ hours (might awaken and fall back to sleep) | 6 | 1 | 2 | ③ | I | A | A |
| 11.05 Comforting self to fall asleep (might use blanket, pacifier to self-regulate) | 6 | 1 | 2 | ③ | E | S | S |
| 11.06 Sleeping for 8–12 hours at night | 12 | 1 | 2 | ③ | I | A | A |
| 11.07 Indicating what he or she wants at bedtime (e.g., pointing, gesturing) gets ponies | 12 | 1 | ② | 3 | S | CM | A |
| 11.08 Indicating understanding a word during bedtime routine (e.g., bed) | 12 | 1 | 2 | ③ | S | CM | K |
| 11.09 Using a sign or word to indicate he or she wants to or does not want to sleep fusses | 18 | 1 | ② | 3 | S | CM | A |
| 11.10 Picking up and carrying larger toy (e.g., stuffed toy, big blanket) | 18 | 1 | 2 | ③ | I | M | A |
| 11.11 Going through the steps in the bedtime routine with caregiver assistance (might even remind caregiver if a step is missed) | 24 | 1 | 2 | ③ | I | S | S |
| 11.12 Joining in to sing a song or say a rhyme (repeating part of it) | 24 | ① | 2 | 3 | E | CG | K |
| 11.13 Staying in bed throughout the night once put to bed (if expected to) good sleeper | 30 | 1 | 2 | ③ | I | A | S |
| 11.14 Cooperating with caregivers' request to go to sleep | 30 | 1 | ② | 3 | S | S | S |
| 11.15 Going to bed fairly quickly (little dawdling) | 33 | ① | 2 | 3 | E | S | S |
| 11.16 Talking about his or her day or what will happen tomorrow | 36 | ① | 2 | 3 | S | CM | K |

A.  Total items scored 3 (Often or Beyond this): __10__

B1. Total items scored for child's age: __12__

B2. Percentage of items mastered by age (A / B1 * 100): __83__ %

C1. Total items scored for full routine: __16__

C2. Percentage of items mastered by routine (A / C1 * 100): __63__ %

*Add scores to the MEISR Scoring Summary page*

19

## 12. Going Out — Participates in going out by . . .

| # | Participates in going out by . . . | Typical starting age in months | Not yet | Sometimes | Often or Beyond this | FuncC | Devb | Out |
|---|---|---|---|---|---|---|---|---|
| 12.01 | Calming when picked up | 0 | 1 | 2 | 3 | E | S | S |
| 12.02 | Settling and being relaxed when held or nestled in carrier | 0 | 1 | 2 | 3 | E | S | S |
| 12.03 | Crying to indicate discomfort | 0 | 1 | 2 | 3 | S | CM | A |
| 12.04 | Smiling purposefully in response to caregiver | 2 | 1 | 2 | 3 | S | S | S |
| 12.05 | Making cooing sounds | 2 | 1 | 2 | 3 | S | CM | K |
| 12.06 | Looking at or watching caregiver move | 3 | 1 | 2 | 3 | E | CG | K |
| 12.07 | Turning head toward a voice (i.e., searching environment for speaker) | 3 | 1 | 2 | ③ | E | CG | K |
| 12.08 | Comforting self with pacifier, thumb, or object | 4 | 1 | 2 | ③ | E | S | S |
| 12.09 | Lifting head when pulled to sitting (e.g., to be placed in stroller) | 5 | 1 | 2 | ③ | I | M | A |
| 12.10 | Responding differently to familiar caregiver versus strangers | 6 | 1 | 2 | ③ | S | S | S |
| 12.11 | Waving or gesturing in response to bye-bye ✩ | 9 | ① | 2 | 3 | S | CM | S |
| 12.12 | Walking with or without help when given the opportunity | 12 | 1 | 2 | ③ | I | M | A |
| 12.13 | Showing understanding of simple questions (e.g., child looks at Mama when asked, "Where's Mama?") | 12 | 1 | ② | 3 | S | CM | K |
| 12.14 | Letting others help (a little stranger anxiety) but still liking constant sight of caregiver | 12 | 1 | 2 | ③ | S | S | S |
| 12.15 | Moving from sitting to standing independently, may use support to pull up | 12 | 1 | 2 | ③ | I | M | A |
| 12.16 | Pointing to show or drawing caregiver's attention to something | 14 | ① | 2 | 3 | S | CM | S |
| 12.17 | Pointing to something in the distance (e.g., outside) to show caregiver | 18 | ① | 2 | 3 | S | CM | S |
| 12.18 | Using a sign or word to say what he or she wants (e.g., cup, bunny) | 18 | ① | 2 | 3 | S | CM | A |
| 12.19 | Finding a way to occupy self for a few minutes while the caregiver is busy | 18 | 1 | 2 | ③ | E | A | A |
| 12.20 | Imitating sounds heard (e.g., animals, vehicles) with or without prompt | 18 | ① | 2 | 3 | S | CM | K |
| 12.21 | Imitating two-word phrase related to going out (e.g., go park, ride car) | 18 | ① | 2 | 3 | S | CM | K |
| 12.22 | Showing affection toward others (e.g., hugging, patting, using affectionate words) | 18 | 1 | ② | 3 | S | S | S |
| 12.23 | Sitting in car seat, leaving the seatbelt fastened for safety undoes fastener ✩ | 24 | ① | 2 | 3 | E | S | A |
| 12.24 | Holding caregiver hand, knowing the social rule to do that | 24 | 1 | ② | 3 | E | S | S |
| 12.25 | Saying "mine" to show ownership of his or her things with others | 24 | 1 | 2 | 3 | S | S | S |
| 12.26 | Climbing into the car or car seat independently | 24 | 1 | 2 | ③ | I | M | A |
| 12.27 | Responding to simple questions (e.g., What's that?) with words | 27 | ① | 2 | 3 | S | CM | K |
| 12.28 | Taking just one of something when told he or she can have only one | 27 | ① | 2 | 3 | E | CG | K |
| 12.29 | Staying with a caregiver when walking (may need frequent reminders) | 30 | ① | 2 | 3 | E | S | S |

(continued)

Measure of Engagement, Independence, and Social Relationships (MEISR™), Research Edition, by R. A. McWilliam and Naomi Younggren.

*(continued)*

## 12. Going Out  Participates in going out by . . .

| | Typical starting age in months | Not yet | Sometimes | Often or Beyond this | Func* | Dev* | Out* |
|---|---|---|---|---|---|---|---|
| 12.30 Responding to "no" or redirection without a tantrum (e.g., *no, we can't have ice cream now; you can play here but not there*) | 30 | (1) | 2 | 3 | S | CG, S | S |
| 12.31 Saying first and last name when asked | 30 | 1 | 2 | 3 | S | CG | K |
| 12.32 Naming familiar people or animals (e.g., *Papa* for grandpa, *kitty* for cat or familiar cat's name) | 30 | 1 | 2 | 3 | S | CM, CG | K |
| 12.33 Experimenting with balance, taking a few steps on curb edge (if safe to do so) | 33 | 1 | 2 | 3 | I | M | A |
| 12.34 Telling others about things not present (e.g., *Mommy goed work*) | 36 | 1 | 2 | 3 | S | S, CM | S |
| 12.35 Waiting during errands (e.g., at cash register) | 36 | 1 | 2 | 3 | E | S | S |

A.  Total items scored 3 (Often or Beyond this): ___15___

B1. Total items scored for child's age: ___26___

B2. Percentage of items mastered by age (A / B1 * 100): ___58___ %

C1. Total items scored for full routine: ___35___

C2. Percentage of items mastered by routine (A / C1 * 100): ___43___ %
*Add scores to the MEISR Scoring Summary page*

## 13. Grocery Shopping — Participates in grocery shopping by . . .

| | Typical starting age in months | Not yet | Sometimes | Often or Beyond this | Func* | Dev* | Out |
|---|---|---|---|---|---|---|---|
| 13.01 Attending to sound of caregiver's voice | 0 | 1 | 2 | ③ | S | S | S |
| 13.02 Looking at caregiver's mouth and eyes when face to face | 2 | 1 | 2 | ③ | E | S | S |
| 13.03 Reaching for items/toys that are given (with an open hand or open hands) | 5 | 1 | 2 | ③ | E | M | A |
| 13.04 Responding to *bye-bye* by looking and might try waving ✫ | 7 | ① | 2 | 3 | S | CM | S |
| 13.05 Sitting independently in the cart | 9 | 1 | 2 | ③ | I | M | A |
| 13.06 Pointing or reaching for named item (e.g., "get apple" when shown two items) | 9 | ① | 2 | 3 | S | CM | K |
| 13.07 Understanding rule to sit in the cart and only occasionally fussing (up to 30 minutes) | 12 | 1 | ② | 3 | E | S | S |
| 13.08 Indicating what he or she wants (e.g., pointing, gesturing) | 12 | 1 | ② | 3 | S | CM | A |
| 13.09 Imitating saying a new word (e.g., *cake, banana, eggs*) | 14 | ① | 2 | 3 | S | CM | K |
| 13.10 Carrying items while walking (e.g., small bag) | 18 | 1 | 2 | ③ | E | M | A |
| 13.11 Recognizing and labeling grocery items (three or more) | 18 | ① | 2 | 3 | E | CM | K |
| 13.12 Understanding yours and mine (e.g., *this is your drink and this is mine*) | 21 | 1 | 2 | ③ | S | CM | K |
| 13.13 Pushing a stroller or pretend shopping cart | 24 | 1 | ② | 3 | I | M | A |
| 13.14 Getting items parents have requested off shelf | 30 | ① | 2 | 3 | S | CM | K |
| 13.15 Showing interest in other children | 30 | ① | 2 | 3 | S | S | S |
| 13.16 Responding appropriately to unknown adults in the grocery store | 33 | ① | 2 | 3 | S | S | S |
| 13.17 Walking around things (small and large), moving, and stepping over | 33 | ① | 2 | 3 | I | M | A |
| 13.18 Walking alongside the cart (staying in safe proximity) | 36 | → 1 | 2 | 3 | I | A | A |

A. Total items scored 3 (Often or Beyond this): __6__

B1. Total items scored for child's age: __13__

B2. Percentage of items mastered by age (A / B1 * 100): __46__ %

C1. Total items scored for full routine: __18__

C2. Percentage of items mastered by routine (A / C1 * 100): __33__ %
*Add scores to the MEISR Scoring Summary page*

22

## 14. Transition Time — Participates in transition times by . . .

| | Typical starting age in months | Not yet | Sometimes | Often or Beyond this | Func[a] | Dev[b] | Out[c] |
|---|---|---|---|---|---|---|---|
| 14.01 Making at least one transition from one routine/activity to another without getting upset or overly fussy | 0 | 1 | 2 | (3) | I | S | S |
| 14.02 Showing awareness of new, strange, different situations by changing behavior (e.g., quieting, looking around more, crying, clinging to caregiver) | 6 | 1 | 2 | (3) | S | S | S |
| 14.03 Listening or attending to caregiver talking without getting distracted | 10 | 1 | 2 | (3) | S | S | S |
| 14.04 Giving toy or object to caregiver upon request | 12 | 1 | (2) | 3 | S | CM | K |
| 14.05 Showing an emotional response that fits the situation (e.g., resisting unwanted change, obvious pleasure with desired transitions) | 15 | 1 | 2 | (3) | S | S | S |
| 14.06 Recognizing funny transitions and laughs (e.g., putting shoes on hands, giving cup upside down, no water in tub) | 15 | 1 | (2) | 3 | E | CG, S | K |
| 14.07 Trying to do things on own and possibly resisting transitions by fussing | 18 | 1 | 2 | (3) | I | A | A |
| 14.08 Showing awareness of familiar routines and proceeding when prompted | 24 | 1 | (2) | 3 | E | S | S |
| 14.09 Showing shyness or caution in new situations | 24 | 1 | (2) | 3 | S | S | S |
| 14.10 Complying, with prompts/support, despite clear reluctance to change | 30 | 1 | (2) | 3 | S | S | S |
| 14.11 Obeying some consistent and familiar rules related to moving from one activity/routine to another | 30 | (1) | 2 | 3 | S | CM, S | S |
| 14.12 Cooperating with if–then rules, such as *first we do ___, then we'll ___* (might protest anyway) | 33 | (1) | 2 | 3 | S | CM, CG | K |
| 14.13 Stating desires about transitions or changes without a tantrum | 33 | (1) | 2 | 3 | S | CM, S | A |
| 14.14 Talking about some feelings about transitions (e.g., *I like Grandma's, I hate going to bed*) | 36 | (1) | 2 | 3 | S | CM, S | S |
| 14.15 Following a number of rules and might remind others of rules (e.g., *you have to wear smock to paint*) | 36 | →1 | 2 | 3 | E | S | S |

A. Total items scored 3 (Often or Beyond this): ___5___

B1. Total items scored for child's age: ___9___

B2. Percentage of items mastered by age (A / B1 * 100): ___56___ %

C1. Total items scored for full routine: ___15___

C2. Percentage of items mastered by routine (A / C1 * 100): ___33___ %
*Add scores to the MEISR Scoring Summary page*

# Amber's Present Levels of Development

## POSITIVE SOCIAL RELATIONSHIPS

Amber wakes up without crying and plays on her own in her bedroom. When Amber's mom or dad wakes her, she looks at them but is not yet saying "mama" or "dada."

Amber shows understanding of the meal time routine by mostly sitting at the table holding her toy ponies and waiting a few minutes for her food. When Amber's parents interact with her, she is mostly quiet and does not always look at them; instead, she stares forward or looks down where she is holding her little ponies. Amber often carries her ponies around, one in each hand, and seems to use them as soothing toys.

When hanging out watching TV, Amber sometimes sits on her dad's lap and plays with his face without giving clear eye contact. Amber pushes her music ball back and forth with her dad and smiles as the music plays, yet she does not respond to her dad or others when they laugh or show excitement.

When the neighbors are over and playing with the music ball or Amber's ponies, Amber will grab them back if another child takes them. When this happens, Amber grabs the toy without saying anything, such as "mine." In the company of other children, Amber mostly plays on her own. However, she shows some interest by going to where the other children are in the house. When they interact with Amber, she looks in their direction, then continues to play on her own.

On the playground, Amber will play without fussing for up to an hour. She will go near to where the other kids are and interacts mostly by letting the older children push her on a swing. When swinging, Amber sometimes says "whee" and "go." Amber separates fairly easily from her parents when in a familiar place, such as at home or at the local fenced-in playground. She'll play by herself for several minutes without a caregiver in her clear sight.

Amber cooperates with familiar caregiving routines, such as brushing hair, putting bath toys away, and going through the bedtime routine, which includes putting her ponies in a box and getting them when she awakens.

During outings, Amber is generally easygoing, although she is not yet pointing or drawing her parents' attention to things that interest her. Amber's parents encourage her to wave "hi" and "bye" by moving her arm in a waving motion. In new situations, such as when the family is traveling, Amber is mostly shy and quiet.

## ACQUIRING AND USING KNOWLEDGE AND SKILLS

Amber is mostly quiet during the day, saying primarily vowel sounds and sing-song sounds and only a few words. The few "real-like" words that she says are in particular situations, such as saying "go" and "whee" on the swings, "popee" sometimes when playing with her little ponies (her favorite toy), and "ipa" when she wants her iPad. At meal times, she sometimes says "no" to mean no. She also seems to understand the difference between "This is your cup, and this is mine." She has a particular cup she likes to drink from at meal times at the table.

During dressing, Amber looks at her shoes when her mom says, "Time to put shoes on," but she's not yet following a direction to go get shoes or to lift her foot or arms or identify other body parts when asked. When given directions or asked to do something, Amber needs several reminders to follow through, unless it is a routine activity, such as putting her diaper in the bin or putting her cup in the sink. Sometimes, when called by her name, Amber seems to stare off or look in the direction of her parents without giving clear eye contact.

Amber's favored toys are her ponies and toys that make music, especially her ball that plays music when it rolls. With the ponies, she'll rub their manes and tails on her face to feel the fur, she'll carry them about, and she'll sometimes stand them up in a line. She also puts them in their toy "bed" (box) when she goes to bed at night. She shows awareness of the basic functions of toys, using many toys purposefully (e.g., dumping sand in and out of containers, putting balls on the ball toy, activating music toys). However, she is not yet engaging in pretend play beyond putting her ponies in their "bed" and stirring in a cup with a spoon. At this time, Amber is not matching colors or shapes or showing interest in coloring beyond using a marker to make marks on the paper and the wall a few times.

Amber climbs on things to get at what she wants, such as getting the iPad from the counter before it was moved to its new hiding place on top of the fridge; she hasn't yet figured out how to get up there. Amber plays with the iPad and can get to her favorite music videos. She smiles when music plays and will sometimes vocalize the tune but is not singing any of the words. For her birthday, Amber made sounds that matched the tune of the "Happy Birthday" song.

When looking at books, Amber shows little interest but will turn a few pages at a time, and when looking at her little pony books, she will look at the pictures and sometimes pat at a picture. She is not yet naming or pointing to pictures in books when asked where something is (e.g., "Where's the pony?").

## TAKING ACTION TO MEET NEEDS

Amber independently moves around by walking, running, jumping, and climbing. She goes up and down the steps at home on her own, putting both feet on each step. At bath time, she stands on one foot for her parents to dry her. When around groups of children, she maintains control by walking around them without bumping into them. She also rarely trips or falls when walking on different surfaces, such as on the playground or on and off curbs. Amber also moves ride-on toys with her feet and goes up the ladder and down the small slide at the local playground.

At meal times, Amber climbs into the adult-sized chair to sit. She uses a spoon to eat and rarely spills. She also drinks from her special pony-themed open cup by picking it up and putting it down without spilling, if she's eating at the table. When not at the table, she uses a sippy cup. Amber is somewhat picky as she rarely eats veggies beyond carrots, but she does like a variety of fruits. For a snack, she gets wrapped fruit candies, and she can unfold the wrappers to get the candy. At meals, she'll push her plate forward to indicate she wants more and stops eating to indicate she is finished. She's not yet saying words like "more" or "all done" or naming foods she wants.

Amber is starting to sit on the potty and will sit there sometimes before bath, but she has not yet gone in the potty. She does stay dry for up to 3 hours at a time and is starting to show discomfort when her diaper is really wet; she shows this by tugging at her diaper.

At dressing, Amber is helpful and can take off her loose shoes and pull up her pants at least up to her diaper. She can also take off her jammies on her own and unzip her jacket.

During baths, Amber rubs the wash cloth on her feet and belly, but this requires some hand-over-hand help. She cooperates when her mom brushes her hair by sitting mostly still. Amber puts the toothbrush in her mouth and will brush with her mom's help, especially if her mom sings the teeth-brushing song.

At nap and bed times, Amber is a pretty good sleeper. She is now taking one nap a day and is sleeping through the night.

Amber is mostly quiet and independent to entertain herself. She stays away from the stove and easily rides in her stroller. She is learning to hold her parents' hands when walking in stores. Amber easily gets into her car seat, but sometimes she undoes the seatbelt during the car ride. Her parents just ordered a seatbelt guard that they think will help.

# CHAPTER 9

# Using the MEISR for Program Evaluation

*How effective is my early intervention program in terms of child functioning?* The MEISR can be used to answer this question. Doing so requires attention to entering data, analyzing data, reporting data, aggregating across residual improvement indices, interpreting data, and showing data.

## ENTERING DATA

From the MEISR form, data can be entered or copied into the MEISR Database 0–36 Months, developed by Catalina Morales Murillo. This database is available as a spreadsheet on the web site for the Evidence-based International Early Intervention Office (EIEIO) at the following address: www.eieio.ua.edu

The first sheet contains instructions. The second sheet, RawData, is where scores for each item on the MEISR are entered. Programs can use the file column for identifying information, such as a name. The ID column is for the child's unique identifier. Date of birth is self-explanatory. Items are organized by time (i.e., which assessment out of multiple assessments) and by routine. T1W1, therefore, indicates Time 1, Waking Up Time, Item 1. In that cell would appear 1 (Not yet), 2 (Sometimes), or 3 (Often or Beyond this), as shown in Figure 9.1.

The fourth sheet, Excel Table Time and Routine, gathers the data from the second sheet, RawData, and displays these data by routines in rows and children in columns. The cells are all formulas linked to the second sheet. The user does not have to do anything. This sheet is mostly to help with other calculations and entry into the Statistical Package for the Social Sciences, now known as SPSS.

## ANALYZING DATA

The third sheet, Count and % 1s, 2s, 3s, provides formulas taken from the RawData sheet. The data are organized by routines (rows) and children (columns) for each assessment time. Within routines, the count of 1s, 2s, 3s, and blanks for the routine is calculated. These, in turn, produce the percentage of 1s, 2s, and 3s. The sheet shows these scores for all children assessed at that time. In Figure 9.2, for example, we see the start of the sheet. At T1 (Time 1), the scores for Child 1 from the RawData sheet appear in Column B. The figure shows the frequency of 1s, 2s, and 3s at waking up time in W1, W2, and W3, and shows the frequency of blanks in Wblanks. Below that, the percentages of 1s, 2s, and 3s appear in W%1, W%2, and W%3, respectively. This continues downward through the remaining

| File | ID | Date of Birth | T1Date | T1Age | T1W1 | T1W2 | T1W3 | T1W4 | T1W5 | T1W6 | T1W7 | T1W8 |
|---|---|---|---|---|---|---|---|---|---|---|---|---|
| | Child1 | | | | | | | | | | | |
| | Child2 | | | | | | | | | | | |
| | Child3 | | | | | | | | | | | |
| | Child4 | | | | | | | | | | | |
| | Child5 | | | | | | | | | | | |
| | Child6 | | | | | | | | | | | |
| | Child7 | | | | | | | | | | | |
| | Child8 | | | | | | | | | | | |
| | Child9 | | | | | | | | | | | |
| | Child10 | | | | | | | | | | | |

**Figure 9.1.** Scores for children by time, routine, and item. (From Murillo, C. M. [n.d.]. *MEISR Database 0–36 Months* [Unpublished database]; reprinted by permission.)

routines and across to the right for the remaining children at Time 1. It all begins again, to the right, for Time 2.

As children enter the program, their first MEISR assessment is always Time 1. Therefore, "time" here is not a date. It is the order of assessments, as in Time 1 is the first assessment, Time 2 is the second assessment, and so on.

The fifth sheet, Time Means, reports, for each routine (e.g., 1. Waking up) and each time (e.g., TI, for Time 1) the percentage of 3s (i.e., mastery) by child in columns. This allows the user to see how the child has increased in percentage of skills for each routine over time.

## REPORTING DATA

Data can be reported with tables or graphs. In the Time Means sheet, at row 105 and following, the data are automatically summarized. The percentages of 3s are averaged across the 14 routines for each assessment time. These are percentages of all the items in a routine, up to 36 months, so they should increase at every assessment time. Users can take this information, click on Home, and Format as Table. They can also select the relevant cells and click on Insert to select an appropriate chart.

## AGGREGATING ACROSS RESIDUAL IMPROVEMENT INDICES

In the Appendix, we describe how we developed the residual improvement index to show how much difference early intervention has made compared to the trajectory the child was on before starting in the program. This index takes the rate of progress (i.e., trajectory) and extends it from Time 1 to Time 2 to calculate the level the child would have reached (regardless of the metric used to assess improvement). The actual level at Time 2 is compared to the predicted level. That difference is what early intervention can be (generously) given credit for. The difference score between the predicted and actual levels is expressed as a percentage of the predicted level, so we can say the child did XX% better than expected.

These percentages—the residual improvement indices (RIIs)—can be entered for each child from one assessment time to the next and can be averaged across children, within and across routines, to report how much better children performed as a function of being in the program. This difference is expressed as a percentage. Once you have three time points, you can use growth curve analyses, which is a multilevel regression technique. It can be done with a number of statistical packages but is more complicated than an Excel analysis. If you can

Note. For the Overall Counts and Percentage of 1s, 2s, and 3s by Time click on the button. [ **Click Here** ]

| Child's Name/ID | 0 | 0 | 0 | 0 | 0 | 0 |
|---|---|---|---|---|---|---|
| **Row labels** | **ChildAverage1** | **ChildAverage2** | **ChildAverage3** | **ChildAverage4** | **ChildAverage5** | **ChildAverage6** |
| **1.  Waking Up** | | | | | | |
| Count | | | | | | |
| W1 | 0 | 0 | 0 | 0 | 0 | |
| W2 | 0 | 0 | 0 | 0 | 0 | |
| W3 | 0 | 0 | 0 | 0 | 0 | |
| Wblanks | 0 | 0 | 0 | 0 | 0 | |
| Percentage | | | | | | |
| W%1 | 0 | 0 | 0 | 0 | 0 | |
| W%2 | 0 | 0 | 0 | 0 | 0 | |
| W%3 | 0 | 0 | 0 | 0 | 0 | |
| **2.  Toileting/Diaper** | | | | | | |
| Count | | | | | | |
| W1 | 0 | 0 | 0 | 0 | 0 | |
| W2 | 0 | 0 | 0 | 0 | 0 | |
| W3 | 0 | 0 | 0 | 0 | 0 | |
| Wblanks | 0 | 0 | 0 | 0 | 0 | |
| Percentage | | | | | | |
| W%1 | 0 | 0 | 0 | 0 | 0 | |
| W%2 | 0 | 0 | 0 | 0 | 0 | |
| W%3 | 0 | 0 | 0 | 0 | 0 | |
| **3.  Meal Times** | | | | | | |
| Count | | | | | | |
| W1 | 0 | 0 | 0 | 0 | 0 | |
| W2 | 0 | 0 | 0 | 0 | 0 | |
| W3 | 0 | 0 | 0 | 0 | 0 | |
| Wblanks | 0 | 0 | 0 | 0 | 0 | |
| Percentage | | | | | | |
| W%1 | 0 | 0 | 0 | 0 | 0 | |
| W%2 | 0 | 0 | 0 | 0 | 0 | |
| W%3 | 0 | 0 | 0 | 0 | 0 | |

**Figure 9.2.**  For each time of assessment, the count and percentage of 1s, 2s, and 3s by child. (rom Murillo, C. M. [n.d.]. *MEISR Database 0–36 Months* [Unpublished database]; reprinted by permission.)

find the resources to use growth curve analyses, we highly recommend you do so, because it eliminates the false linear projection in the RII: Taking a single data point to project future performance is subject to error. However, the simplicity of the RII is helpful when showing a program's effectiveness in a fairly nonscientific environment, such as to stakeholders who might not be impressed with fancy although credible statistics.

**Table 9.1.** Example of disaggregating MEISR data by child age

| Routine | Age Bracket in Months | | |
| --- | --- | --- | --- |
| | 0–12 | 13–24 | 25–36 |
| Waking Up | 0.45 | 0.35 | 0.32 |
| Toileting/Diapering | 0.56 | 0.48 | 0.52 |
| Meal Times | 0.54 | 0.44 | 0.42 |
| Dressing Time | 0.87 | 0.63 | 0.77 |
| Hangout – TV – Books | 0.80 | 0.64 | 0.60 |
| Play With Others | 0.81 | 0.60 | 0.53 |
| Nap Time | 0.76 | 0.59 | 0.71 |
| Outside Time | 0.93 | 0.80 | 0.83 |
| Play by Him- or Herself | 0.68 | 0.64 | 0.53 |
| Bath Time | 0.73 | 0.68 | 0.60 |
| Bedtime | 0.60 | 0.35 | 0.60 |
| Going Out | 0.71 | 0.51 | 0.63 |
| Grocery Shopping | 0.65 | 0.65 | 0.61 |

## INTERPRETING DATA

To interpret the data for program evaluation, programs might consider disaggregating the data, reporting performance up to the child's age, and reporting performance to 36 months. What are the variables on which to disaggregate, and what are the implications for demographic data collection?

Variables on which to disaggregate can be child or family sociodemographic or child or family-measured characteristics. Table 9.1 shows some of these possibilities. An example of disaggregating data would be showing the percentage of under-1s, 1-year-olds, and 2-year-olds who mastered their skills by routine or overall. If a program has data on enough children, a user can combine disaggregated data in cross-tabulations. For example, a user could report the percentage of under-1s, 1-year-olds, and 2-year-olds who mastered the items, divided into two groups, boys and girls. If the user is reporting the data by routines, disaggregating by more than one variable like this, however, can be cumbersome.

An example from the family sociodemographics might be by socioeconomic status (SES), if those data are available. The user can report the percentage of children mastering MEISR skills, by routine and in total, by low, medium, and high SES. An example from child characteristics could be disaggregating the data by severity, if those data are available. We used the ABILITIES Index (Simeonsson & Bailey, 1991); write to McWilliam at ramcwilliam@ua.edu for a copy.

An example of disaggregating by a family characteristic might be to report the percentage of items mastered on the MEISR by low, medium, and high levels of family quality of life. We use the Families in Early Intervention Quality of Life Scale (McWilliam & García Grau, 2017), also available from McWilliam. If you think you will want to disaggregate data by any of these variables, you obviously will need to decide on the variables and on how to collect the data.

## SUMMARY

One of the main purposes of the MEISR is to monitor children's progress, which is important for intervention, so teams can adjust interventions. Child progress is also an indicator of program effectiveness, so MEISR data can be a good, functional indicator. This chapter has summarized how to enter data, analyze them, report them, aggregate them, and interpret them. It is helpful to have meaningful data for reporting our effectiveness.

# References

Aguiar, C., & McWilliam, R. A. (2013). Consistency of toddler engagement across two settings. *Early Childhood Research Quarterly, 28*, 102–110.

Almqvist, L., & Granlund, M. (2005). Participation in school environment of children and youth with disabilities: A person-oriented approach. *Scandinavian Journal of Psychology, 46*, 305–314.

Almqvist, L., Hellnäs, P., Stefansson, M., & Granlund, M. (2006). "I can play!" Young children's perceptions of health. *Developmental Neurorehabilitation, 9*, 275–284.

Bailey, D. B., Jr. (2002). Are critical periods critical for early childhood education? The role of timing in early childhood pedagogy. *Early Childhood Research Quarterly, 17*, 281–294.

Bagnato, S. J. (2007). *Authentic assessment for early childhood intervention: Best practices.* New York, NY: Guilford Press.

Bagnato, S. J., Macy, M., Salaway, J., Lehman, C. (2007). *Research foundations of authentic assessments ensure accurate and representative early intervention eligibility.* Pittsburgh, PA: TRACE Center for Excellence in Early Childhood Assessment, Early Childhood Partnerships, Children's Hospital/University of Pittsburgh; US Department of Education, Office of Special Education Programs, and Orelena Hawks Puckett Institute.

Bagnato, S. J., Smith-Jones, J., Matesa, M., & McKeating-Esterle, E. (2006). Practice-based research synthesis of child find, referral, early identification, and eligibility practices and models. *Cornerstones, 2*(3).

Barton, L., Taylor, C., Spiker, D., & Hebbeler, K. (2016). Validity of the data from the Child Outcomes Summary process: Findings from the ENHANCE project. Menlo Park, CA: Center for IDEA Early Childhood Data Systems and Early Childhood Technical Assistance Center. Retrieved from https://ectacenter.org/~pdfs/calls/2016/ENHANCEbrief_03-02-16Final.pdf

Bayley, N. (1993). *Bayley Scales of Infant Development: Manual.* San Antonio, TX: Psychological Corporation.

Bernheimer, L. P., & Keogh, B. K. (1995). Weaving interventions into the fabric of everyday life: An approach to family assessment. *Topics in Early Childhood Special Education, 15*(4), 415–433.

Bernheimer, L. P., & Weisner, T. S. (2007). "Let me just tell you what I do all day . . .": The family story at the center of intervention research and practice. *Infants and Young Children, 20*, 192–201.

Billett, S. (2002). Toward a workplace pedagogy: Guidance, participation, and engagement. *Adult Education Quarterly, 53*, 27–43.

Birbili, M., & Tzioga, K. (2014). Involving parents in children's assessment: Lessons from the Greek context. *Early Years, 34*, 161–174. doi:10.1080/09575146.2014.894498

Björck-Åkesson, E., Wilder, J., Granlund, M., Pless, M., Simeonsson, R., Adolfsson, M., . . . Lillvist, A. (2010). The International Classification of Functioning, Disability and Health and the version for children and youth as a tool in child habilitation/early childhood intervention: Feasibility and useful-ness as a common language and frame of reference for practice. *Disability & Rehabilitation, 32*, S125–S138.

Boavida, T., Aguiar, C., & McWilliam, R. A. (2014). A training program to improve IFSP/IEP goals and objectives through the Routines-Based Interview. *Topics in Early Childhood Special Education, 20*, 200–211. doi:10.1177/0271121413494416

Boavida, T., Aguiar, C., McWilliam, R. A., & Correia, N. (2016). Effects of an in-service training program using the routines-based interview. *Topics in Early Childhood Special Education, 36*, 67–77.

Boavida, T., Akers, K., McWilliam, R. A., & Jung, L. A. (2015). Rasch analysis of the Routines-Based Interview Implementation Checklist. *Infants & Young Children, 28*, 237–247. doi:10.1097/IYC.0000000000000041

Bowman, B. T., Donovan, M. S., & Burns, M. S. (Eds.). (2001). *Eager to learn: Educating our preschoolers.* Washington, DC: National Academies Press.

Boyce, W. T., Jensen, E. W., James, S. A., & Peacock, J. L. (1983). The family routines inventory: Theoretical origins. *Social Science & Medicine, 17*, 193–200.

Bronfenbrenner, U. (1986). Ecology of the family as a context for human development: Research perspectives. *Developmental Psychology, 22*, 723–742.

Bruckner, C., McLean, M. & Snyder, P. (2011) Building a comprehensive assessment system in early intervention/early childhood special education. In S. M. Eidelman, S. Maude, & L. Kacxmarek (Vol. Eds.) & C. J. Groak (Set Ed.), *Early childhood intervention: Shaping the future for children with special needs and their families.* Santa Barbara,CA: Praeger Publishing Co.

Carroll, J. B. (1989). The Carroll model. *Educational Researcher, 18*, 26–31.

Casey, A. M., & McWilliam, R. A. (2008). Graphical feedback to increase teachers' use of incidental teaching. *Journal of Early Intervention, 30*(3), 251–268.

Casey, A. M., McWilliam, R. A., & Sims, J. (2012). Contributions of incidental teaching, developmental quotient, and peer interactions to child engagement. *Infants & Young Children, 25*, 122–135. doi:10.1097/IYC.0b013e31824cbac4

Center for IDEA Early Childhood Data Systems (DaSy) & Early Childhood Technical Assistance Center (ECTA). (2017). *Definitions for Child Outcomes Summary (COS) ratings.* Retrieved from http://ectacenter.org/eco/assets/pdfs/Definitions_Outcome_Ratings.pdf

Cole, K. N., Dale, P. S., & Mills, P. E. (1992). Stability of the intelligence quotient-language quotient relation: Is discrepancy modeling based on a myth? *American Journal on Mental Retardation, 97*, 131–143.

de Kruif, R. E. L., & McWilliam, R. A. (1999). Multivariate relationships among developmental age, global engagement, and observed child engagement. *Early Childhood Research Quarterly, 14*, 515–536.

de Kruif, R. E. L., McWilliam, R. A., Ridley, S. M., & Wakely, M. B. (2000). Classification of teachers' interaction behaviors in early childhood classrooms. *Early Childhood Research Quarterly, 15*, 247–268.

Division for Early Childhood (DEC). (2014). *DEC recommended practices in early intervention/early childhood special education 2014.* Retrieved from http://www.dec-sped.org/recommendedpractices

Doke, L. A., & Risley, T. R. (1972). The organization of day-care environments: Required vs. optional activities. *Journal of Applied Behavior Analysis, 5*, 405–420.

Dunst, C. J., & Bruder, M. B. (1999). Family and community activity settings, natural learning environments, and children's learning opportunities. *Children's Learning Opportunities Report, 1*, 1–2.

Dunst, C. J., Bruder, M. B., Trivette, C. M., & Hamby, D. W. (2006). Everyday activity settings, natural learning environments, and early intervention practices. *Journal of Policy and Practice in Intellectual Disabilities, 3*, 3–10. doi:10.1111/j.1741-1130.2006.00047.x

Dunst, C. J., Hamby, D., Trivette, C. M., Raab, M., & Bruder, M. B. (2000). Everyday family and community life and children's naturally occurring learning opportunities. *Journal of Early Intervention, 23*(3), 151–164.

Dunst, C. J., McWilliam, R. A., & Holbert, K. (1986). Assessment of preschool classroom environments. *Diagnostique, 11*, 212–232.

Dunst, C. J., Trivette, C. M., & Hamby, D. W. (2007). Meta-analysis of family-centered helpgiving practices research. *Families of Children with Developmental Disabilities, 13*(4), 370–378.

Early Childhood Technical Assistance Center (ECTA). (2017). *State approaches to child outcomes measurement Part C APR Indicator 3: FFY 2015 (2015-2016).* Chapel Hill, NC: FPG Child Development Institute of the University of North Carolina. Retrieved from http://ectacenter.org/eco/assets/pdfs/map_partC3.pdf

Early Childhood Technical Assistance Center (ECTA). (2019). Instrument crosswalks. Retrieved from http://ectacenter.org/eco/pages/crosswalks.asp

Early Childhood Technical Assistance Center (ECTA) & Center for IDEA Early Childhood Data Systems (DaSy). (2018a). *Age anchoring guidance for determining child outcomes summary (COS) ratings: Guidance for EI/ECSE practitioners and trainers.* Retrieved from http://ectacenter.org/~pdfs/eco/COS_Age_Anchoring_Guidance.pdf

Early Childhood Technical Assistance Center (ECTA) & Center for IDEA Early Childhood Data Systems (DaSy). (2018b). *Decision tree for summary rating discussions.* Retrieved from http://ectacenter.org/eco/assets/pdfs/Decision_Tree.pdf

Elliott, R. (2003). Executive functions and their disorders: Imaging in clinical neuroscience. *British Medical Bulletin, 65*, 49–59.

Fiese, B. H., Tomcho, T. J., Douglas, M., Josephs, K., Poltrock, S., & Baker, T. (2002). A review of 50 years of research on naturally occurring family routines and rituals: Cause for celebration? *Journal of Family Psychology, 16*, 381–390.

García-Grau, P., McWilliam, R. A., Martínez-Rico, G., & Grau Sevilla, M. D. (2018). Factor structure and internal conistency of a Spanish version of the Family Quality of Life (FaQoL) Scale. *Applied Research in Quality of Life, 13*, 385–398.

Gladwell, M. (2005). *Blink: The power of thinking without thinking.* New York, NY: Little, Brown and Co.

Harbin, G. L. (2005). Designing an integrated point of access in the early intervention system. In M. J. Guralnick (Ed.), *The developmental systems approach to early intervention* (pp. 99–131). Baltimore, MD: Paul H. Brookes Publishing Co.

Hart, B., & Risley, T. R. (1974). Using preschool materials to modify the language of disadvantaged children. *Journal of Applied Behavior Analysis*, *7*, 243–256.

Hewett, V. M. (2001). Examining the Reggio Emilia approach to early childhood education. *Early Childhood Education Journal*, *29*, 95–100.

Horwitz, S. M., Chamberlain, P., Landsverk, J., & Mullican, C. (2010). Improving the mental health of children in child welfare through the implementation of evidence-based parenting interventions. *Administration and Policy in Mental Health and Mental Health Services Research*, *37*, 27–39.

Individuals with Disabilities Education Act (IDEA) of 1990, PL 101-476, 20 U.S.C. §§ 1400 *et seq.*

Individuals with Disabilities Education Improvement Act (IDEA) of 2004, PL 108-446, 20 U.S.C. §§ 1400 et seq.

Jung, L. A., & Baird, S. M. (2003). Effects of service coordinator variables on individualized family service plans. *Journal of Early Intervention*, *25*, 206–218.

Jung, L. A., & McWilliam, R. A. (2005). Reliability and validity of scores on the IFSP Rating Scale. *Journal of Early Intervention*, *27*, 125–136.

Macy, M., & Bricker, D. (2006). Practical applications for using curriculum-based assessments to create embedded learning opportunities for young children. *Young Exceptional Children*, *9*(4), 12–21.

McWilliam, R. A. (1992). *Family-centered intervention planning: A routines-based approach*. Tucson, AZ: Communication Skill Builders.

McWilliam, R. A. (2006). What happened to service coordination? *Journal of Early Intervention*, *28*, 166–168.

McWilliam, R. A. (2010). *Routines-based early intervention: Supporting young children and their families*. Baltimore, MD: Paul H. Brookes Publishing Co.

McWilliam, R. A. (2014). *Classroom Measure of Engagement, Independence, and Social Relationships (ClaMEISR)*. Chattanooga, TN: Siskin Children's Institute.

McWilliam, R. A. (2016a). Metanoia in early intervention: Transformation to a family-centered approach. *Revista Latinoamericana de Educación Inclusiva*, *10*, 155–173.

McWilliam, R. A. (2016b). *RBI with ecomap checklist*. Tuscaloosa, AL: Evidence-based International Early Intervention Office, The University of Alabama.

McWilliam, R. A. (2016c). The Routines-Based Model for supporting speech and langauge. *Logopedia, Foniatría y Audiología*, *36*, 178–184.

McWilliam, R. A., & Bailey, D. B. (1992). Promoting engagement and mastery. In D. B. Bailey & M. Wolery (Eds.), *Teaching infants and preschoolers with disabilities* (2nd ed., pp. 229–256). Columbus, OH: Merrill.

McWilliam, R. A., & Bailey, D. B. (1995). Effects of classroom social structure and disability on engagement. *Topics in Early Childhood Special Education*, *15*, 123–147.

McWilliam, R. A., & Casey, A. M. (2008). *Engagement of every child in the preschool classroom*. Baltimore, MD: Paul H. Brookes Publishing Co.

McWilliam, R. A., Casey, A. M., & Sims, J. L. (2009). The Routines-Based Interview: A method for assessing needs and developing IFSPs. *Infants & Young Children*, *22*, 224–233.

McWilliam, R. A., Ferguson, A., Harbin, G. L., Porter, P., Munn, D., & Vandiviere, P. (1998). The family-centeredness of individualized family service plans. *Topics in Early Childhood Special Education*, *18*, 69–82.

McWilliam, R. A., & García-Grau, P. (2017). *Families in Early Intervention Quality of Life Rating Scale*. Tuscaloosa, AL: Evidence-based International Early Intervention Office, The University of Alabama.

McWilliam, R. A., & Hornstein, S. (2007). *Measure of Engagement, Independence, and Social Relationships* [Instrument]. Nashville, TN: Vanderbilt University.

McWilliam, R. A., Scarborough, A. A., & Kim, H. (2003). Adult interactions and child engagement. *Early Education and Development*, *14*, 7–27.

McWilliam, R. A., & Scott, S. (2001). A support approach to early intervention: A three-part framework. *Infants & Young Children*, *13*, 55–66.

McWilliam, R. A., Trivette, C. M., & Dunst, C. J. (1985). Behavior engagement as a measure of the efficacy of early intervention. *Analysis and Intervention in Developmental Disabilities*, *5*, 59–71.

McWilliam, R. A., & Ware, W. B. (1994). The reliability of observations of young children's engagement: An application of generalizability theory. *Journal of Early Intervention*, *18*, 34–47.

Murillo, C. M. (n.d.). *MEISR Database 0–36 Months* [Unpublished database].

National Association for the Education of Young Children (NAYEC) & National Association of Early Childhood Specialists in State Departments of Education (NAECS/SDE). (2002). Early learning standards: Creating the conditions for success: A joint position statement of the NAYEC and the NAECS/SDE. Retrieved from http://www.naeyc.org/files/naeyc/file/positions/position_statement.pdf

Neisworth, J. T., & Bagnato, S. J. (2004). The mismeasure of young children: The authentic assessment alternative. *Infants & Young Children*, *17*(3), 198–212.

Newborg, J. (2005). *Battelle Developmental Inventory, Second Edition*. Itasca, IL: Riverside Publishing.

Parks, S., Furuno, S., O'Reilly, K., Inatsuka, T., & Hosaka, C. M. (1997). *Hawaii Early Learning Profile*. Palo Alto, CA: VORT Corporation.

Parks, S., Furuno, S., O'Reilly, K., Inatsuka, T., Hoska, C., & Zeisloft-Falbey, B. (1992). *Hawaii Early Learning Profile (HELP)*. Palo Alto, CA: Vort Corp.

Pessanha, M., Aguiar, C., & Bairrao, J. (2007). Influence of structural features on Portuguese toddler child care quality. *Early Childhood Research Quarterly, 22*, 204–214.

Quilitch, H. R., & Risley, T. R. (1973). The effects of play materials on social play. *Journal of Applied Behavior Analysis, 6*, 573–578.

Rapport, M. J. K., McWilliam, R. A., & Smith, B. J. (2004). Practices across disciplines in early intervention. *Infants & Young Children, 17*, 32–44.

Rasmussen, J. L., & McWilliam, R. A. (2010). RBI implementation checklist. In R. A. McWilliam (Ed.), *Working with families of young children with special needs* (pp. 44–47). New York, NY: The Guilford Press.

Raspa, M. J., McWilliam, R. A., & Ridley, S. M. (2001). Child care quality and children's engagement. *Early Education and Development, 12*, 209–224.

Ray, R. A., & Street, A. F. (2005). Ecomapping: An innovative research tool for nurses. *Journal of Advanced Nursing, 50*, 545–552.

Ridley, S. M., McWilliam, R. A., & Oates, C. S. (2000). Observed engagement as an indicator of child care program quality. *Early Education and Development, 11*, 133–146.

Robbins, T. A., Smith, S., Stagman, S. M., & Kreader, J. L. (2012). *Practices for promoting young children's learning in QRIS standards*. New York, NY: Columbia University Academic Commons.

Shelden, M. L., & Rush, D. D. (2013). *The early intervention teaming handbook: The primary service provider approach*. Baltimore, MD: Paul H. Brookes Publishing Co.

Shepard, L., Kagan, S.L., Wurtz, E. (Eds.). (1998). *Principles and recommendations for early childhood assessments*. Washington, DC: National Education Goals Panel.

Shonkoff, J. P., & Phillips, D. A. (2002). From neurons to neighborhoods: The science of early childhood development. *Journal of the American Academy of Child and Adolescent Psychiatry, 41*, 625–626.

Simeonsson, R. J., & Bailey, D. (1991). *The ABILITIES Index*. Chapel Hill, NC: Frank Porter Graham Child Development Center.

Squires, J. (2015). Guiding principles for accurate and efficient decision making. In *Division for Early Childhood (DEC) Recommended Practices: Enhancing Services for Young Children with Disabilities and their Families* (DEC Recommended Practices Monograph Series No. 1). Los Angeles, CA: DEC.

SRI International. (2013, February 19). *ENHANCE: Team decision-making study: Content coded in videos*. SRI International, Menlo Park, CA. Retrieved from http://enhance.sri.com/datacollection/data.html

Tennessee Department of Education. (2013). *Revised Tennessee Early Learning Developmental Standards: Birth–48 Months*. https://www.tn.gov/content/dam/tn/education/standards/tnelds/std_tnelds_birth-4yo.pdf

U.S. Department of Health and Human Services. (2014). *Child care and development block grant act (CCDBG) of 2014: Plain language summary of statutory changes*. https://www.acf.hhs.gov/occ/resource/ccdbg-of-2014-plain-language-summary-of-statutory-changes

Vygotsky, L. S. (1978). *Mind in society: The development of higher psychological processes*. Cambridge, MA: Harvard University Press.

Weisner, T. S., Matheson, C., Coots, J., & Bernheimer, L. P. (2005). Sustainability of daily routines as a family outcome. In M. I. Martini & A. E. Maynard (Eds.), *Learning in cultural context: Family, peers, and school* (pp. 41–73). New York, NY: Kluwer Academic/Plenum Publishers.

Wolery, M. (1997). *Individualizing inclusion of young children with disabilities in child care: A model demonstration project*. Chapel Hill, NC: U.S. Department of Education.

Wolery, M. (2012). Voices from the field. *Young Exceptional Children, 15*, 41–44. doi:10.1177/109625612466379

Workgroup on Principles and Practices in Natural Environments. (2008). Agreed upon practices for providing early intervention services in natural environments. Retrieved from http://www.nectac.org/~pdfs/topics/families/AgreedUponPractices_FinalDraft2_01_08.pdf

World Health Organization. (2002). *Towards a common language for functioning, disability, and health: ICF* [WHO/EIP/GPE/CAS/01.3]. Geneva, Switzerland: Author.

World Health Organization. (2007). *International classification of functioning, disability and health: Children and youth version: ICF-CY*. Geneva, Switzerland: Author.

Younggren, N., Barton, L., Jackson, B., Swett, J. & Smyth, C. (2016). *Child Outcomes Summary–Team Collaboration (COS-TC) quality practice checklist and descriptions*. Menlo Park, CA: SRI International.

# Psychometric Properties of the MEISR

The MEISR is a list of skills children birth to 36 months of age might use to participate in their everyday home activities. In this appendix, we describe the development and field testing of the MEISR and present some information on the psychometric and usability properties of the tool.

## DEVELOPMENT AND FIELD TESTING

The MEISR was first developed in 2007. The process for generating items, field testing the tool, revising items, and continuing this process is described in the following sections.

### Generating Items

In 2006, when the need for a list of skills for children, organized by typical home routines, became clear to me (McWilliam), I conscripted a doctoral student to watch video recordings or RBIs; look through common skill sets, such as curricula and tests, for newborns through children age 5 years; and propose skill sets for routines. We deliberately repeated skills across routines, as necessary, so each routine would have a list of skills for engagement, independence, and social relationships (EISR) as well as those for communication, motor, and social skills.

By 2007, we had the first version (McWilliam & Hornstein, 2007). We sent it to expert early interventionists around the country and overseas to get their feedback. Reviewers were favorable and noted that no other instrument had skills organized by home routines. They made some suggestions for individual items but endorsed the overall organization. In the intervening years, a number of changes have been made—much too often for some implementers.

We have always resisted turning this profile into a developmental tool, partly because we didn't think the field of early intervention needed yet another such instrument, and we weren't interested in seeking the items that would best identify a child's developmental or mental age. But, users were asking for guidance about the typical ages at which to expect the skills described in different items. Although we feared this was an indication they were turning the profile into a curriculum, I (McWilliam) asked a graduate student to find similar items on curricula and tests and insert the age range. One interesting discovery was that some items were hard to find on other tools, such as participating in waking up by calling out for caregivers (1.16), participating in going out by finding a way to occupy self for a few minutes while the caregiver is busy (12.19), and participating in play with others by playing without messing up others' creations (6.35). This discovery might have been an indication of those tools' lack of functionality. That should not be seen as a problem for developmental tests, however, because they are designed for best measuring developmental or mental ages or quotients. It was a bit jarring to find that curricula (i.e., what adults should be teaching children) often did not include functional, home routine skills, such as participating in meal times by remaining calm (at least briefly) while waiting for feeding when hungry (3.07), participating in toileting by indicating need to go in enough time to get to the bathroom (2.14), participating in play time by knowing safe play boundaries (9.35), and participating in transitions by showing an emotional response that fits the situation (14.05). We have always cautioned users not to consider the age guide as scientifically precise until and unless someone norms the instrument empirically.

The need to check the ages we'd assigned items became serious when, against our better judgment, we found the need to have fairly accurate age references. When I (McWilliam) was running an early intervention program, where, traditionally, early interventionists had used the Hawaii Early Learning Profile (HELP) (Parks et al., 1992) to monitor child progress, I wanted to monitor child progress with the MEISR because 1) it matched the needs assessment process, consisting of the RBI; 2) progress on functional skills seemed more important than progress up the developmental scale; and 3) the MEISR made possible summaries by functional EISR areas and the national child outcomes. Using both the MEISR and the HELP was overkill, however, so I asked the state for permission to use the MEISR. They said we could do so, but only if we were able to age reference the tool. I argued that age referencing was unnecessary: We could judge the accumulation of skills by routines. If we wanted numbers, we could use the same quantification we used for program evaluation: percentage of items mastered within and across routines. The state wouldn't budge, however: They admitted they wanted the tool to estimate percentage of delay for children already in the program. So, I set about revising the age guidelines, by consulting the sources—tests and curricula—and using other scientific accounts of child development and developmental progressions when necessary. This time, instead of age ranges, I used expected (i.e., normal) *starting* ages for the functional routines-based skills. Further, the age anchoring is important for reporting progress on the national child outcomes.

Routines are times of day. They are not skill areas.

## Field Testing the Tool

At Siskin Children's Institute, we used the MEISR with over 500 families. This allowed for ongoing field testing. As problems with items were identified, such as users' difficulty in understanding the meaning of an item, we modified the tool. This implementation of the MEISR, every 6 months per family, provided a rich data bank, so we are now confident that the item set is adequate for our purposes. At Siskin Children's Institute, every 6 months, families rated their children's mastery of functional skills commonly found in everyday home routines on the MEISR. After 1 year in the program, the standardized difference in the average scores across children was 65% of a standard deviation, which is a noteworthy effect. Figure A.1 shows the mean percentage of correct items over multiple assessments for 244 (at Time 1) children. Children come into early intervention programs at different ages, so only a small number received six MEISRs.

## Residual Improvement Index

Results showed that children's mastered skills increased over time while children were in the program, which would be expected by maturation alone. We have developed a *residual improvement index* for calculating the improvement that can be attributed to the program, after taking maturation into account. First, we calculate the slope of the child's projected improvement on the MEISR using the first score. For example, assume we have a child come into the program at age 12 months, mastering 50% of the items for his age on the MEISR, as shown in Table A.1. If he masters half the items, his MEISR developmental age is 6 months. At that rate of progress, 6 months later (Time 2), we would expect him to master skills up to 9 months [(6 months × 50% rate = 3 months' gain) + 6 months skills at Time 1]. But, at Time 2,

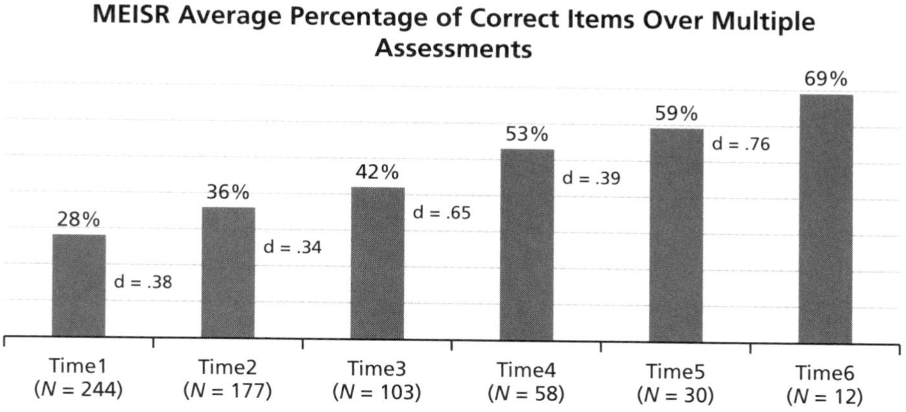

## MEISR Average Percentage of Correct Items Over Multiple Assessments

Figure A.1. MEISR average percentage of correct items over multiple assessments; MEISR's sensitivity to change over time.

instead, he mastered 70% of the skills for his age: 70% skills × 6 months = 4.2 months' gain. Compare 4.2 months' gain (actual) to 3 months' gain (expected). The difference is 1.2 months, which is 11.76% better than expected (100/b × c or 100/10.2 × 1.2). See Figure A.2.

In other words, first, professionals need to calculate the slope to predict later scores. Then they calculate the actual change at the next data point. Finally, they calculate the difference between the actual change and the predicted later score. This difference is expressed as a percentage better (or worse) than expected.

## Different Versions

Younggren reorganized the MEISR items by the three national outcomes to make the reporting of progress on those outcomes easier. This cross-referencing and use of the MEISR to assist with measurement of these outcomes is described in Chapter 5. Previous versions of the MEISR have been translated into Portuguese, Spanish, Chinese, and Polish.

## Organization

The current MEISR was revised from the 2007 version by adding a transition section, including clarification and examples to items that were interpreted differently across early intervention providers, clarifying starting ages, and restating the items to be participation based. Essential to the MEISR is the assessment of children's participation in the everyday routines of their homes. These routines have been selected on the basis of 30 years of experience in asking families about their daily lives. Each routine is discussed with reference to the kinds of skills needed for EISR in it. As noted earlier in this manual, routines are times of day. They are not skill areas. The MEISR is organized around 14 commonly reported family routines, as reported in the book.

Table A.1. Hypothetical data for calculating the residual improvement index

| Age | Expected | Actual DA |
|-----|----------|-----------|
| 0 | 0 | 0 |
| 12 | 6 | 6 |
| 18 | 9 | 10.2 |

Key: DA, developmental age.

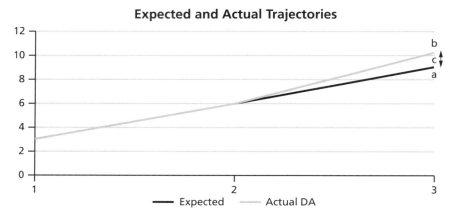

**Figure A.2.** Residual improvement index: expected and actual trajectories of developmental age (DA).

Not all the routines in the MEISR will be equally meaningful to any one family perhaps, and other routines, not included in the instrument, might be more meaningful. Nevertheless, the 14 common family routines should provide enough information to be able to develop a functional profile of the child in his or her home environment.

## Distribution of Items Across Crosswalk Categories

MEISR items are nearly equally distributed across crosswalked areas, as shown in Figure A.3.

## PSYCHOMETRIC AND USABILITY PROPERTIES

The version of the MEISR published in this book is the product of data and experience. Were we to repeat these analyses with the final version, we might see some differences, but the changes we've made are unlikely to alter the results drastically. The addition of some items to some routines to balance out the functional-skill areas and the addition of the transition "routine" probably have not weakened the instrument, in terms of psychometric properties and usability—quite the opposite—although it's an empirical question, obviously.

The MEISR was designed as a tool to help families and the professionals working with them understand and monitor children's progress in functional living and to discuss potential targets for intervention. Even though it was intended as a profile and not a developmental test, it is a quantitative measure, items are averaged, and means can be compared across time. Therefore, we examined the internal consistency of the items, the sensitivity and specificity of the scores, the sensitivity to population differences, and usability and social validity.

## Internal Consistency

To determine the extent to which the items hang together to produce reliable scores, we conducted an analysis of internal consistency. For example, when we say that a child scores a mean of 1.9 on a scale of 1 to 3 in play time with others, we need some assurance that that score really is scoring a single dimension (i.e., competence during play with others). If internal consistency is low, it means the items score a variety of things, so the score cannot be trusted to be as reliable as we would like.

Table A.2 shows Cronbach's alpha for the total score as well as for each of the routines. These data show that, indeed, the items on the MEISR measure a unitary construct, which might be labeled "functional competence." The full scale has remarkably strong internal consistency, and all individual routines have Cronbach's alpha > .85.

## MEISR – Engagement – Independence – Social Relationships Distribution

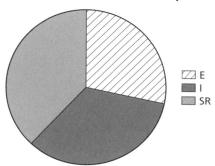

E
I
SR

## MEISR – Developmental Domain Distribution

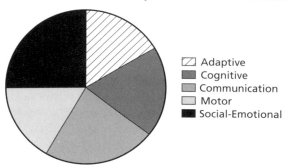

Adaptive
Cognitive
Communication
Motor
Social-Emotional

## MEISR – Child Outcomes Distribution

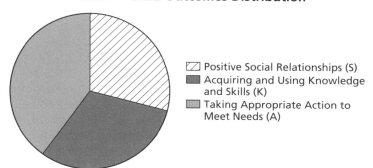

Positive Social Relationships (S)
Acquiring and Using Knowledge and Skills (K)
Taking Appropriate Action to Meet Needs (A)

**Figure A.3.** Distribution of MEISR items across three crosswalked areas. E, engagement; I, independence; SR, social relationships.

## Sensitivity and Specificity

Sensitivity refers to the tool's ability to identify children correctly, based upon a stated eligibility criterion. Specificity is the tool's ability to exclude children who do not meet the eligibility criterion correctly. Although the MEISR is not designed for teams to use it alone in eligibility determination, it is important to consider these dimensions in a psychometric property review.

The MEISR has been used in one state to estimate the percentage of delay. To determine whether the estimation of delay would substantially differ from HELP scores, decisions for 10 children with different characteristics were compared. All decisions were the same using both tools. Sensitivity was easier to measure, because these were children already in early

**Table A.2.** Cronbach's alpha values for the total score as well as for each of the routines (earlier version of the MEISR)

| Scale | Number of Valid Cases | Number of Items | Cronbach's Alpha |
|---|---|---|---|
| Full MEISR | 138 | 308 | .994 |
| Waking Up | 215 | 21 | .950 |
| Toileting/Diapering | 255 | 21 | .917 |
| Meal Times | 228 | 38 | .971 |
| Dressing Time | 246 | 23 | .931 |
| Hangout – TV – Books | 247 | 31 | .958 |
| Play With Others | 233 | 27 | .949 |
| Nap Time | 247 | 13 | .864 |
| Outside Time | 252 | 20 | .975 |
| Play by Him- or Herself | 251 | 23 | .962 |
| Bath Time | 242 | 28 | .952 |
| Bedtime | 253 | 14 | .886 |
| Going Out | 246 | 32 | .943 |
| Grocery Shopping | 247 | 17 | .919 |

intervention. Eight of the children were found still to have delays with both instruments, and two children were found to have delays below the cutoff (i.e., not delayed enough) with both instruments. In other words, with this small sample, specificity was 100%.

## Sensitivity to Change Over Time

For one early intervention program, the MEISR was completed every 6 months. Figure A.1 shows that the longer children were in the program, the greater the percentage of functional skills they acquired. We recognize that maturation alone could account for this trend, but these data do show that the MEISR overall (or "total") percentage score is sensitive to differences in time in program.

## Usability

Usability is, of course, another important consideration in tool development. To measure this, 13 professionals using the MEISR completed a usability scale. Ten had been using the MEISR with families for 2 years, and the remaining three were using it for the first time, when they completed the usability scale. Five used the MEISR to develop IFSPs, 10 used it to monitor child progress, 8 used it to describe children's functioning, and 1 used it for another purpose. One person did not report how the MEISR was used. In all but three use scenarios, family members completed the MEISR alone: Two completed it with professionals, and one provided no information on who completed it. We asked these professionals to respond to the following statements as being not at all true, somewhat true, true, or very true.

1. Most early interventionists would find the MEISR suitable for helping develop IFSP outcomes/goals.

2. Most early interventionists would find the MEISR suitable for monitoring children's progress.

3. Most early interventionists would find the MEISR suitable for describing present levels of development.

4. Most early interventionists would find the MEISR suitable for helping rate federal child outcomes.

5. The MEISR is an acceptable tool for helping develop IFSP outcomes/goals.

6. The MEISR is an acceptable tool for monitoring children's progress.

7. The MEISR is an acceptable tool for describing present levels of development.

8. The MEISR is an acceptable tool for helping rate federal child outcomes.

9. Overall, the MEISR would be beneficial for families.

10. I would be willing to use the MEISR.

11. I would recommend the MEISR to other early interventionists.

12. The MEISR would not result in negative side effects for the family.

13. The MEISR is practical in the amount of time required to complete.

14. The MEISR would not be difficult to implement with 30 other families.

15. Early interventionists are likely to use the MEISR because it requires little technical skill.

16. Early interventionists are likely to use the MEISR because it requires little training.

The responses to these statements (identified as Q1 to Q16) are reflected in Figure A.4.

The responses in Figure A.4 show that the respondents found the MEISR suitable for many purposes. They were a little less positive about the amount of time required to complete it and the feasibility of implementing it with 30 other families. Most of them said it was true (but not very true) that early interventionists were likely to use it. In general, these few respondents endorsed the usability of the MEISR. Furthermore, it has been used successfully with all families in one particular early intervention program in southeast Tennessee. Over 4 years, about 500 families completed it with no reported problems.

## Social Validity

Beyond provider usability, social validity is an important aspect to consider. Social validity in this instance refers to family member acceptability and satisfaction with the tool. To measure this, 46 families completed a social validity scale. The items they rated on a 4-point Likert-type scale were as follows:

1. It was easy to understand.

2. It was easy to score what my child can do.

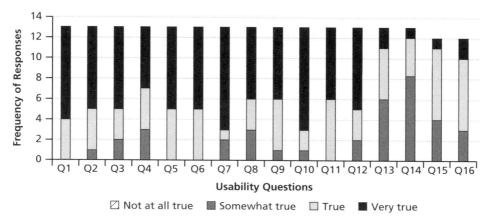

**Figure A.4.** Results of usability questions posed to professionals (N = 13).

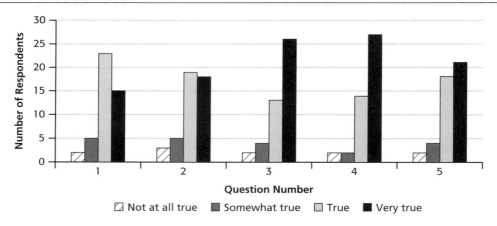

**Figure A.5.** Number of families (N = 46) reporting the acceptability of, and their satisfaction with, the MEISR.

3. Filling this out helped me see all the things my child can learn throughout the day.

4. Talking about my completed MEISR with my early interventionist was helpful.

5. Overall, I think it's a good idea for parents to complete the MEISR.

Results of the questionnaire are depicted in Figure A.5. These results indicate the MEISR was helpful in seeing all the things the child can learn throughout the day and that talking about it with the early interventionist was helpful. Still true, but not very true, was the MEISR is easy to understand. In general, families were positively disposed toward the MEISR.

## CONCLUSION

The MEISR shows promise as a tool producing reliable and valid scores. It should never be used for high-stakes purposes, such as determining eligibility or frequency and intensity of services. It should be used for what it was designed for: to monitor child progress, to help with outcomes ratings, and to help with the RBI. These purposes do not require sophisticated psychometrics. Nevertheless, the tool has been successfully field tested over a number of years, we have developed the residual improvement index, and we have some data indicating professionals consider the MEISR usable in their practice.

# Index

References to tables and figures are indicated with *t* and *f*, respectively.